Affective Intensities and Evolving Horror Forms

Affective Intensities and Evolving Horror Forms

From Found Footage to Virtual Reality

Adam Daniel

EDINBURGH
University Press

Edinburgh University Press is one of the leading university presses in the UK. We publish academic books and journals in our selected subject areas across the humanities and social sciences, combining cutting-edge scholarship with high editorial and production values to produce academic works of lasting importance. For more information visit our website: edinburghuniversitypress.com

© Adam Daniel, 2020, 2021

Edinburgh University Press Ltd
The Tun – Holyrood Road
12(2f) Jackson's Entry
Edinburgh EH8 8PJ

First published in hardback by Edinburgh University Press 2020

Typeset in 11/13 Adobe Garamond Pro
IDSUK (DataConnection) Ltd

A CIP record for this book is available from the British Library

ISBN 978 1 4744 5635 7 (hardback)
ISBN 978 1 4744 5636 4 (paperback)
ISBN 978 1 4744 5637 1 (webready PDF)
ISBN 978 1 4744 5638 8 (epub)

The right of Adam Daniel to be identified as the author of this work has been asserted in accordance with the Copyright, Designs and Patents Act 1988, and the Copyright and Related Rights Regulations 2003 (SI No. 2498).

Contents

List of Figures	viii
Acknowledgements	ix
Introduction	1
Evolving Forms, Evolving Affects	1
Affect and Horror Media	3
Horror Media and the 'Lived Body'	6
Deleuze, Embodiment, Neuroscience and Horror:	
A 'Machinic Assemblage'	7
The Book	9
1. From the Semantic to the Somatic: Affective Engagement with	
Horror Cinema	13
Cognitivist Frameworks of Spectatorship	14
Towards the Somatic	18
The Phenomenology of Horror	23
2. From Identification to Embodied Spectatorship in the	
Found Footage Horror Film	30
To Look (or Not to Look)	30
Technologies of Perception in Horror Film	30
Bleeding Binaries: When a Screen Becomes a Portal	33
The Birth and Emergence of 'Found Footage'	
Horror Cinema	38
The Unreal Reality of Found Footage	41
Found Footage and the Embodied Spectator	45
3. Camera Supernaturalis	54
The Out-of-Frame of Found Footage	54
Into the Woods: *Willow Creek* and *The Blair Witch Project*	56
The 'Empty' Frame of Found Footage Horror	63
Cinematic Dread and the Camera of *Paranormal Activity*	66
The Monster as Visual and Aural Intensification	71

4. Perception and Point of View in the Found Footage Horror Film: New Understandings via Deleuze's Perception-Image ... 74
   How Do We Get 'Inside' a Movie? ... 75
   'Becoming-with' the Film ... 79
   Deleuzian 'Spectatorship' ... 81
   The Perception-Image ... 82
   Found Footage Horror and 'Camera Consciousness' ... 88
   Deleuze and Representation ... 91

5. Horrific Entwinement: Affective Neuroscience and the Body of the Horror Spectator ... 97
   The Question of Empathy ... 97
   Empathic Identification and 'Embodied Simulation Theory' ... 101
   Mimetic Innervation ... 106
   Foraging through Found Footage: Panksepp's SEEKING Instinct ... 109

6. What Hides behind the Stream: Post-Cinematic Hauntings of the Digital ... 116
   The Affect of Apocrypha: *Suicidemouse* and *11bx1371* ... 117
   The Soundscapes of Post-Cinematic Horror ... 127
   Denson and the 'Horror of Discorrelation' ... 128

7. The Evolving Screen Forms of New Media Horror ... 132
   Always Watching: The Evolving Screen Form of Horror and *Marble Hornets* ... 133
   The Embodied Experience of New Media Artefacts ... 136
   The Aesthetics of Distortion: Synaesthetic Qualities of Sound and Image ... 144
   New Modalities, New Tensions ... 147
   'Screenlife' Horror and *Unfriended* ... 149
   On the Threshold ... 154

8. The Embodied Player of Horror Video Games ... 157
   Fear in the First Person ... 157
   Lo-fi, High Tension: *Marginalia* and *Anatomy* ... 159
   Deleuze and the Video Game ... 164
   Spatial and Temporal Apertures in *Alien: Isolation* ... 165

9. The Spectator-Interactor of Virtual Reality Horror ... 171
   The Meeting Place of Virtual Reality and Horror Cinema ... 173
   Virtual Reality and Presence ... 178
   Virtual Reality and Cinema: Strange Bedfellows? ... 180

The Melding of Spectator and Interactor	186
The Radical Potential of Virtual Reality	190
What Cinema Can Return to VR	192
The Future of Cinematic VR	194
Conclusion	200
Bibliography	206
Books, Articles and Websites	206
Videos	216
Films	217
Television	219
Games	219
Index	220

Figures

2.1	Samara crawling out of the television in *The Ring*	36
3.1	Inside the tent in *Willow Creek*	58
3.2	Heather fleeing the tent in *The Blair Witch Project*	63
3.3	Katie sleepwalks in *Paranormal Activity*	70
4.1	Aaron's point of view in *Creep*	87
4.2	Josef takes out the trash in *Creep*	89
5.1	Becca's filmed reflection	98
5.2	Hide and seek in *The Visit*	108
6.1	*Suicidemouse* by Nec1	119
6.2	*11bx1371*'s 'Birdman'	120
6.3	Spectrogrammetric analysis of *11bx1371*	121
6.4	*Cursed Kleenex Commercial*	123
7.1	ARE YOU ONE OF THEM, in *Conversion*	133
7.2	A glimpse of The Operator	134
7.3	The 'obscured' Operator of *Marble Hornets*	136
7.4	Camera attached to sternum in *Marble Hornets*	139
7.5	Corrupted imagery in *File*	145
7.6	Facial distortion in *Unfriended*	152
7.7	*Unfriended*'s screens within screens	153
8.1	A floating tape recorder in *Anatomy*	163
8.2	*Alien: Isolation* motion sensor	166
9.1	The woman in *11:57*	172
9.2	*VR Noir*	175
9.3	*Catatonic VR*	183
10.1	The woman in the graveyard in *#Screamers*	201

Acknowledgements

Thanks to my family and friends for your love, encouragement and support. Special thanks to Marty Murphy, Duncan McLean, Matthew Campora and Maija Howe for your support and friendship. To Brett Hendry and Kevin Thompson: two passionate teachers who opened my eyes through their love of education, literature and art. To all of the horror creators cited within, thank you for the potent thrills of the work you create. To the Sydney Screen Studies Network, particularly Phoebe Macrossan, Jessica Ford and Melanie Robson for their encouragement and camaraderie. To Alex Ling: for your wisdom, good humour and constant encouragement. To both Shane Denson and Erin Harrington: for your kindness and intellectual generosity as friends and peers. To Edinburgh University Press and the skilled editorial assistance of Gillian Leslie and Richard Strachan. To Angela Ndalianis and Anna Powell: for their insight and support, and for inspiring me through their work. To Anthony Uhlmann and Sara Knox: for the generosity of their feedback and guidance. To Anne Rutherford: for your constant mentorship, encouragement and generous professional guidance, and for always championing me. To Lara: my very own person, my number one supporter, my best friend. Thank you for being patient, supportive and loving as I have wrestled with this monster.

Introduction

> Like an expired body that blends with the dirt to form new molecules and living organisms, the body of cinema continues to blend with other image/sound technologies in processes of composition/decomposition that breed images with new speeds and new distributions of intensities. The cinema does not evaporate into nothingness, but transmutes in a becoming that has no point of origin or completion.[1]
>
> – Elena del Rio, 'Cinema's Exhaustion and the Vitality of Affect'

Evolving Forms, Evolving Affects

At the time of writing this, horror cinema is alive and well. Indeed, many argue it is currently experiencing another cycle of expanded popularity. The critical and commercial success of films such as *Get Out* (2017), *Hereditary* (2018), and *The Conjuring* series (together with its spinoffs), for example, indicates a renewed appreciation of horror cinema *in the cinema*, with each producing box office returns that have dramatically surpassed expectations. The rise of streaming services and the accessibility of on-demand video have also played a significant role in horror film's current popularity. Recently, the Netflix original *Bird Box* (2018) set a record for streaming within the company, with 45 million individual streams over a seven-day period. Horror as a genre, however, has never been contained within a predominant media form. Instead, it has historically infected both emerging forms and the technologies which deliver them, parasitically preying upon the fears that emerge from these developments. Accompanying these advances in technology and the concomitant evolution in form are mutations in how horror operates, not only at the level of the diegetic content, but also in its reconfiguration of the spectatorial experience. There is something different in the way horror works once it begins to move outside of the borders of horror cinema's traditional form and content.

This 'something different' is at the heart of this book. In these nine chapters I will explore the transgressions of these boundaries across a variety of media, as well as the fluctuating experience of horror spectatorship this entails. Central to the book's various investigations are questions of what modern horror media is capable of, and how contraventions of the boundaries described above may reveal to us the capacities (and possible limitations) of cinema itself. I also ask how horror as a genre can explore questions of perception and affect in our increasingly technologically mediated society. While academic studies in the field of horror cinema are often focused around critically assessing why horror appeals to the spectator, in this book I instead pose the question from a different perspective, by asking what it is that horror film (and horror media more broadly) does differently to other genres: what kinds of experience can it produce and more specifically, how is it that the aesthetic choices made within the genre generate a spectatorial engagement that may differ from that of classical cinema? The understandings that emerge from this examination of horror illuminate the experience of spectatorship more generally and explain how it is that we may become engaged with film in a manner that cannot be fully explained by understandings of the spectatorial experience as one that is primarily predicated upon cognitive assessment of the film and its contents.

We live in a culture that is increasingly reshaped by transformations in audio-visual media. Since the beginning of the twenty-first century, our definition of cinema and its presence in everyday life has transformed rapidly – the theatrical experience is now but one element of a larger, ever-shifting human interaction with technologies of perception and expression. The ubiquity of the smartphone has availed us of the capacity to watch audio-visual media, and even make our own, at a moment's notice. Gaming culture has intensified with the predominance of screens, leading to an explosion in both independent and commercial game production. Consumer level technologies of augmented and virtual reality (VR) have become mainstream if not yet widely adopted. While this acceleration in the production and distribution of audio-visual media has effects across all genres, it is the field of horror that is my explicit focus.

The increasing velocity of audio-visual culture since the turn of the twenty-first century has led to the production of what Marshall McLuhan describes as new 'sense ratios' amongst its consumers. In explaining this term, McLuhan contends that new inventions and technologies produce variations in sensory input that customarily require adjustments from our sense organs.[2] Crucially, these modifications to the way we experience audio-visual media, at the level of the senses, have effects that transcend variations in narrative content or structure. In order to best understand the intensification of experience these modifications produce for a viewer, this book builds upon existing scholarship that has examined the limitations of cognitive appraisal as the primary foundations for spectatorship. This scholarship, in the field of embodied spectatorship, sees the sensory-affective properties of cinema as foundational to the viewing experience, and argues that they produce a bodily engagement between spectator and film. This book seeks to extend upon these models by synthesising them with concepts drawn from the philosophical work of Gilles Deleuze. By testing and applying these concepts in an exploration of emerging new media, new insights can be offered into how the spectatorial experience alters across the spectrum of these technologies.

Given its transgressive concerns, horror as a genre is often the first site to interrogate evolving technologies, both within the narrative and through the formal properties of the medium within which it exists. However, any investigation into how horror responds to or evolves with new media forms needs to be accompanied by an analysis of how they reconfigure experience. With the emergence of new media forms come not only new methods to construct audio-visual horror narratives, but also alterations in the ways in which spectators process and experience these images. As William Brown argues, 'digital technology has expanded cinema and the psychological sciences have expanded our understanding of perception to such a degree that new theories of cinema and our perception(s) of it are urgently required'.[3]

The theoretical examination of the 'post-cinematic' is of vital importance to my approach. Shane Denson and Julia Leyda identify numerous ideas, concepts, technologies and properties as qualities of the post-cinematic, which includes works that are 'digital, interactive, networked, ludic, miniaturized, mobile, social, processual, algorithmic, aggregative, environmental, or convergent, among other things'.[4] In their edited collection on post-cinema, Denson and Leyda draw on a variety of scholarly approaches to examine how the shift away from cinema and television as the dominant media of the twenty-first century has shaped and reflected new 'cultural sensibilities'.[5] Denson observes that post-cinematic horror 'trades centrally on a slippage between diegesis and medium; the fear that is channelled *through* moving-image media is in part also a fear *of* (or evoked *by*) these media'.[6] This contention is central to the expanded approach I take in analysing the works within this book. Similarly, the sources of affective excess I identify herein can be connected to Denson's provocative and compelling post-phenomenological consideration of the 'Horror of Discorrelation', whereby images are disconnected from human embodied subjectivities.[7] Post-cinema theory provides valuable tools to analyse the transition from cinema's photographic ontology to the digital temporality of modern screens and networks.

Affect and Horror Media

In order to more fully understand divergent 'post-cinema' media forms, these new realms require a synthesis of broader conceptions of cinematic affect with one that considers the primacy of the non-representational content of the sound and image as vital to its production. Emergent forms of horror, such as the found footage horror film, streaming video horror, web-series, horror video games, and virtual reality horror cinema, provide a location where this non-representational content is often foregrounded.

Horror film has a long history of destabilising the semantic content of the image to increase its capacity to terrify. Robert Wiene's *The Cabinet of Dr Caligari* (1920), for example, broke with the conventions of cinematographic realism in favour of a heavily stylised mise-en-scène that visually reproduced the inner landscape of insanity.[8] This revealed cinema's capacity to be not only a reflective medium, but also one that was capable of a poetics that allowed for a more expressive means of storytelling. There are, however, inadequacies in scholarship that contend that such poetics emerge by simply undermining the processes of cognitive or reflective mechanisms that supposedly lie at the foundations of how we process the cinematic sound and image; these theories neglect the primacy of the embodied experience.

The modern forms of horror media that are investigated in this book further this destabilisation of the image's semantic content. They are often less reliant on structures of narrative as their basis; in the place of the de-emphasised narrative, these works utilise distinct strategies of sound and image, such as placing emphasis on the out-of-frame, on visual and aural distortion, or on the image's synaesthetic or haptic qualities, in place of a coherent image. Consequently, they activate a distinct concurrent embodied response for the viewer. This book posits that affect is at the origins of this corporeal response, and that, importantly, this affect is not necessarily coterminous with the presence of on-screen bodies.

This approach is a departure from the psychoanalytic, representational and hermeneutic models that have previously been used to understand horror film. These foundational approaches, by scholars such as Noël Carroll, Carol Clover, Barbara Creed, and Robin Wood, while offering crucial insight, have limitations in that they are largely focused on unpacking the semantic elements of film. This book reframes an approach to horror around the somatic response, using theories of affect to elucidate the foundations of this corporeal interface.

Affect Studies consists of a diverse and wide-ranging number of scholarly approaches. In *The Affect Theory Reader*, Melissa Gregg and Gregory J. Seigworth tentatively categorise eight 'orientations' in approaches to affect, orientations that often 'undulate' or 'overlap'.[9] These include: phenomenologies of embodiment; assemblages of the human/machine/inorganic, drawing on neuroscience, artificial intelligence, robotics and bio-engineering; nonhumanist Spinozist philosophical approaches; psychological or psychoanalytic inquiries; the politics of feminist, queer and disability studies; approaches that counter the 'linguistic turn' in the humanities; critical discourses in emotions outside of interiorised subjectivity; and finally, science studies.[10] The definition of affect I am applying within this book is drawn primarily from the work of scholar Brian Massumi, who broadly understands affect as intensity, and emotion as the qualification of this intensity.[11] For Massumi, the term 'affect' also describes the work of various intensities in relation to each other, the way they translate or transform each other. In this conception, sounds and images carry an affective charge for the viewer, but this charge is not equivalent to a codified emotional response. Affect is the non-conscious experience of intensity, the unformed and unstructured potential that later becomes sedimented in 'semantically and semiotically formed progressions, into narrativizable action-reaction circuits, into function and meaning'.[12] This book draws on Massumi's conception of affect to articulate how it is that horror cinema can work to produce responses in excess of cognitive appraisal or emotional codification, precisely because its affective components are not always directly correlated with the semantic content of the image, such as the on-screen body.

This work shares a similar phenomenological approach with scholars who posit the spectatorial body at the foundations of the viewing experience. Xavier Aldana Reyes, for example, argues for the spectatorial body as an 'anchoring point' in moments of 'visceral contact between the viewer's [body] and the character's [body], as foregrounded in examples of graphic horror, mutilation or torture'.[13] Reyes positions the occasions when the viewer's body is moved by the bodies seen on screen as 'the epitome of the moment of affect'.[14] Where our approaches diverge is in Reyes's focus on the somatic alignment between the viewer and the threatened, harmed or tortured body. In many of the works I analyse, the bodies of the protagonists, while in danger, are rarely explicitly mutilated or tortured, and as such, do not generate the same kind of 'anchoring'. The marginalisation of the on-screen body is a marked feature of found footage horror films, but this book argues that found footage horror nonetheless relies on embodiment as central to the spectatorial experience. My account also departs from Alexandra Heller-Nicholas's comprehensive and cogent examination of found footage, which theorises that the engagement produced by the subgenre is primarily reliant on the viewer's cognitive appraisal; instead, I focus on the embodied response of the viewer as a primary driver of the intensification of experience.

Similarly, the new media works I examine also commonly de-emphasise the presence of the on-screen body: the horror games I analyse feature no on-screen avatars during their gameplay, and I explicitly wrestle with the possibilities of the viewer as unseen diegetic participant (in other words, their point of view and presence as an unseen 'body' in the diegetic world) in many works of virtual reality cinema. This raises particular questions about the insufficiencies of theories which prioritise identification, alignment or mimetic communication with on-screen bodies as central to affective exchange.

Horror Media and the 'Lived Body'

My engagement with theories of film phenomenology is strongly motivated by the reconstitution of experience brought on by the rise of new media technologies. The novel states of bodily involvement in the consumption, production and distribution of these new media forms bring to the fore a type of sensuous charge that forces us to reconsider the links between consciousness and corporeality. The move towards interactivity and immersion has to some degree dissolved the boundaries that may have been conceived between a viewer-subject and media products as objects of experience. There is little doubt we now *participate* more explicitly with the media we experience.

In an attempt to reconcile the somatic, emotional and cognitive responses of the viewer, scholar Julian Hanich has advanced a comprehensive account of the phenomenology of horror spectatorship, one that attempts to reinstate the importance of the lived body in the moment of viewing.[15] His work develops a typology of cinematic fear that articulates the distinctions between shock, dread, terror and direct or suggested horror. My own approach echoes this move towards thinking the experience of viewing from the perspective of a 'lived body', and expands Hanich's methodology outside of the realm of traditional horror cinema, applying his concepts to media such as video games and virtual reality.

Horror is unabashedly a 'body genre', as scholar Linda Williams has argued.[16] However, it is important to distinguish that this corporeal response is not simply the outcome of a cognitive reaction to on-screen bodies under threat. A persuasive field of scholarship has emerged in the last twenty-five years that understands the viewing experience as necessarily embodied. Often underpinned by a phenomenological conception of the film–viewer encounter, this scholarship has offered diverse accounts for how this embodiment occurs. This book draws from a range of these academic approaches to embodied spectatorship in order to support my contention that the horror viewer is necessarily intertwined with the sound and image in a bodily way.

The emergent forms of horror media examined here, such as found footage horror, streaming video and virtual reality, often have deficits in relation to narrative and its components, such as the incomplete construction of compelling characterisation or, as in the case of virtual reality, an equation between the VR camera and the protagonist, which implies that the spectator is a diegetic character. This leads to a lack in spectatorial identification as it is traditionally understood. Interrogating this conventional account of identification, I instead propose a more robust account of the engagement between spectator and film, by drawing on the foundations of embodied spectatorship theory.

The spectrum of horror media examined in this book provides several valuable sites for expanding the study of embodiment and affect in relation to horror, because accompanying this reduction in the semantic content of the image is an attendant increase in the somatic aspects of cinematic experience. While many theoretical frameworks that examine horror texts decode the meaning of the monster, this book instead addresses the somatic response to the form itself from a phenomenological perspective. Examining how it is that horror cinema intensifies this embodiment can reveal new understandings about why horror affects a viewer in a way that can often transcend their intellectual or vicarious distance.

A movement beyond simply analysing the imbrication of horror and technology at the narrative level is crucial to this study. Instead, the book examines what these new technological forms do: how they alter the dynamics of spectatorship, how they traverse the material distinction between image and viewer, how they intensify the embodied experience. The exploration of these new forms is staged across several distinct new modes: first, the generic shift from conventional cinematic horror stories to found footage horror film, the movement into the new media world of streaming video (in the form of YouTube horror shorts and the web series *Marble Hornets*), the rise of independent horror video games, and finally, the rapidly expanding world of cinematic virtual reality horror.[17] Building on studies of embodied spectatorship theory and expanded understandings of perception offered by modern neuroscience that have crucially debunked the Cartesian logic of the mind–body dualism, in this book I will examine horror texts not only for their content and meaning, but also for the manner in which their form affects viewers on a bodily level.

Deleuze, Embodiment, Neuroscience and Horror: A 'Machinic Assemblage'

Throughout this book there are multiple occasions where I draw on the work of philosopher Gilles Deleuze (and, on occasion, his collaborations with Félix Guattari). However, I would encourage the reader to consider these explorations of Deleuzian theory as a form of synthesis and not a wholesale application. This synthesis often involves attempts to draw together the wide-ranging considerations of Deleuzian theory with analysis of the exemplar audio-visual works, reflections on embodiment theory and broader film theory, and in the case of one chapter, elements of neurocognitive research. I consider this concerted embrace of Deleuze's concept of a 'machinic assemblage', where the potential resonance of the ideas within each field and how they act upon each other provides greater insight than the isolated conceptual domains.

For Deleuze, cinema and philosophy are similar endeavours: both are practices of thought, involved in a reciprocal process of generating concepts that can produce shared insight between the two, rather than cinema simply illustrating philosophy, and vice versa. Deleuze conceived of directors, artists, musicians and philosophers as all essentially 'thinkers' – the only difference being that the 'artists create percepts and affects', where 'the philosopher constructs concepts'.[18] This book works with Deleuzian concepts through what Robert Sinnerbrink calls an aesthetic-hermeneutic circle, where 'aesthetic experience precedes and informs philosophical reflection', bringing about novel means of expression.[19] This involves a consideration of how films themselves, much like philosophy, have the capacity to pose questions about the experience and meaning of being human.

Deleuze sees the concept of 'brain-screens' as being crucial to investigating not only how we process cinematic images, but also the processes of thought itself. In an interview with *Cahiers du Cinema* in 1986, Deleuze said:

> The brain is unity. The brain is the screen. I don't believe that linguistics and psychoanalysis offer a great deal to the cinema. On the contrary, the biology of the brain – molecular biology – does. Thought is molecular. Molecular speeds make up the slow beings that we are . . . Cinema, precisely because it puts the image in motion, or rather endows the image with self-motion, never stops tracing the circuits of the brain.[20]

Given that neuroscientific research has, in the years since this interview, illuminated the indivisibility of the brain and body as a cohesive unit, it is vital that we continue to also further expand our understandings of the interaction between the brain/mind/body assemblage and the cinematic image. Much recent neuroscientific scholarship has claimed an indivisible conception of brain and body, and sees the development of this research as fundamentally key to understanding how human experience is produced. Grouped under the term '4EA', these scientists have adopted a phenomenological philosophical framework from the works of Husserl, Heidegger and Merleau-Ponty. They see cognition as embodied, embedded, enactive, extended and affective, an approach which assumes an inseparability between cognition and affect. In this field of scholarship, brain, body and world are inexorably linked in interactive loops.[21] This has considerable relevance to understandings of the experience of the cinematic image, in that it may lend credence to approaches that similarly consider spectatorship as a continual reciprocity between image, mind and body.

The phenomenologically informed stance of 4EA scholars finds a considerable ally in Deleuze's cinematic philosophy, despite his own objections to characterisations of his cinema work as 'phenomenologically' informed. Cinema is an art both of time and of space and examining the space of the lived body is crucial to understanding how cinema works. In order to explicate my own understandings of how these evolving forms of horror media are altering the spectatorial experience, the following chapters offer a detailed reading of exemplar works in light of the potential interaction and overlap between embodied spectatorship, Deleuzian cinematic theory and developing understandings of the mind–body relationship from neuroscience. This intersection opens up vital new ground for questioning the experience of spectatorship.

THE BOOK

This book is structured to be a progression through several different forms of emergent horror media, analysing the dynamics of embodiment produced by each, and how these dynamics are altered by the particulars of the various modes. Most of the chapters open with a short subjective description of one of the audio-visual texts examined. These anecdotal tales often describe my initial experience with the media in question, and are designed to pique the reader's curiosity in much the same way I was drawn in to the work. They also provide a brief introduction to texts that may be unfamiliar to the mainstream reader, such as the streaming horror videos and virtual reality examples. The audio-visual texts I have chosen are largely publicly available (see the Bibliography for links to access YouTube playlists for both *Marble Hornets* and the YouTube shorts discussed).[22]

Chapter 1, 'From the Semantic to the Somatic: Affective Engagement with Horror Cinema', begins with an examination of some of the conventional theoretical frameworks that have been applied to analysing the origins of horror film's affect, and a critical assessment of the limitations of these existing notions.

Chapter 2, 'From Identification to Embodied Spectatorship in the Found Footage Horror Film', assesses the inadequacies of a purely hermeneutic approach to understanding horror film's effects. Turning to the horror subgenre of found footage, exemplified by films such as *The Blair Witch Project* (1999), *Paranormal Activity* (2007) and *Willow Creek* (2013), this chapter examines how these films push the experience of modern horror spectatorship to its limits in terms of what Kimberly Jackson calls the 'undecidable relation between reality and image' that often emerges in the nexus of technology and horror.[23] Found footage horror films highlight the insufficiency of frameworks that contend that identification is our main form of engagement with the horror film, given that the films often reject the hallmarks of characterisation deployed in most conventional Hollywood narratives, and that they are, for the most part, presented as a record of events by a witness who remains largely unseen by us.[24]

An interrogation of the embodied experience of the out-of-frame is the focus of Chapter 3, 'Camera Supernaturalis'. Given that the threat of the out-of-frame is a frequently utilised generic element of found footage horror, it is essential to examine what occurs in the spectatorial experience of said moments. I do so by taking into account Hanich's concept of 'cinematic dread' and its affective properties for the spectator, while also reconciling these phenomenological considerations with some aspects of Deleuzian theory, including Anna Powell's examination of the genre.

In Chapter 4, 'Perception and Point of View in the Found Footage Horror Film: New Understandings via Deleuze's Perception-Image', Deleuze's cinematic 'perception-image' is considered as a way to understand how found footage horror may destabilise a hierarchical concept of film-object and viewer-subject. Here I argue that found footage horror does so specifically through its ability to catalyse both the subjective and objective properties of the cinematic image, a process Deleuze argues is inherent to the perception-image, a particular type of image in his taxonomy of images.[25] Examining the film *Creep* (2014), this chapter unpacks the premise of the so-called subjective camera of found footage and asks if the distinction between the subjective view of the character and the diegetic camera of these films is as clear as we would initially assume.

'Theory of mind' and 'embodied simulation theory' are two speculative propositions that are often used to explain an empathic engagement not only with the characters of the film, but with the image itself. In Chapter 5, 'Horrific Entwinement: Affective Neuroscience and the Body of the Horror Spectator', I critically contrast these theories and, through an analysis of *The Visit* (2015), argue that a more productive pathway may be found in rethinking the process of spectatorship through the affective neuroscience theory of the SEEKING system, proposed by neuroscientist Jaak Panksepp.

The development of horror narratives in the space of internet video and the modalities of the third and fourth screens of media theory – computers and tablets/smartphones – has had dramatic effects for the spectator. Chapter 6, 'What Hides Behind the Stream: Post-Cinematic Hauntings of the Digital', looks at the shifting nature of spectatorship in relation to these modalities.

Examining a variety of YouTube short horror videos that borrow the tropes of non-fiction, this chapter argues that this new mode of delivery appropriates many of the qualities of 'post-cinematic' media, clearly differentiating themselves in their form as an evolution from both conventional horror films and the subgenre of found footage horror films. In order to examine how these works alter our embodied relationship, I focus on their distinct synaesthetic and haptic qualities, and the 'aesthetics of distortion' which accentuate these qualities at both the visual and aural levels.

Chapter 7, 'The Evolving Screen Forms of New Media Horror', further develops the work of the previous chapter through a study of the YouTube found footage series *Marble Hornets*, to interrogate the differences between conventional found footage horror and post-cinematic works. It then turns to the film *Unfriended* (2014), which takes place entirely on a computer screen in the film's diegetic world, to unpack the effects of the blurring of boundaries in new delivery modalities.

Chapter 8, 'The Embodied Player of Horror Video Games', examines two experiential horror works by independent game designers Kitty Horrorshow and Connor Sherlock, *Anatomy* (2016) and *Marginalia* (2017). It argues that the aesthetics of each exemplar operates to produce a defined embodied experience for the player, one that is altered from the dynamics of cinema spectatorship but one that can be explained by drawing on similar foundational approaches. Finally, this chapter turns to the console and VR experience of the game *Alien: Isolation* (2014) to explore the expanded perceptual experience of virtual reality in the realm of horror gaming.

The final chapter addresses the burgeoning space of VR technology and those who are pioneering the integration of the cinematic form with the nascent potential of VR. This chapter, entitled 'The Spectator-Interactor of Virtual Reality Horror', asks what the potential ramifications are for the experience of horror spectatorship in this new realm, and how the redefinition of the cinematic 'frame' in VR opens up new understandings about our embodied relationship to sound and image. The chapter examines a variety of virtual reality horror projects, such as *The Black Mass Experience*, *Catatonic VR*, *Escape the Living Dead* and *11:57*. It also considers the implications of the new cinematic space for narrative and interactivity, and the phenomenological implications of the temporal and spatial capacities of virtual reality, particularly in relation to the production of cinematic dread. Virtual reality cinema also offers us a compelling site to examine the ideas about identification, empathy and embodied experience that are laid out over the preceding chapters, as the form itself demands that creatives reconceive the narrative processes that have been thought to be at the foundation of spectatorial engagement.

From found footage to cinematic virtual reality, these new domains of horror demonstrate that the somatic elements of experience are intensified in relation to a reduction in the semantic content. Given that the genre of horror largely relies upon this undermining or disruption of the viewer's processes of meaning-making, horror cinema scholarship can benefit from this examination of embodied experience as the bedrock of the viewer's engagement with the image.

Notes

1. Del Rio, 'Cinema's Exhaustion and the Vitality of Affect'.
2. McLuhan, *Understanding Media*, p. 66.
3. Brown, *Supercinema*, p. 8.
4. Denson and Leyda, 'Perspectives on Post-Cinema', p. 1.
5. Ibid. p. 1.
6. Denson, 'The Horror of Discorrelation'.
7. Ibid.
8. Skal, *The Monster Show*, p. 39.
9. Gregg and Seigworth, *The Affect Theory Reader*, pp. 8–9.
10. Ibid. pp. 8–9.
11. Massumi, *Parables for the Virtual*, pp. 23–45.
12. Ibid. p. 28.
13. Reyes, *Horror Film and Affect*, p. 2.
14. Ibid. p. 3.
15. Hanich, *Cinematic Emotion in Horror Films and Thrillers*.
16. Williams, 'Film Bodies', p. 3.
17. A growing body of work on stereoscopic 3D horror media may offer some productive links to the new media forms examined here; however, these connections remain outside of the scope of this book.
18. Deleuze, cited in Flaxman, *The Brain Is the Screen*, p. 3.
19. Sinnerbrink, 'Questioning Style', p. 43.
20. Deleuze, cited in Flaxman, *The Brain Is The Screen*, p. 366.
21. Protevi, *Life, War, Earth*, p. 102.
22. Based on videos that were accessible at the time of publication.
23. Jackson, *Technology, Monstrosity, and Reproduction in Twenty-First Century Horror*, p. 35.
24. For example, Hud, the camera operator in *Cloverfield* (2008), appears on screen for only a few minutes of the film's 85-minute run time.
25. Deleuze, *Cinema 1*, pp. 71–6.

CHAPTER ONE

From the Semantic to the Somatic: Affective Engagement with Horror Cinema

Horror cinema has a long history of affecting spectators in profound and often unsettling ways. Its impact is often catalysed in the way it produces a reluctant bodily response for a viewer. While an intellectual consideration of its content may shock and unnerve, there is also often a coincident corporeal action on the spectator; this sometimes emerges in involuntary somatic responses, such as the startle or the freeze, or the capacity to nauseate the viewer. But is this response truly coincident? Or is there something fundamental in the coalescence of our bodily experience of sound and image that requires that we reassess arguments regarding horror spectatorship that understand this somatic response as a simple parallel to semantic appraisal?

A range of scholarly approaches, many drawn from film scholarship more broadly, have been employed to attempt to fully comprehend and interrogate the intensity of the spectatorial experience of horror cinema. These frameworks have necessarily evolved over time: as the nature of the approach of horror films has changed, so too has the nature of the analysis required to understand it. A cornerstone text in the discourse of horror, Noël Carroll's *The Philosophy of Horror, or, Paradoxes of the Heart*, attempts to articulate the underlying premises of horror through a philosophical investigation into horror's paradoxical appeal. This seminal treatise on horror's genesis, function and capacities underpins many early theoretical approaches to the genre. In the work, Carroll first separates 'art-horror' from horror, specifying the latter as the outcome of real-world effects. His 'art-horror' requires that an audience evaluate the central monster for two particular components: its potential threat and its impurity. Carroll contends that if either element is missing, the evaluation will be incomplete; a monster without impurity generates only fear, whereas a monster without threat produces only disgust.[1]

Building upon Mary Douglas's classic study, *Purity and Danger*, Carroll infers that the impurity present in horror emerges from what Douglas defined as 'the transgression or violation of schemes of cultural categorisation'.[2] In Carroll's terms, horror as a genre does not only require a 'monster', be it the literal titular monster of MGM's horror classics, such as Dracula or the Wolfman, or the faceless, nameless monster of creature films such as *Slither*

(2006); in his understanding, beings or creatures only fully become monsters when they are defined as 'categorically interstitial, categorically contradictory, incomplete or formless'.[3]

The presence of these monsters is, for Carroll, the intellectual hook which draws in a spectator: he claims that horror narrative works 'because it has at the center of it something which is given as in principle *unknowable*'.[4] Deploying Hobbes's contention that curiosity is the 'appetite' of the mind, horror fiction is presented as an intellectual desire for the process of discovery, revelation and ratiocination of the 'putatively unknowable'.[5] Disgust is affiliated with disclosure of the impure: this impurity manifests through monsters that are 'categorically interstitial' (half-man, half-fly, for example), 'categorically contradictory' (alive and dead, as in the vampire or zombie), 'incomplete' (a severed hand acting on its own, for example), or 'formless' (such as ghosts or demons). In this understanding, the experience of horror relies on a concerted cognitive evaluation of the horrific content by the viewer.[6]

COGNITIVIST FRAMEWORKS OF SPECTATORSHIP

This concept of the monster as an intellectual 'hook', when applied to cinema, frames the viewer's primary experience with the horror film as one of comprehension of the semantic content of the image. It is unsurprising that Carroll's consideration of how horror works aligns with his broader understanding of cinema spectatorship as a process whereby viewers primarily decode filmic images as representations. Carroll is a key proponent of the cognitivist branch of film theory that arose in the latter half of the twentieth century and is exemplified in his work, along with scholars David Bordwell, Murray Smith, Greg Currie, Carl Plantinga, and others.

The cognitivist approach involves an attempt to counter the positing of 'unconscious desires' at the heart of the viewing experience with understandings of perception and cognition that could be framed and tested with empirical hypotheses. This approach identifies horror film as a genre that is dependent on a specific consideration of the monster's transgressive qualities by the spectator: an act of decoding and appraisal.[7] In his work with William Seeley, Carroll argues that filmmakers 'direct us to perceptually categorize an object or event', leading to an 'intended emotion' in the viewer.[8] For horror film, he identifies two crucial aspects:

> First, local narrative and visual cues are used to categorize the behaviour of a character as unnatural, and thereby disgusting. Second, global narrative cues are used to generate the long-term expectation that a negative outcome is highly probable, and likely inevitable, for the protagonist. The result is an intermingling of hopelessness, fear and revulsion that we delight in experiencing at the movies.[9]

Cognitivist film theory looks to examine the experience of film through an analytical frame that applies analogous real-world cognitive procedures and relies on rigorous 'logical reflection' and 'empirical research' to account for film spectatorship as a process.[10] Bordwell and Carroll prefer to categorise cognitivism not as a theory but as a mode which 'seeks to understand human thought, emotion and action by appeal to processes of mental representation, naturalistic processes, and (some sense) of rational agency'.[11] Countering the approaches to horror made by scholars such as Julia Kristeva, Barbara Creed and Robin Wood, among others, a cognitivist understanding does not outright reject the practicality of applying psychoanalytical theory to film study, but instead limits its usefulness to the aspects of films that are irrational; as Bordwell asserts, there is 'no reason to claim for the unconscious any activities which can be explained on other grounds'.[12]

Cognitivist theory relies on what Bordwell calls the 'contingent universals' of viewers: in other words, the 'hard-wired' physiological and cognitive systems of all human beings.[13] Cognitivist frameworks suggest that the principal process in the act of spectatorship is the viewer's use of 'narrative schema' to build a dynamic cognitive model of the events of the film as they unfold, a model that adapts and adjusts with the presentation of further novel information through the film's choice of shots and sequences.

Theories that draw conceptual links between the filmic image and thought have historical antecedents as far back as the inception of the cinematographic device. From the very advent of cinema there arose philosophical concerns regarding how the filmic image works on its subject. Hugo Münsterberg instigated the study into the connection between mental processes and cinema in his 1916 book, *The Photoplay: A Psychological Study*, which provided the foundations for what we refer to currently as spectator theory and narrative theory. Münsterberg argued that film's effectiveness was the result of its ability to mimic psychological processes, and that it required the mental cooperation of the spectator in order to achieve its full potential.[14] He proposed that film is particularly adept at expressing the consciousness of fictional characters when the cinematic devices used to do so are analogous to 'the mechanisms of the mind'. Comparisons could be drawn, for example, between the close-up and our acts of attention outside of the film, the flashback and our processes of memory, and the flash-forward and our facility to imagine or hypothesise. These then novel devices became, in Münsterberg's account, metaphors for synchronising the thought process of a character with intrinsic human thought processes.[15]

Münsterberg's foundational research into questions of cognitive engagement is still very much at the heart of some contemporary theories that attempt to explain how a viewer processes a film. Carl Plantinga, for example, sees the 'narrative information' of the film as the key driver of audience emotional response.[16] Likewise, Todd Berliner utilises Bordwell to argue that the central component of the aesthetic pleasure of film is storytelling: 'the process by which an artwork selects, arranges and renders its narrative information in order to stimulate the perceiver to perform cognitive activities'.[17] In this understanding it is cognition that is the inevitable terminus into which our cinematic experience is channelled. This rationale is supported by Steven Pinker, who argues that the true act of artistry is the creation of 'human mental representations' or the 'cascade of neural events that begin with the sense organs and culminate in thoughts, emotions, and memories'.[18]

Carroll argues that film is uniquely equipped to elicit this cognitive activity, due to the 'pictorial recognition' that underlies its form, a universal 'biological capability' that all humans use to recognise objects and events.[19] He contends that the conventions of classical Hollywood cinema utilise narrative, editing and framing to harness a viewer's attention, particularly in the manner in which the shots, scenes or events of the film raise questions or answer them: this he calls the 'erotetic model' of narrative.[20] This approach, however, raises the question of how cognitivist models account for the affective power of film. Within the typical cognitivist model, affect is elicited by the sound and image and is simultaneously cognitively processed. Plantinga, for example, proposes a typology of affect that separates it into three forms: 'moods', 'emotions' and 'various automatic body responses'.[21] Moods are considered as 'diffuse' forms of emotions, with 'causes but not reasons'. Emotion, for Plantinga, is typically a 'concern-based construal': something that occurs when we make an appraisal of a situation based on our own concerns.[22] Plantinga argues that our investment in the narrative leads to our desire for various outcomes. For instance, when we construe that a character is in jeopardy, the emotion elicited is fear; when we construe that the character has escaped jeopardy, the emotion elicited is relief or happiness. The important distinction to make here is that emotion, in the cognitivist framework, is the outcome of thought. Regarding the 'automatic body responses', Plantinga largely equates these to 'baseline affective charges' that arise from a viewer's pre-reflective response to movements, sounds, colours and textures; he uses the example of a physiological reflex action, like the startle effect, which occurs from the sudden appearance of visual stimuli.[23]

While Plantinga acknowledges that affect and cognition generally 'work together in a holistic and mutually dependent interplay', he also asserts that a viewer's cognitive activity 'may sometimes run independent of affective experience', and it is evident that he locates affect in a hierarchical relationship to cognition, where affect, outside of 'automatic body responses', is inevitably channelled into mood or emotion through cognition.[24] He writes, for example, of how the elicitation of emotion typically comes about through a viewer's identification with the characters or events of the filmic narrative. Torben Grodal describes this process as 'a viewer-activation of affects and emotions in identification with the interests of a fictive being'.[25] This notion argues that cinema produces a 'prolonged cognitive identification', of which empathic engagement will be a result.[26] Ultimately, under this broad conception, our engagement with the film is primarily a result of the film/filmmaker manipulating the spectator's 'emotional trajectory' through cinema's capacity to 'elicit sympathies, antipathies, allegiances, and other responses to fictional characters'.[27] Various scholars have contributed to this model in different ways: Smith in relation to recognition, alliance and allegiance; Currie in relation to simulation; and Carroll in terms of narration and point of view.[28] Plantinga extends these theories into a more pluralist approach, attempting to integrate the perceptual, cognitive, intentional and embodied responses of the viewer. However, while acknowledging cinema's affective power, his emphasis remains on the role of cognition in how we process the image.

Plantinga contends that the viewer is never so deluded as to believe what they are seeing is real, and draws on Smith's term 'twofoldedness' to explain the dual response of a spectator's appraisal of cinema characters as both 'real' (which Plantinga equates to having desires, goals and emotions that are equivalent to those of real people) and 'fictional constructs'.[29] Our experience of viewing, he argues, 'is always tempered by a background awareness of the fictional and conventional nature of the movie-going experience'.[30] Plantinga may be correct in asserting that we do not respond to cinematic events such as an alien invasion in the same manner we would in real life by, for example, fleeing the cinema. However, to assert that the movie-going experience is always 'tempered' in such a way leaves no space for the experiences of spectatorship that are affectively intense in ways that seem to exceed this delineation.

While accounts such as those discussed above do, in part, explain the cognitive pleasures experienced by spectators of horror film, and highlight an important dimension of the appeal of horror, the cognitive approach cannot encompass all dimensions of spectatorship, and ignores an element that is vital to the experience of cinema: the pre-cognitive, affective power of film in the 'lived-body' experience of the spectator. In Plantinga's conceptual model, the pre-cognitive aspects of affect are limited to automatic bodily responses to sensory stimuli. Through the processes of cognition, affect is codified into mood or emotion based on the viewer's understanding of the representational content of the film.

This model is inadequate to fully account for instances when, in the moment of cinematic experience, our affective response exceeds or contradicts that which our semantic understanding of the image presents. Anna

Powell speaks to this when she argues that 'film theory [that] treats images as static, symbolic components of underlying representational structures [...] abstracts them from their moving, changing medium'.[31] Drawing on Deleuzian theory, she argues that film's 'affective power' is something which 'exceeds the symbolic properties of both language and image'.[32] Filmic affect 'vibrates intensively rather than extensively' and it stimulates a kind of thought that moves towards 'non-symbolic ideation', something more akin to Bergsonian 'intuition' (emerging from the philosophical work of Henri Bergson).[33] This accords with the understanding advanced by Steven Shaviro, who argues against the overemphasised bodily detachment of an engagement with film's representational elements by citing the cinematic event as a location of 'affect, excitation, stimulation and repression, pleasure and pain, shock and habit'.[34]

Acknowledging cinema's capacity to generate affect that may exceed the spectator's cognitive appraisal of the image requires an interrogation of an understanding of cognition and affect outside of a hierarchical model. If we constrain our understanding of the appeal of horror film to the potential of a sharply defined central monster, or a narrative drive to know the unknowable, we neglect to consider that cinema has effects that go beyond intellectual evaluation of potential threat and impurity, and we disregard the full dimensions of the experiential moment of spectatorship, and how it is the somatic components of the film–viewer relation that play a pivotal role in how we experience this excess.

Towards the Somatic

By reframing the study of horror cinema spectatorship towards an emphasis on the somatic relationship between film and viewer, rather than the semantic components of the image, we can open up ways of thinking through how cinema works, as Powell argues, to '[bypass] the cognitive and reflective faculties [of the viewer]'.[35] This is a conception of spectatorship akin to that proposed by Shaviro: 'cinema [as] a kind of non-representational contact, dangerously mimetic and corrosive, thrusting us into the mysterious life of the body'.[36]

The visceral nature of horror undeniably brings our bodily response to the fore – the word horror, from an etymological perspective, is derived from the Latin *horrere*, which means to shudder or bristle – but, crucially, this response should not be comprehended simply as a reaction to cognitive appraisal of the monster or the horrifying situation: it is also a pre-cognitive feedback to horror's sensory intensification, in which the senses can no longer be considered entirely discrete. Redirecting our understanding of the primacy of this experience occurring through sensory intensification challenges existing theories that attempt to comprehend the viewing experience in terms of 'top-down processing', where the structures of perception and cognition simply codify sensory intensification into cognitive appraisal. These structures place the body as secondary to cognition in our understanding of the film viewing event. This understanding potentially abrogates the capacity for bodily responses that run counter to cognitive conceptualisation.

The top-down processing model not only places cognition and corporeal response in a hierarchical binary, but it also conceives of the experience of spectatorship in terms of a strict delineation between film and viewer: on one side is a specific combination of sounds and images representing a monster or monstrous situation, arranged in such a way as to provoke and sustain audience attention and elicit this emotional response, and on the other side is the receptive viewer, whose perceptual processes result in an ongoing cognitive appraisal of these sounds and images, transforming this representation into the intended comprehension. However, horror as a genre continually reminds us of the impossibility of hermetic distinction, between film/viewer, true/false, inside/outside, self/other, and the untenable nature of each of these binaries within the heterogeneity of both the filmic world and the lived world. Much like the lived world, within the filmic world the boundaries between these entities are constantly under negotiation, which leads to supposedly singular entities, like the body, being susceptible to transformations and reconfigurations.[37] Acknowledging this process of negotiation in the act of spectatorship is important, as it destabilises the subject–object dichotomy which underlies some of the existing theoretical frameworks that examine the effects of horror on the viewer (for example, those theories that focus primarily on the representational aspects of the monster).

Reframing the primary interface between viewer and image to that of the spectator's pre-cognitive, affective, corporeal engagement allows us to understand how horror may produce experiences that contradict or undermine our evaluative cognitive processes. This conception of affect, drawn from the work of Brian Massumi, differs from that posited by Plantinga: Massumi argues for an understanding of affect in the Spinozist sense, as the body's capacities for affecting or being affected. Massumi defines affective engagement as the 'passing of a threshold, seen from the point of view of [this] change in capacity'.[38] He goes on to clarify:

> A body's ability to affect or be affected – its charge of affect – isn't something fixed [. . .] [D]epending on the circumstances, it goes up and down gently like a tide, or maybe storms and crests like a wave, or at times simply bottoms out. It's because this is all attached to the movements of the body that it can't be reduced to emotion. It's not just subjective, which is not to say that there is nothing subjective about it. Spinoza says that every transition is accompanied by a feeling of the change in capacity. The affect and the feeling of the transition are not two different things. They're two sides of the same coin.[39]

In *Parables for the Virtual*, Massumi argues for a framework of affective primacy by drawing on the research into psychological and physiological responses to the so-called emotional content of images.[40] Massumi contends that the event of image reception is 'multi-levelled' and that at least two of those levels consist of, separately, the semantic content of the image and its intensity. As he explains, 'the strength or duration of an image's effect is not logically connected to the content in any straightforward way'.[41] Content and intensity are non-correspondent, but can have relations of 'resonation or interference, amplification or dampening'.[42] Importantly, Massumi's concept of emotion is separate from affect: emotion, in his comprehension, is 'the socio-linguistic fixing of the quality of an experience'; or 'intensity owned and recognised'.[43] However, prior to this semantic codification, there is a pre-reflexive bodily intensity that is unassimilable to language. This intensity, which Massumi defines as affect, opens up the potential for relational responses to the image that resist clear demarcation into codified meaning. These responses would run counter to those proposed by a cognitivist understanding of how we process a film.

Massumi's concept of affect returns the body to a central position in our understanding of how we experience images. Here corporeal experience becomes more than merely an 'add-on' to our cognition of the image and its meaning: it is instead at the very basis of it. Shaviro builds on Massumi's work in his conception of 'post-cinematic' affect. I will return to this notion of the 'post-cinematic' in later chapters; however, here I want to note that, of the distinction between emotion and affect, Shaviro, drawing on Massumi, argues that 'behind every emotion, there is always a certain surplus of affect that "escapes confinement" and "remains unactualised, inseparable from but unassimilable to any *particular*, functionally anchored perspective"'.[44] Shaviro adds an acknowledgement of the inevitable proposition of this surplus remaining outside of cognition: '[o]ur existence is always bound up with the affective and aesthetic flows that elude cognitive definition or capture.'[45]

Eugenie Brinkema concurs with this understanding of affect's capacity to elude cognition, writing that affect

> disrupt[s], interrupt[s], reinsert[s], demand[s], provoke[s], insist[s] on, remind[s] of, agitate[s] for: the body, sensation, movement, flesh and skin and nerves, the visceral, stressing pains, feral frenzies, always rubbing against: what undoes, what unsettles, that thing I cannot name, what remains resistant, far away (haunting, and ever so beautiful); indefinable, it is said to be what cannot be written, what thaws the critical cold, messing all systems and subjects up.[46]

There are productive links here to a Deleuzian concept of affect and its production through cinema. In her explication of 'the aesthetics of affect' in relation to horror cinema, Powell unpacks the Bergsonian foundations of Deleuzian affect. She writes that, '[f]or Bergson, all perceptions are prolonged into movement, and movement is the key to understanding perception. He locates affect in those bodily sensations and physical symptoms by which we evaluate the intensity of stimuli.'[47] This link between movement and perception underpins the Deleuzian movement-image, which is composed of three varieties: perception-image, action-image and affection-image.[48] The movement-image, importantly, is not conceptually bound to the cinema screen; as Powell notes, it 'occurs both on screen and in us at the same time, and actually blurs any such distinction between inside and out'.[49]

Bergson's consideration of sensation, as an evaluation of intensity, is vital to the workings of Deleuze's affection-images. As well as carrying representational meaning, images operate as material forces that contain shades of colour, intensities of light and timbres of sound. Each of these stylistic components has an affective gradation. These elements of the image interact at both a micro level between themselves and at a macro level with the broader aspects of the film, and the gradations of intensity they contain is at the root of the complexity of affect. The flux of these gradations contributes to the manner in which affect, to some degree, resists codification. Powell explains this concept by returning to Bergson; she elucidates how Bergson 'locates intensity at the junction between "the idea of extensive magnitude from without" and "the image of an inner multiplicity" that arises from "the very depths of consciousness." Such multiplicity exists in complex intensive layers that constantly interweave.'[50] Powell then clarifies how this multiplicity becomes overthrown by language when we attempt to communicate experience: 'the complexity of these shifting qualitative sensations is difficult to quantify, because their milieu *is* quality itself, not quantity'.[51] This is adequately captured in the way Bergson describes the experience of the shift in sensations: 'we feel a thousand different elements which dissolve into and permeate one another without any precise outlines, without the least tendency to externalise themselves in relation to one another; hence their originality'.[52]

This concept of affect's relation to perception and sensation has, for Deleuze, a cinematic equivalent. The example he provides is from G. W. Pabst's *Pandora's Box* (1929):

> There are Lulu, the lamp, the bread-knife, Jack the Ripper: people who are assumed to be real with individual characters and social roles, objects with uses, real connections between these objects and these people – in short, a whole actual state of things. But there are also the brightness of the light on the knife, the blade of the knife under the light, Jack's terror and resignation, Lulu's compassionate look. These are pure singular qualities or potentialities.[53]

For Deleuze, these 'potentialities' are singularities, which, when placed in 'virtual conjunction' then 'constitute a complex entity'.[54] He describes them as 'like points of melting, of boiling, of condensation, of coagulation'.[55] Powell expands on this, describing affection as being in 'dynamic motion', something which 'surges in the subjective centre of indetermination, between a troubling perception and a hesitant action'.[56] These conceptions of affect, like Massumi's, are less about the demarcation of states of being and more about the relations that occur in the interval between them. Both Bergson and Deleuze understood human perception as the integration of our movement through broader vibrations of matter with our neuronal processes. This concept sees the body/brain as embedded in the flow of images that constitute the universe. Recent developments in neuroscience both support this and contest a cognitivist approach that hierarchises mind and body. These developments, emerging from the work of neuroscientists such as Alva Noë, Antonio Damasio, Andy Clark, and Francisco Varela, Evan Thompson and Eleanor Rosch, posit an 'enactive' theory of perception, which contends that perception necessarily involves the interaction between the activity of a body and its environment.[57] As Noë states in his book, *Action in Perception*:

> Perception is not something that happens to us, or in us. It is something we do. Think of a blind person tap-tapping his or her way around a cluttered space, perceiving that space by touch, not all at once, but through time, by skilful probing and movement. This is, or at least ought to be, our paradigm of what perceiving is. The world makes itself available to the perceiver through physical movement and interaction [. . .] [A]ll perception is touch-like in this way: Perceptual experience acquires content thanks to our possession of bodily skills. What we perceive is determined by what we do (or what we know how to do); it is determined by what we are ready to do [. . .] [W]e enact our perceptual experience; we act it out.[58]

While cognitivist theory does not completely elide the body in its understandings of the cinema experience, it does to a degree bracket the bodily experience as secondary. However, the enactive theory of perception argues that this is a flawed notion, in that all cognition arises from the interaction between body and environment. Shaun Gallagher and Dan Zahavi, for instance, note that 'perception is not a passive intake of information. Perception involves activity—for instance, the movement of our body.'[59]

This conception replaces cognition with the concept of the embodied mind. It argues that our bodies and our consciousness are inexorably entwined and always present in/with the world around us. As Gallagher and Zahavi stress, '[c]ognition is not only embodied, it is situated and, of course, it is situated because it is embodied.'[60] This means that there is no 'objective' or detached position from which consciousness observes the world, but rather consciousness emerges from the relation of the body–brain as a singular entity and the world it exists in. This is a stance that aligns closely with a phenomenological approach to film analysis.

Phenomenological accounts do not consider the body as one object among others: rather, the body is regarded as a constitutive principle, vital to the very possibility of experience, and implicated profoundly in mind–world relation.[61] The phenomenological model presents a direct challenge to the notions of a stable and unchanging cinematic subjectivity. Jenny Chamarette concurs, arguing for a model that allows for the dynamics and fluctuations of the cinematic encounter, when she writes:

> [I]f the mind is not the site of consciousness, but rather consciousness unfolds through an intertwining of mind, body and world, then bodies and bodily responses, such as sensation, are also involved in processes of experience. This reasserts the significance of the senses to the cinematic encounter – that notions of embodiment and the sensory permeate and interpenetrate the bodies of the film, the spectator and the screen. In short, embodiment and sensory theories of film are a means of thinking the cinematic with relation to slippery, unfixed subjectivity.[62]

This 'slippery, unfixed subjectivity' recurs throughout horror works, and demands conceptual models that can unpack and explain the spectatorial experience in light of this.

THE PHENOMENOLOGY OF HORROR

Returning to horror scholarship, a phenomenological model is central to the work of scholar Julian Hanich, whose argument for both the paradoxical pleasure of horror and the techniques by which it achieves its power on the experiential level are more persuasive than cognitivist accounts. Hanich posits a phenomenological entanglement between film and viewer that is specifically charged by the five modes of cinematic fear he postulates: direct horror, suggested horror, cinematic shock, cinematic dread and cinematic terror.[63] Each of these modes operates in a unique way, but all of them rely on the dynamic entwinement of film-as-aesthetic-object and viewer-as-experiencing-subject. Although this entwinement fluctuates in every unique experience of spectatorship, Hanich contends that horror films manipulate this engagement, and that the fear produced can bring about gradual or sudden transformation of ourselves and our relation to the world around us. He identifies the origins of this breach in a contracted focus of attention that

> comes with a phenomenological (not geographical!) closeness of the intentional object that seems to press in on us and that we wish to flee.[64] At the same time, the lived-body is experienced differently; we literally feel it foregrounded in a specific way.[65]

Phenomenology, and more specifically the existential form of phenomenology drawn from the work of Maurice Merleau-Ponty, reframes the processes of perception in a manner that requires that we necessarily interrogate the distinction between film-as-object and viewer-as-subject. A phenomenological framework can offer valuable insight into the experience of spectatorship, because it not only provides us with certain methods that may question this dualistic dichotomy, as Chamarette argues, but also allows us to, as she suggests, cleave a 'middle way' between subjectivism (reality constructed through the subject) and empirical objectivism (artefact as stable object-of-enquiry).[66] From a phenomenological perspective, we cannot conceptualise the act of spectatorship as simply the outcome of a thinking subject or the empirical qualities of the object being watched: there is, as Vivian Sobchack stresses, always a 'dialogue' in the 'dialectic of perception' that is shared between film and viewer.[67] The 'act of viewing' that the film performs, as an object, merges with the viewing activity of the spectator in an operation of reciprocity.

One explanation for why film theory has long wrestled with this notion of 'subjects' and 'objects' is the ephemerality of the experience of film watching. As David Rodowick notes, whereas the 'reassuring ontological stability' of painting, sculptures or books within modern aesthetic theory is self-evident, this stability is often in question within cinema studies, despite the 'apparent solidity of the celluloid strip' and the 'continuities in the experience of watching projected motion pictures'.[68] This anxiety regarding cinema's aesthetic value he attributes to its hybrid nature as 'an art of space *and* an art of time'; cinema's temporal aspect highlights its immateriality.[69]

Phenomenological accounts of cinema, such as that advanced by Chamarette, recognise that films are not only 'objects of and for interpretation', but they are also 'objects and moments of experience'.[70] This approach draws attention to film's status as a perceptual object and its direct sensory-affective features. As Daniel Yacavone points out, phenomenological accounts no longer reside at the margins of film theory, but are close to its centre, mainly due to the way these explanations, while recognising films as 'cognitive, narrative or cultural-ideological [objects]', also offer us a way of interpreting the *experience* of film.[71] Through the description of the phenomena of lived experience provided by a phenomenological account, we can more fully understand the spectatorial experience of a stable and unchanging aesthetic work. Simon Glendinning describes the approach of phenomenological theory as the work of 'elucidation, explication or description of something we, in some way, already understand, or with which we are already, in some way, familiar, but which, for some reason, we cannot get into clear focus for ourselves without more ado': it is 'description' and not simply 'explanation or analysis'.[72] However, in revealing what is often obscured by institutionalisation and habituation, the description involved in a phenomenological account can produce new insights about the experience of spectatorship, revelations that are commonly unnoticed as our awareness is primarily focused on the filmic world and not necessarily the lived body.

A phenomenological approach reframes our experience of the world, self and others through embodiment, while also interrogating some of the earliest Cartesian distinctions that defined the mind–body concept. Edmund Husserl, for example, differentiated the objective body, *Körper*, from the lived body, *Leib*, as a method of explicating the two different ways we can experience and understand the body.[73] This distinction is of a phenomenological kind, rather than an ontological one. The crucial point made by this differentiation is that any account of the body from an observer's point of view, as something that can be analysed and dissected objectively, ignores the reality that the only way we can make such observations (or any observation) is through an experiencing, lived body. Gallagher and Zahavi, drawing on Husserl, expand on this concept:

> The body is not a screen between me and the world; rather, it shapes our primary way of being-in-the-world. This is also why we cannot first explore the body by itself and then subsequently examine it in its relation to the world. On the contrary, the body is already in-the-world, and the world is given to us as bodily revealed.[74]

Our sense of our body is ultimately in what it accomplishes for us: its actions and perceptions. This includes tacit awareness of our position in space in relation to other objects or bodies, but also attunement with mood and feeling that manifests as something that is felt bodily. These aspects of embodiment also shape our perception of the world. If I feel claustrophobic, the world itself feels claustrophobic: this comes about through the way my lived body is in constant contact with the world through the embodied self as the grounds of perception. Unlike Husserl's concept of *Körper*, which conceives of the body's contact with the world as a distinction of surface of skin to surface of world, the lived body is in rapport with the world in a way that constantly makes new meaning through the body itself; the dynamics of perception necessarily alters each side of this dualistic consideration of body/world in the moment of experience.

The cognitivist approach advanced by theorists such as Bordwell and Carroll to understanding how we process images inserts a hierarchical structure into the model of the lived body. In this model, while there are various automatic bodily responses to sensory input, it is cognition which restructures all sensory data into models of meaning. For example, Carroll and Seeley propose that

> affective responses in general, and emotional responses in particular, are evolved means for appraising the behavioral significance of environmental stimuli. We can think of our affective responses to the environment as being divided into two types: involuntary, automatic reflexive responses like the startle response, and more cognitively nuanced emotional responses.[75]

These approaches cannot account for the way in which affective responses may be in excess of, or antithetical to, our means of appraisal or evaluation. Yet it is these kinds of affective responses that are crucial to the power of horror film, and also cinema itself more generally. A large body of work has emerged in cinema theory to address this disparity and systematically challenge the model of cinema spectatorship as primarily a process of cognitive assessment: this collection of interrelated scholarship investigates spectatorship as necessarily 'embodied'.[76]

Embodied spectatorship theory synthesises our understandings of film viewing through this notion of the lived body. Thinking about the lived body is central to the phenomenological project, and its consideration of material presence, perception and sensory engagement informs many of the approaches within this book. The phenomenological approach is also significant in relation to an examination of the reinscription of cinematic possibilities into the new forms and technologies, given their potential to alter the lived-body experience. Vivian Sobchack, drawing on Merleau-Ponty's conceptual approach, frames the importance of phenomenology in relation to new technologies, when she writes of how the

> relatively novel [. . .] materialities of human communication, photographic, cinematic, and electronic media [. . .] have not only historically *symbolized* but also historically *constituted* a radical alteration of the forms of our culture's previous temporal and spatial consciousness and of our bodily sense of existential 'presence' to the world, to ourselves, and to others.[77]

These alterations of temporal and spatial consciousness and of our bodily sense of 'presence' become apparent to us when we hone our description of the cinematic experience in relation to the lived body. What is evident, however, is that the phenomenological approach has been disregarded by some aspects of horror scholarship, which have focused more fully on the representational or hermeneutic dimensions of horror texts. In the following chapter I shall look to how our comprehension of the cinematic experience can be more fully 'fleshed out' by integrating embodied spectatorship theory with all the aspects that contribute to the moment of viewing: the viewer's cognitive assessment, their physiological response, their emotional state, the environmental factors (including those with whom they may be sharing the experience), and the phenomenological presence that manifests in the experience of spectatorship.

Notes

1. Carroll, *The Philosophy of Horror*, p. 28.
2. Ibid. p. 31.
3. Ibid. p. 32.
4. Ibid. p. 182.
5. Ibid. p. 184.
6. Ibid. p. 32.
7. Ibid. p. 28.
8. Carroll and Seeley, 'Cognitivism, Psychology, and Neuroscience', p. 68.
9. Ibid. p. 69.
10. Bordwell and Carroll, *Post-Theory*, p. xiv.
11. Ibid. p. xvi.
12. Bordwell, *Narration in the Fiction Film*, p. 30.
13. Bordwell, 'Convention, Construction, and Cinematic Vision', p. 91.
14. Münsterberg, *The Photoplay*, p. 44.
15. Moure, 'The Cinema as Art of the Mind', p. 24.
16. Plantinga, 'The Affective Power of Movies', p. 106.
17. Bordwell, *Narration in the Fiction Film*, p. xi, cited in Berliner, 'Hollywood Storytelling and Aesthetic Pleasure', p. 195.
18. Pinker, *The Blank Slate*, p. 417.
19. Carroll, 'The Power of Movies', p. 84.
20. Carroll, *Theorizing the Moving Image*, p. 98; 'erotetic' meaning pertaining to questions.
21. Plantinga, 'The Affective Power of Movies', p. 95.
22. Plantinga, *Moving Viewers*, p. 57.
23. Plantinga, 'The Affective Power of Movies', p. 102.
24. Ibid. p. 95.
25. Grodal, *Moving Pictures*, p. 93.

26. Ibid. p. 93.
27. Plantinga, 'The Affective Power of Movies', p. 104.
28. Smith, *Engaging Characters*; Currie, *Image and Mind*; Carroll, *Theorizing the Moving Image*.
29. Smith, 'On the Twofoldedness of Character', cited in Plantinga, 'The Affective Power of Movies', p. 98.
30. Plantinga, 'The Affective Power of Movies', p. 98.
31. Powell, *Deleuze and Horror Film*, p. 10.
32. Ibid. p. 10.
33. Ibid. pp. 11–12.
34. Shaviro, *The Cinematic Body*, p. 27.
35. Powell, *Deleuze and Horror Film*, p. 22.
36. Shaviro, *The Cinematic Body*, p. 258.
37. Representations of this possibility, in films such as *The Exorcist* (1973), bring to light the fallacy of these binaries.
38. Massumi, *Politics of Affect*, pp. 3–4.
39. Ibid. p. 4.
40. Massumi, *Parables for the Virtual*, pp. 23–46.
41. Ibid. p. 24.
42. Ibid. p. 24.
43. Ibid. p. 28.
44. Shaviro, 'Post-Cinematic Affect', p. 4, citing Massumi, *Parables for the Virtual*, p. 35; original emphasis.
45. Shaviro, 'Post-Cinematic Affect', p. 5.
46. Brinkema, *The Forms of the Affects*, p. xii; original italics.
47. Powell, *Deleuze and Horror Film*, p. 110.
48. Deleuze, *Cinema 1*, pp. 61–6.
49. Powell, *Deleuze and Horror Film*, p. 111.
50. Ibid. p. 111.
51. Ibid. p. 111.
52. Bergson, *Time and Free Will*, p. 132.
53. Deleuze, *Cinema 1*, p. 102.
54. Ibid. p. 103.
55. Ibid. p. 103.
56. Powell, *Deleuze and Horror Film*, p. 118.
57. See for example Clark, *Being There*; Gallagher, *How the Body Shapes the Mind*; Varela et al., *The Embodied Mind*.
58. Noë, *Action in Perception*, p. 1.
59. Gallagher and Zahavi, *The Phenomenological Mind*, p. 109.
60. Ibid. p. 150.
61. Ibid. pp. 147–70.
62. Chamarette, *Phenomenology and the Future of Film*, p. 63.
63. Hanich, *Cinematic Emotion in Horror Films and Thrillers*, pp. 18–24.
64. 'Intentional object' is a term related to mental phenomena, and is taken from the work of Franz Brentano in *Psychology from an Empirical Standpoint*. It refers to

the directed-ness of consciousness: that in the act of perceiving, feeling or thinking, our mental state is always 'about' or 'of' something.
65. Hanich, *Cinematic Emotion in Horror Films and Thrillers*, p. 22.
66. Chamarette, *Phenomenology and the Future of Film*, p. 53.
67. Sobchack, *The Address of the Eye*, p. 141.
68. Rodowick, *The Virtual Life of Film*, p. 13.
69. Ibid. p. 14; original emphasis.
70. Chamarette, *Phenomenology and the Future of Film*, p. 3.
71. Yacavone, 'Film and the Phenomenology of Art', p. 159.
72. Glendinning, *In the Name of Phenomenology*, p. 17.
73. Husserl, *Zur Phänomenologie der Intersubjektivität II*, p. 57.
74. Gallagher and Zahavi, *The Phenomenological Mind*, p. 155.
75. Carroll and Seeley, 'Cognitivism, Psychology, and Neuroscience', p. 67.
76. Among these scholars: Barker, *The Tactile Eye*; Elsaesser and Hagener, *Film Theory*; Marks, *The Skin of the Film*; Sobchack, *The Address of the Eye*; Shaviro, *The Cinematic Body*; Rutherford, *What Makes A Film Tick?* Chapter 2 examines these varied conceptual frames around embodiment in greater detail.
77. Sobchack, *Carnal Thoughts*, p. 136; original emphasis.

CHAPTER TWO

From Identification to Embodied Spectatorship in the Found Footage Horror Film

To Look (or Not to Look)

In a darkened room I lie awake, watching the digital numerals of the bedside clock taunt me as they flip past 12:00, a new day announcing its presence far too early. Unable to sleep, I turn to what has now become for many a habitual reaction to insomnia: staring into the digital abyss of an iPhone.

Bored with social media, I load up the application called CamViewer, a remote viewing program that is connected to my home security cameras. I scroll through each of the exterior views. In the neon green glow of the night vision, the tree branches tremble softly in the night air. I switch to the interior view: our front door, and the alcove where the dogs sleep at night. The two golden retrievers are in their beds, mocking me with their blissful slumber. Using the buttons on the screen, I turn the camera 360 degrees. The sleeping dogs remain still, unaware of the electronic eye watching them.

The silence is abruptly broken by a noise coming from outside my bedroom: a heavy thud. One of the dogs is still sleeping. The other is not. He's now standing at attention, rigid, looking into the guest bedroom adjacent to the entrance. His tail is raised, signalling focused attention, if not danger. I can see only the doorway to this bedroom, but no further. Whatever has caught his attention is unknown, unseen. Out-of-frame.

I strain to hear, my body taut like a piano string, the slightest new sensation promising a discordant reaction. Was that a shifting of weight? The creak of the floor boards? An ineffable sense tells me someone – something – is in that room. But why isn't Bentley barking? Why is he so still?

In the glow of the electronic screen, I watch the empty doorway, and hold my breath.

Technologies of Perception in Horror Film

The small tale that prefaces this chapter highlights some of the elements that have drawn me to explore the field of new forms of cinematic horror: the pervasive presence of cameras, our need to watch and/or record, and the capacity of the actual (or even virtual) image to produce affective bodily responses. It is this emerging relationship between technologies of perception and expression, such as cameras and screens, and the genre of horror that generates novel forms of cinema, the apogee of which can be found in the subgenre of found footage horror.

Given that horror cinema as a genre has always been a site of radical fluctuations in phenomenological presence, it is understandable that newer forms of audio-visual technology have produced modifications in experience that have perhaps been overlooked, or have been mistaken for the pre-existing correspondences between various forms of horror and the concomitant bodily experience. At the core of this and subsequent chapters are the following questions: how is the diegetic interface between horror and the technologies of cameras and screens producing an innovative experience of horror spectatorship? What is it that the aesthetic choices of the subgenre of found footage horror enable that the conventions of older genres of horror do not? By examining these questions, we can further interrogate the existing understandings of spectatorship raised in the previous chapter and ask whether approaches that consider a phenomenological engagement between viewer and image allow for a more complete comprehension.

Horror cinema's efficacy comes not only from its narrative contents, but also from the particular affective force generated by its sensory and sensual capacities, capacities that are being transformed by the genre's direct engagement with technologies of perception and expression such as screens and cameras, particularly in the subgenre of found footage horror. The imbrication of these technologies has had profound consequences on our experience of horror. In particular, it has accentuated and intensified the push/pull of attraction and repulsion, which scholars such as Carroll, Clover, and Hanich have identified as pivotal to the genre. That horror generates both attraction and repulsion is central to my claims in this chapter; however, what is at stake is a more nuanced understanding of how the movement between these poles is not regulated merely by scopophilia and fear, but more fully by the intensification of the lived-body experience of the spectator. Drawing on Freud's conception of scopophilia as an unconscious desire to take others as objects of pleasure through a controlling gaze, Laura Mulvey argues that one of the intrinsic pleasures provided by film is that it provides a location for this 'voyeuristic phantasy'.[1] However, scopophilia in Mulvey's sense, understood as visual pleasure motivated by unconscious desires, is insufficient to fully account for horror film's appeal and power, as is any theoretical conception of the gaze that elides the presence of a fully embodied spectator.[2] While these conceptions of the gaze offer valuable insights, the ocularcentrism that underpins them elides the importance of the other senses; a more complete understanding acknowledges the integration of the range of perceptual, cognitive and bodily ways in which we are drawn into the image.

In horror, the bodily components of this engagement are predicated upon the unique spatial and temporal affects generated by cinematic fear, in combination with elements of mise-en-scène that are affectively charged. The viewer's proximity to the image differs from the literal distance they take from the screen, as does their experience of cinematic duration differ from that of 'clock time'. I argue that this heightened corporeal engagement emerges, in part, from how found footage horror films utilise the sensory aspects of the image in ways that are both concurrent with and contradictory to cognitive appraisal.

'Found footage' is a term that refers to 'the conceit that the movie was filmed not by a traditional, omniscient director, but by a character that exists within the film's world – and whose footage was discovered sometime after the events of the film'.[3] The most common trope is that the film was compiled after the events portrayed on screen, from recovered tapes and film. It can be composed of footage from diegetic cameras operated by the characters, or from surveillance footage in the diegetic world of the film, or more recently, from recordings of computer screens. A more inclusive definition of found footage would also allow for the 'mockumentary' components of films such as *The Last Broadcast* (1998) and *The Last Exorcism* (2010), in which the film is presented as a documentary complete with interviews, voice-overs and other documentary techniques, where the fictional content of the film, while crafted into documentary form, still makes the same claims to authenticity as unadulterated footage that has been 'found'. Peter Turner prefers to employ the term 'diegetic camera horror film', which encompasses any horror film that features a diegetic camera as the source of the images presented to the audience.[4]

Horror cinema as a genre has a long history of exploring emerging technologies within the film's diegetic world.[5] However, a shift can be identified at the turn of the twenty-first century in terms of the way horror films began to explore these technologies at the formal level by integrating them into the diegetic world. In his comparison of found footage horror and the 'killer POV' (point of view) of earlier horror film, Adam Charles Hart contends that 'in the twenty-first century, [horror] has shifted to an alignment with more vulnerable modes of looking'.[6] The incorporation of technologies of perception like the camera within the found footage subgenre also afforded these films the opportunity to examine the terrifying potential of mediation itself: that both the message and the medium could be sites of a parasitic haunting.[7]

Horror as a genre is constantly evolving, and the presence of technology in horror is co-constituted by the evolution of technologies in the surrounding culture. The most basic level at which we can consider the imbrication of technologies of perception and the horror film is to look at how this entanglement has been traditionally represented: through the diegetic employment of screens and cameras within the narrative.

BLEEDING BINARIES: WHEN A SCREEN BECOMES A PORTAL

The history of horror film demonstrates that large-scale technological shifts inevitably warrant investigation within the genre. As Jeffrey Sconce observes in *Haunted Media: Electronic Presence from Telegraphy to Television*, '[t]ales of paranormal media are important [. . .] not as timeless expressions of some underlying electronic superstition, but as a permeable language in which to express a culture's changing social relationship to a historical sequence of technologies.'[8]

By engaging with emerging technologies in both form and content in their fullest expression, horror film (and in particular found footage horror film) is often the first genre to pose questions for scholars regarding the changing nature of the viewing experience *vis-à-vis* our connection to cameras and screens, the effects of cameras and screens on subjectivity, and the possible new modes of perception and experience that may arise from the transformative powers of this new compact with screens (and images). As these technologies attempt to replicate the process of human consciousness and perception in their expression, they are also imbued with ghostly traces of the information that passes through them: the ineffable presence that these images have, despite their ephemerality, becomes an incubator of sorts for metaphysical questions about the nature of that which we can and cannot perceive. The residue of this presence is a haunting of sorts, and to see the effects of this haunting one need only examine how quickly each of the 'new' media of their times – photography, radio, the telegraph and the telephone – was soon imbricated with the paranormal.[9] This contention that there is a paranormal occupation of sorts in new technology is furthered by the way that television and film consistently self-reflexively present themselves as sites of this occupation: the screen, for example, becomes a tabula rasa upon which our supernatural anxieties recur in various guises. Television shows such as *The X-Files* (1993–2018) and *The Twilight Zone* (1959–64) have employed the diegetic television screen as the location of the horrific, and films have also similarly engaged with an assortment of screens in different ways: television as a site of haunting (*Poltergeist*, 1982) or brainwashing (*Videodrome*, 1983), projected 16mm film as portal to demonic possession (*Sinister*, 2012), and the chat windows of a computer screen as the site of a conversation with an angry and vengeful deceased teenager (*Unfriended*, 2014; covered in greater detail in Chapter 7).

The compact between horror film and technology has also been examined in detail by scholars seeking to understand the interchange between the two from the perspective of their contemporaneous evolution. Blake and Reyes's edited collection on 'digital horror' offers a comprehensive study of that which they define as 'any type of horror that actively purports to explore the dark side of contemporary life in a digital age governed by informational flows, rhizomatic public networks, virtual simulation and visual hyper-stimulation',[10] while Brian Duchaney argues that improvements in technology necessitate new forms of horror, and that horror as a genre acts out our distrust of the concurrent social advances that new technology brings.[11] Caetlin Benson-Allott's work further develops this concept, contending that the specific intersection of cultural and technological anxiety present in the horror genre makes it the ideal location for studying the shifting process of spectatorship, as it moves from the containment of the auditorium to what can now be the palms of our hands.[12] Benson-Allott's analysis of spectatorship statistics identifies 1988 as the year in which video consumption (which she expands over the timeline to today to include VHS, DVD, Blu-ray, Video on Demand, and streaming media) overtook the in-theatre experience.[13] Drawing on Jean-Louis Baudry and Christian Metz, among others, she proposes that

> the meaning-making process of watching a movie necessarily includes the mechanics of viewing, from the architecture of the theater to the location of the projector and the size of the screen, not to mention its constitutive components: the motion picture being screened and the human viewer.[14]

For Benson-Allott, each viewing medium produces its own specific qualities of experience, which, especially when coordinated with the diegetic content of the film, allows for the spectator to be more pervasively 'infected' by the film's content: by having the titles smash through what appears to be glass at the conclusion of the title sequence of *Friday the 13th* (1980), she argues, the film is embracing its predominant location of consumption, the television screen (via VHS), in an effort to more extensively join the medium with the content, and thus, more fully immerse the viewer.[15]

Gore Verbinski's film, *The Ring* (2002) is an apt case in point for examining the evolution of integration of medium and concept. Although not a found footage horror film, *The Ring* offers a potent illustration of how the horror genre can appropriate the dynamics of our regular interactions with modern screen culture, directly implicating television and video as the source of the film's diegetic haunting. *The Ring* tells the story of Rachel Keller, a journalist investigating the mysterious death of her niece and three other teenagers who all watched a particular videotape a week prior to their deaths. In the process of her investigation, Rachel also watches the tape, as does her ex-husband Noah and their child, Aiden. Initially sceptical, Rachel finds herself 'infected' by the tape, the contamination leading to nightmares, nose bleeds and supernatural phenomena. As she attempts to locate the origins of the video, she discovers the story of Samara Morgan, a young girl whose electro-telepathic abilities led to her tragic death at the hands of her mother. Far from stopping her abnormal powers, Samara's death instead facilitated her ability to haunt electronic media from beyond the grave: to inhabit the cursed videotape and the screens upon which its contents are displayed. Rachel discovers that the only escape from Samara's affliction is to copy and propagate the tape, and in doing so saves her son's life – but also continues the spread of Samara's destructive epidemic.

Adapted from the Japanese *Ringu* series (1998), co-created by Hideo Nakata and Koji Suzuki (whose novel is the source material), *The Ring* (2002) was at the time the most commercially successful and, arguably, the most aesthetically successful Hollywood adaptation of what has been deemed 'New Asian Horror'. As Jay McRoy points out in *Nightmare Japan*, this genre has allowed artists 'an avenue through which they may apply visual and narrative metaphors in order to engage aesthetically with a rapidly transforming social and cultural landscape'.[16] Although the social and cultural landscapes of Japan and the United States are vastly different, they are both privileged locations in terms of the prominence and velocity of their uptake of electronic media and media technologies. Thus, it is to be expected that Japanese horror's specific preoccupation with ghostly technology is effectively translated in its Hollywood adaptation.

The diegetic narrative of *The Ring* allows for an explicit investigation of haunted media. As Benson-Allott puts it, '*The Ring* uses VCRs and videocassettes as sponges, which it saturates with recurring industry anxieties and then wrings out onto its spectator, who is already being wrung out by its horrors.'[17] However, the most compelling aspect of *The Ring* is its ability to force us to question our separation from the image, and in turn the related binaries of body and world, at a narrative, thematic and affective level. For Jeremy Tirrell, culture is progressively moving towards the use of binaries as a way of categorising and hermetically isolating elements; the breakdown of binaries in *The Ring* illustrates how a 'messy, variable and heterogeneous' conception of the world inevitably 'bleed[s] through'.[18] Among the specific binaries that Tirrell refers to are those of the body and world (a division that is traversed by infection, which he equates to Samara's parasitic movement); the supernatural world and the empirical world; and the observer and the image. He argues that *The Ring* specifically threatens the distinction and separation that are usually entailed by vicarious identification with on-screen characters: by forcing us as viewers to watch the same images that cause the haunting of

Rachel Keller, *The Ring* removes the apparent safety of our distance as spectators and directly implicates *us* in the haunting.

Tirrell's understanding echoes Carroll's notions of threat and impurity as the foundations of horror, recapitulating the notion that underlying all horror is the recurring thematic of the persistent human desire to enforce a binary structure of purity (true/false, inside/outside, self/other, for example) onto bodies and worlds that are inexorably intertwined, and that it is our failure to secure this demarcation that produces fear, disgust and revulsion for the spectator. However, while Tirrell does not limit this demarcation to a cognitive appraisal, in that he argues for the broader possibilities of contamination between binaries (such as 'biology' and 'technology', for one example), his consideration of film is still one of a monologic, 'one-way' medium, where there is little to no reciprocity between film and viewer.[19] What limits Tirrell's account is that he primarily conceives of this ongoing breakdown as a conceptual or metaphorical one.

Horror films have often presented similar metaphorical accounts of the failure to maintain these limits through the infiltration of supposedly impenetrable boundaries by the 'monster': David Cronenberg's *The Fly* (1986), Roman Polanski's *Repulsion* (1965) and David Lynch's *Eraserhead* (1977) are paradigms of this collapse at the level of narrative. *The Ring* presents the same thematic, but in a manner that targets our superstitious insecurities and fears regarding technologies of the image. A particularly vivid example is that of the ghost of the young girl Samara crawling out of the television (Figure 2.1). This nightmarish vision, of the monster escaping the confinement of the TV is a potent one for horror viewers.

Figure 2.1 Samara crawling out of the television in *The Ring*.

The television, in *The Ring*, becomes, at one level, a gateway for infiltration: in its most memorable sequence, the film explicitly explores this crossing of boundaries, as the ghostly Samara, coated in static, enters the real world through the portal of the television screen, crawling towards Noah in his final moments. In an earlier sequence, an on-screen fly is plucked into reality by Rachel's hand – she reaches out to the buzzing two-dimensional image of a fly on the screen and it instantly becomes a three-dimensional 'real' fly – a demonstration within the film itself of the potential breakdown of this division between screen content and the world external to the screen. These unambiguously symbolic moments and their entwinement with technology metaphorically capture the manner in which this type of horror escapes the containment of our supposedly safe spectatorial 'distance' from it, rupturing the implied separation between what we are watching and the world outside of the viewing experience. This type of hermeneutic analysis is one way of analysing the uptake of technological shifts within the genre of horror. It is, however, perhaps the most superficial method of analysis, as it does not take into account the lived-body experience of watching these films: while the forged bridge between the image and the 'real' is metaphorical within the diegesis, it is, on the level of actual spectatorship, decidedly material and corporeal. As viewers, we are literally 'touched' by the image, in terms of it affecting us in a bodily way, at varying levels of depth – the skin, the muscles and the viscera.

For a viewer, there is also a second, more subtle affective shift that occurs in the complex interaction between character/screen/viewer: this second shift is the creation of a liminal space for a spectator, in which their conceptions of cinematic reality and unreality are unmoored by the complex relations we have with screens and cameras. This produces a cinematic experience that upends the spectatorial disbelief that is more easily summoned in standard horror genre films. As Kimberly Jackson claims in her study on the relationship between technology and monstrosity, by focusing on how inextricably linked we are to our technologies, these films introduce a hyperawareness of 'the undecidable relation between reality and image'.[20] Jackson contends that this irresolution 'becomes horrific and affective rather than desensitizing and anaesthetic'.[21]

The diegetic world of *The Ring* explores one version of a liminal space, through Samara's escape from the confines of the screen, but the film itself also plays with an 'undecidable relation between reality and image' in the unwelcome pact that occurs between viewer and image when the cause of Samara's curse is presented on screen. As Rachel views the tape, we too see the same collection of macabre and chilling images within the frame of a television screen in the diegetic world, and the larger frame of our own screens, be they cinema, TV, computer or other. The diegetic screen flickers as the images coalesce, a flash many viewers would recognise from the days of analogue video and cathode ray tubes, and then finally the sequence of images ends with the also familiar static hiss of white noise. The film cuts to Rachel only twice in this sequence, very briefly, as she stares directly at the screen, mirroring the stare of the viewer. As screen technology provides for the presence and propagation of malevolent images in the diegetic world of the film, so too does it confront the viewer in the non-diegetic world, making us complicit with those who are infected – and perhaps 'infecting' us as well. This sequence and the consequences of viewing the tape established by the narrative set up the possibility of a fusion between reality and fictional representation.

William Egginton draws attention to how this narrative trope of blurring between representation and reality has increased in prevalence in contemporary film, and he specifically examines its relation to found footage. Egginton pinpoints this 'bleeding' as a natural concern for writers since the invention of theatre in the sixteenth century, as theatre, and other subsequent cultural forms such as television and film, is inevitably drawn to the question of the ontological distinction between 'reality' and that which represents it.[22] To distinguish how this confusion can occur, he outlines two methods of 'making represented realities "realistic"': 'illusionism' and 'realism'.[23] 'Illusionism' works to assure viewers that the medium – in this case, the film – *is* an aesthetic object. The common outcome for a spectator of 'illusionism' is that the images are still perceived as 'framed' object, seemingly realistic but never taken as real. Realism, in Egginton's conception, presents the object *as if it were* the medium. The snuff film is its most extreme example, Egginton proposes, stating that 'the viewer takes what is in fact the object—images of a human being's death—as a medium, as a trace of a further, "real" death, a mysterious and terrifying (or titillating, depending on the viewer) event'.[24] This conception of realism necessarily requires the eradication of the distinction between object and medium. The realism of the found footage horror film has the potential to produce the same dissolution of this distinction and fuse the audience with the film in a manner that exceeds the cognitive process of the 'pact' described above. It does so through the way its distinct aesthetics intensify the liminality of the division between illusionism and realism and bring to the fore the embodied experience of the viewer.

THE BIRTH AND EMERGENCE OF 'FOUND FOOTAGE' HORROR CINEMA

The modality of the camera/screen dyad has become an inescapable aspect of contemporary life. One glance at any crowded urban space and it is self-evident, with hundreds of people engaged in the act of either viewing or recording. Catherine Zimmer identifies the genre of found footage as the best representation of 'the increasing ubiquity of visual recording technologies in the hands of the "average" person and the drive to *record*, on such consumer level technologies, virtually everything: to document, represent, share and spectacularize the world as it unfolds before each individual'.[25]

The consequences of this large-scale shift to the ubiquitous tethering of humans and cameras/screens are bound to filter into cultural products like television and cinema, and vice versa. In his study of the blurred lines between visibility, reality and fiction, Joel Black contends that cinema itself holds much of the burden of responsibility for the compulsion people feel to render every element of their daily lives as a visible spectacle.[26]

This ubiquitous presence of screens and cameras in real life emerges in fictional form in the increasing prevalence of found footage films in the first decade of the twenty-first century. The prevalent cinematic home of found footage appears to be the horror genre, although it should be noted that the subgenre has in recent years been adopted by a variety of other genres.[27] Key exemplar films of the horror subgenre include the *Paranormal Activity* series, the *[REC]* series (2007–14), *Cloverfield* (2008), *Willow Creek*, *V/H/S* (2012) and *V/H/S 2* (2013), among many others, but few would disagree with Alexandra Heller-Nicholas's contention that it was the commercial success of 1999's *The Blair Witch Project* that ignited the rebirth of what has become a prolific, popular and profitable subgenre within contemporary horror film.[28] Although there were previous entries in the canon, none was as successful with mainstream audiences as *The Blair Witch Project*.[29] Most horror film scholars point to Ruggero Deodato's *Cannibal Holocaust* (1980) as the progenitor of the modern-day found footage horror film, but Heller-Nicholas points back to more tangential origins, such as Orson Welles's radio broadcast of *War of the Worlds* (1938) and the road safety films of the 1950s.[30] Heller-Nicholas also argues that *Man Bites Dog* (1992) played a significant role in the development of the found footage conceit, melding the mockumentary format with the turgid violence of a serial killer film.[31]

Perhaps the most vital achievement of *The Blair Witch Project* directors, Daniel Myrick and Eduardo Sánchez, was a transition from the more controversial and underground uses of found footage in arthouse and grindhouse cinema, such as *Man Bites Dog* and *Cannibal Holocaust*, to a mainstream appeal that was fostered on the development of a burgeoning millennial fascination with 'reality' television. Kevin J. Wetmore argues that reality television's fusion of documentary and entertainment was pivotal to naturalising the aesthetic of the documentary form in modern horror.[32] It was in this intersection between horror and 'reality' that found footage took hold of the imagination of horror audiences worldwide. Accounting for this appeal, Heller-Nicholas states:

> The pleasure of found footage horror in part stems from the spectatorial knowledge that something we rationally know not to be true (the supernatural) can momentarily be reimagined (consciously or otherwise) as 'real' because the vehicle in which that information is delivered is one we otherwise trust to provide reliable information.[33]

Another potential explanation for the subgenre's growing appeal in the post-millennial years following *The Blair Witch Project* is that after being confronted with the real horror of the September 11 terrorist attacks, and the subsequent media coverage that prompted many to describe the shocking footage as 'like a movie', some American audiences sought out corners of the genre that steered clear of the explicitly graphic imagery of pre-9/11 horror films.[34] What Myrick and Sánchez had coincidentally achieved prior to 9/11 with *The Blair Witch Project* was, in the words of James Keller, to create 'a sense of actuality by systematically repudiating virtually every feature of the film industry's formula for realistic drama'.[35] As Keller says, 'they have achieved realism by rejecting realism'.[36] Keller claims that the directors had produced the veneer of reality by embracing unconventional techniques, such as allowing the camera to be reflexively seen, or presenting images that obscure rather than reveal the source of the terror, such as those sequences in *The Blair Witch Project* where the characters flee from an unseen threat, the cameras recording only a blur of movement.

In this way, the directors demonstrated a formula that post-9/11 filmmakers could emulate, one that presented horror films in a manner that was '[un]like' a movie. Indeed, a central aspect of the capacity of these films to produce a mode of terror that differed sharply from the slasher or torture porn subgenres was their embrace of methods of generating suspense that strategically mimic how apprehension and dread occur in the non-cinematic world. By dwelling on the quiet, the incongruous, the odd or the seemingly innocuous, found footage is where, in the words of Heller-Nicholas, 'nothing seems to happen [. . .] in strategic ways'.[37] The *Paranormal Activity* series is an ideal example of this concept, as much of the film is composed of static surveillance-style footage designed to prompt the spectator to search the frame for any presence of the supernatural entity.

A major influence on the emergence of these films was the increasing prominence of reality TV and the accompanying prevalence of amateur video in the broader culture. Found footage horror trades on the explicit consciousness of form that ghost-hunting shows, such as *Most Haunted*, began to establish in the early 2000s. This referential familiarity carried over to the subgenre and bestowed on these films a superficial claim to authenticity. The apparent 'reality' of these films, moreover, is also predicated upon the viewer's existing relationship with documentary form and its claims to authenticity. These claims have, however, been problematised by a postmodern society that questions the notion of the visual record ever holding a stable claim to indexical truthfulness. The anxiety that belies this potential inconsistency between authenticity and the documentary form plays a vital role in the power of found footage, opening up a space for the 'unreal'.

The Unreal Reality of Found Footage

Horror film as a genre has long made claims to the veracity of the events depicted, for the purposes of deepening a viewer's curiosity and interest. The opening narration of *The Texas Chainsaw Massacre* (1974), for example, falsely claims that the film's victims were based on real people and that 'the events of that day were to lead to the discovery of one of the most bizarre crimes in the annals of American history, The Texas Chain Saw Massacre'. Similarly, *Wolf Creek* (2005) opens with the assertion, 'the following is based on actual events', a claim that can only be based on its tangential relation to the backpacker murders by serial killer Ivan Milat, and the unrelated terrifying ordeal of British tourists, Peter Falconio and Joanne Lees.[38] Haunted house films *The Amityville Horror* (1979) and *The Conjuring* (2013) are also tenuously based on real events, employing claims of authenticity to heighten the immersive properties of the narrative.

Found footage goes beyond these claims. These films are not 'inspired by' events, but are presented as actual documentation of real people, not characters standing in for real people. Cecilia Sayad describes these films as being presented as 'a fragment of the real world', with the implication that their content has tangible connections to the world outside of the film. This contention explores the dissolution in modern media of clear demarcations between fiction and reality, which Sayad describes as 'the increasingly tenuous boundaries separating representation from real life, the popularity of reality TV being this phenomenon's clearest illustration'.[39] Since the release of *The Blair Witch Project*, the prevalence of this realist impulse in the horror genre is clearly apparent, as evidenced by the large increase in the proportion of found footage films produced within the genre.

Horror is not the only genre to display this movement from fictionality to realism. Scholars such as Lucia Nagib and Cecilia Mello have noted this return of realist tendencies in film since the turn of the twenty-first century, offering a wide variety of sources for this shift, from the popularity of the Dogme 95 manifesto, to the explosion of various world cinemas that embraced this mode as a tool that aspired to reveal unknown or concealed political, social or psychological dimensions of reality.[40] This realist shift could also be seen as a concerted counter-response to the hyper-reality afforded by computer-generated imagery, a way of regrounding film in what Bazin referred to as an unmediated relation to objective reality.[41] Within the realm of found footage, the increasingly ubiquitous presence of cameras and screens in the modern world has produced a knotty web of technology, viewer and film, and raised questions about the authenticity effects of perceptual realism. Stephen Prince describes perceptually realistic images as those which 'structurally [correspond] to the viewer's audiovisual experience of three-dimensional space'.[42] However, he also points out that this correspondence does not prevent perceptually realistic images from being 'referentially unreal'.[43]

The 'unreality' of found footage horror images is often ameliorated by their engagement with documentary tropes. Employing what Bill Nichols describes as the 'observational mode' in documentary, found footage horror relies on the viewer's understanding that the camera captures events as they really are.[44] This supposed fidelity to real events in the documentary genre is an assumption that, as Nichols points out, relies heavily on 'the indexical capacity of the photographic image, and of sound recording, to replicate what we take to be the distinctive visual or acoustic qualities of what they record'.[45] As viewers, we anticipate that documentaries will marshal evidence and present a perspective on that world – that they are, in John Grierson's words, 'a creative treatment of actuality' – but nonetheless, we still generally accept that these are actual occurrences that are being documented.[46] This is due to documentary's privileged position as genre, in that we assume that documentary harnesses a direct relationship between image and referent, and thus accesses and portrays reality. This privileged position has arisen from the concept of the camera as an 'apparatus through which the natural world could be accurately documented and recorded'.[47] This authenticity is also promoted by generic stylistic conventions, like the handheld camera, the self-reflexive presence of the recording devices, and the imprecise or 'messy' composition of the image.

However, the verisimilitude implied using documentary codes, combined with the knowledge that the events depicted are often not of this world, produces an oscillation in terms of our conception of the film's realism or fictionality, with each concept destabilising the status of the other. Barry Keith Grant concurs, arguing that 'the realist aesthetic of these films, in combination with their fantastic and frightening elements, reveals a postmodern anxiety about the indexical truthfulness of the image that has been exacerbated by the ubiquity of digital technology'.[48] Labelling this current cycle of found footage films 'new verité horror', Grant contends that they '[exploit] our psychic investment in the power and truth status of documentary images to generate emotional affect'.[49] However, Grant also acknowledges the complexity of this truth status when he identifies the capacity of this new verité horror to express 'a postmodern vacillation' between the concurrent faith we hold in the authenticity claims of documentary images, and our fear of their falsification, a fear he locates in our awareness of the 'unlimited possibilities regarding the manipulation of digital images'.[50]

Despite this awareness, most viewers still ultimately place faith in the documentary's claims to be a truthful record of reality. This power stems from the observational documentary tradition, which came to prominence in the French cinéma vérité movement and the North American Direct Cinema movement. In their work on documentary and mockumentary, Jane Roscoe and Craig Hight note that both of these movements were motivated by the pursuit of an objective and evidential insight into reality itself for the spectator.[51] Heller-Nicholas, however, contends that the convention of realism is, for the found footage genre, only a clever ruse intended to hook an audience. She asserts that found footage is intentionally crafted only to have the *appearance* of documentary realism, and that the films rely on a tacit agreement between film and viewer to acquiesce in the belief that the film is a documentary in form but not in truth status. The dynamic of this documentary influence has shifted over time, and Heller-Nicholas argues that 'generic saturation' is responsible for audiences who 'no longer assume [that] the signs that once denoted authenticity refer to anything but a specific (and fictional) horror style'; however, it could also be argued that, for viewers who are less acquainted with the conventions of documentary, an implied claim to authenticity is also absent.[52] While she is careful to note that this absence does not rob the subgenre of its pleasures, Heller-Nicholas does, however, contend that these films invite media-savvy audiences to 'indulge in an active horror fantasy, one where [they] can knowingly accept and embrace the real-seeming film frame while never fully suspending disbelief'.[53]

Tethering found footage's efficacy to its appropriation of the relative authenticity of the documentary form cannot fully explain the generation of a deep and penetrating experience for a viewer. It is not only this relative authenticity, but also the specific engagement generated by the aesthetics of the found footage form, that underpins the experience. In the viewer's experience of the image, there is an interaction that operates prior to their cognitive evaluation of the image and its narrative contents, one that powers this engagement. Although many contemporary audiences have become savvy to the codes and customs of the subgenre, and are complicit in a pact between creator and viewer to experience these films only 'as if' they were authentic records of the experience they purport to be, there can be a surplus to this collusion that exceeds the boundaries of the spectator's imaginative engagement: returning to Massumi, an intensity that does not necessarily correspond to our appraisal of the semantic content of the image.

The surplus is produced by adopting the tropes of our ever more visual culture, such as our predilection to record, and transforming them into horror through the intensification of image and sound allowed by the vagaries of the documentary form. The supposed realism allows the inclusion of that which would normally be eliminated to maintain the clear chain of causality and coherence of the classical Hollywood style, such as 'empty' frames, unidentified sound sources, indistinct spatial geography, and aberrant shot durations. Untethered to the demand that each shot of the film carry semantic content in an orchestrated narrative progression, found footage can utilise sounds and images that halt, contradict, or confound the kind of processing on which cognitivist theory predicates a viewer's engagement. Contrary to notions that argue that found footage's effects rely on an implied authenticity of the image, this spectatorial surplus can emerge with or without the spectator's acquiescence to this supposed authenticity, because it resides not only in a cognitive appraisal of the image, but in the pre-cognitive manner in which the viewer's body is affectively imbricated with the filmic image.

Vivian Sobchack argues for a similar dynamic understanding of a bodily engagement that is not entirely predicated on semantic content, in her writing on Haskell Wexler's *Medium Cool* (1969) and Peter Jackson's mockumentary film, *Forgotten Silver* (1995).[54] Sobchack suggests that the way in which fictional film content intersects with documentary in these works arouses a 'documentary consciousness' in the viewer, which she defines as 'a particular mode of embodied and ethical spectatorship that informs and transforms the space of the irreal into the space of the real'.[55] While Sobchack is referring specifically to the use of actual documentary footage within a fictional diegesis, the vital notion is how an image can be 'charged' with an 'embodied' and 'subjective' sense of what counts as the 'objective' real.[56] Sobchack points out that our engagement with cinematic representations is 'more dynamic and labile' than that which formal or generic conventions would seek to preclude: for example, the disparate elements of fiction and documentary, when integrated in a single film, may be experienced by the viewer in a manner that resists any clear demarcation.[57] She contends that, in the contingency of the actual viewing experience, 'our engagement with and determination of film images as fictional or real may be experienced either preconsciously or consciously, idiosyncratically or conventionally, momentarily or for relatively sustained periods of time'.[58] Sobchack's 'charge of the real', her term to describe the mode elaborated above, is a form of affective surplus which brings to the surface our corporeal presence, despite a viewer's general awareness of the fictional status of the film. It occurs when we suddenly (or, in some cases, subtly) experience the emergence of our extracinematic and extratextual knowledge of the world, bringing with it the foregrounding of the viewer's body, in the space where previously they were engaged with the irreal fictional world in the transparent way encouraged by conventional cinematic fictions. In Sobchack's words, when this occurs, the fictional elements are no longer 'typical particulars', but instead become 'specifically particular, real and embodied as other'.[59]

FOUND FOOTAGE AND THE EMBODIED SPECTATOR

Found footage horror film's explicit playfulness with the truth status accorded to the documentary style combines with what Grant describes as the 'postmodern vacillation' of a viewer's credulity to facilitate this transition from the irreal to the real in ways that other genres rarely do. This transitional moment encourages this 'bringing to the surface' of bodily affect; however, this production of affect is also heightened by the intensification of the sensory in found footage horror film. Reframing engagement around bodily affect provides an alternative approach to the key question of how horror cinema, despite the inconceivability of its fictional content, can genuinely affect a spectator. This question is referred to in film scholarship as the 'paradox of fiction': how is it that we can come to be emotionally or affectively engaged with content we know is fictional? Colin Radford summarises the paradox thus: if the human emotional response is predicated on the actuality of the stimulus, and fiction presents us with characters and situations that we do not believe to be actual, how is it that we nonetheless respond emotionally to these characters and situations?[60]

Robert Sinnerbrink takes issue with Radford's contention that such a response is, in essence, irrational, and describes the various competing responses that have emerged to account for our response to fiction: '[p]retence theory', 'illusion theory' and 'thought theory'.[61] Pretence theory posits that we have only a 'quasi-emotional' engagement through imaginative interaction; our emotional response is only a simulation, based on 'make-believe' (pretence theory essentially denies the third premise, that the viewer's response is *genuinely* emotional). Illusion theory maintains that we come to believe that the characters or situations of fiction are, in some sense, real. This negates the second component of the paradox, that we do not believe the characters and events to be actual. Thought theory, advocated by Carroll and extended in Greg Currie's 'simulation theory', is premised on the notion that we mentally simulate in imagination the ideas of characters and situations, and that, in doing so, we arrive at an empathetic understanding of each of the characters' subjective state, a process we continue throughout the film.[62]

Sinnerbrink argues that these theories cannot account for the totality of our engagement. He writes:

> Our affective and emotional engagement [...] cannot be reduced simply to the thought being expressed, or to simulating the emotional responses of characters, but involves sensuous, bodily and aesthetic elements that heighten our receptivity to, and resonance with, the emotions portrayed on screen.[63]

Each of these attempts to reconcile our response to the paradox of fiction has its limitations, particularly when we consider audio-visual content which strains the credulity of the viewer. However, if we reframe our understanding in light of the primacy of an embodied response to the cinematic experience, we have another way to understand how the cinematic experience itself can overwhelm an intellectual label of authenticity/inauthenticity. This is particularly pertinent to found footage horror. While the viewer may intellectually classify the film being watched as only fiction, the designated fictionality of horror is constantly under threat from the vividness of experience that is generated by the way we process the image corporeally. Thus, an understanding of embodied experience circumvents the various accounts for the paradox of fiction, because the bodily experience of a viewer can be in excess of, or contradictory to, cognitive appraisal.

This contention runs counter to the way many scholars approach found footage. Heller-Nicholas, for example, argues that found footage never escapes its generic placement as an artificially produced fiction. She writes:

> On one hand, the formal construction of these films encourages a sense of verisimilitude and suggests that what is being shown is raw, unprocessed 'reality'. At the same time, however, it does this by making it impossible to forget that we are watching a film: If the shaky camera and the regular glitches in sound and vision fail to remind us of this, then the appearance of and references to filmmaking technologies in many of these films [make] it inescapable.[64]

This assumption that the viewer's conscious critical awareness of 'filmmaking technologies' extracts them from the 'reality' of the experience does not match the experience of many viewers, particularly when the sounds and images presented are exceptionally intense. At a phenomenological level, our experience of the filmic moment vacillates between proximity and distance, and the intensity of the sounds and images is often at the origin of our movement towards either pole. Exceptionally intense sounds and images can produce horror that fascinates rather than repels, and generate dread or terror that can draw the viewer into the film. Moments of shock or overwhelming horror occur when the film becomes 'too close' for the viewer, to the point where they may extricate themselves (by closing their eyes, or leaving the cinema).

The realism that is vital to fantastic horror emerges from an audience's sensory rather than intellectual knowledge, and, in the words of Angela Ndalianis, horror's powerful ability 'to be able to affect the sensorium in such a way that it perpetually collapses the boundaries between reality and fiction'.[65] The sensorium that Ndalianis attributes this sensory knowledge to is the indivisible integration of the senses, the body and cognition. While I have previously argued that our conceptions of the real and fictional in found footage horror are potentially unmoored by the complex existing relations we have with screens and cameras, this concept goes beyond that, emphasising the viewer's sensory responses as pivotal to their experience of the film. This is a direct challenge to the 'top-down' model utilised by many of the cognitivist theories, and instead sees our experience as inextricably grounded in the interrelation between our sensory processes and our bodies. By understanding this affective process as a pre-cognitive function, we can explain how the found footage horror film generates moments of intensification of experience that belie our attempts to classify them as merely 'unreal'. While much existing horror theory proposes a cognitive distance in how viewers successfully 'process' horror, reducing it to the outcome of viewer imagination, emotional response and mental representation, this top-down model of processing ignores the primary interface between viewer and image: that of the affective, corporeal response, one that may contradict or undermine these evaluative processes. The concept of the embodied spectator instead embraces the notion that our bodies and our consciousness are entwined and always present in/with the world around us. This concept is supported by the phenomenological accounts of embodiment outlined in Chapter 1, and the insights into enactive perception provided by neuroscience: that there is no 'objective' or detached position from which consciousness observes the world, but rather consciousness emerges from the relation between the body–brain as a singular entity and the world it exists in. The affective complexity that arises from this embodied response allows for the possibility of relational responses to the image that may be in excess of, or counter to, the intended codified meaning. In turn, we may respond to found footage horror film in a manner that goes beyond identification with its protagonists and their situation, as proposed by the cognitivist theorists.

This distinction can be illustrated with a brief example from *The Blair Witch Project*. Watching the compiled footage of the trio's tragic journey into the woods, we gradually come to know each of the characters, their desires, and their fears about their situation. We come to know of fragments of the myth of the Blair Witch, which imbues the situation with dread. We are even privy to the story of Rustin Parr, a man convicted of the murder of seven children in the 1940s, who claimed to be acting under the command of the Blair Witch: a vital element of his story is how he would tell one of his victims to stand facing the corner of a room while he would kill the other.

At the film's denouement, as Heather and Mike stumble upon an old house in the middle of the woods, the viewer is of course engaged in some sense by an imaginative assessment of the desperation of the duo's plight and of the terror of their dimly lit passage into the dark, rotting, dilapidated old house. Later, upon reflection, the viewer may come to a logical conclusion about how the film's final images can be read: Heather finds Mike in the basement of the house facing into the corner. Her camera is struck down, with the implication that she is also, and the film ends on the blurry, flickering recording of the broken camera. The viewer has witnessed someone, or something, replicating the Rustin Parr murders.

However, this retrospective reflection is completely insufficient to explain precisely *why* these final moments are so intensely freighted for a viewer. We see no explicit action of violence against either character. We see no monster, or witch, or murderer. What we are presented with are the manifold textures and inky black shadows of the house, its incongruous, maze-like spatial dimensions (it is nearly impossible for a viewer to get their bearings), Mike's ragged breathing, and the frenzied screams of Heather. All of these sensory aspects contribute to an intensity of *bodily* experience that belies the film's limited depth of narrative or characterisation.

While I agree broadly with Turner's contention that found footage horror films 'create a sense of increased immediacy and alignment with the characters through various techniques associated with the diegetic camera trend', his emphasis on cognitivist theory to explain spectatorial engagement negates the centrality of the body of the viewer to experience.[66] At the root of cinema's distinctive powers is the capacity to generate an affective event that has its foundations in the sensorium. Echoing the broader shift in film scholarship, recent horror scholarship has emphasised the return of the body to the moment of spectatorship, prompting equal consideration of the affective and sensorial power of cinema on the body with the film's semantic content. Anna Powell, drawing on Deleuze, sees the vital importance of reframing the experience of cinema around the interaction between the film and the body, in her consideration of the genre of horror cinema. Noting that Deleuze's conception of cinema involves the 'flux of corporeal sensation and sensory perception' in opposition to accounts that see cinema as a 'purely visual, specular experience', Powell argues that horror deliberately stresses the 'visceral, sensory nature of viewing'.[67]

This understanding of horror's 'visceral, sensory nature' is shared by the work of Ndalianis, who argues that our encounters with horror operate across the full range of both sensory and intellectual responses. She does so to counter what she sees as existing homogenous models of understanding horror, ones that are predicated on a hierarchical model where vision is prioritised and interpretations that are outside of a specific theoretical orthodoxy are less valid.[68] Her approach seeks to reconcile 'the sensory mechanics of the human body' with the 'intellectual and cognitive functions connected to it'.[69] Like Reyes, Ndalianis focuses on the presence of an on-screen body, particularly in her examination of New Horror, where she argues that 'the mental, psychological and sensory impact on the bodies of the characters who suffer at the hands of the monsters are not only depicted explicitly but this trauma also thrusts itself onto the body of the spectator'.[70] The presence of the on-screen body is also vital to her examination of the avatars of horror video games, which become vehicles for embodiment relations.[71] For Ndalianis, this foregrounding of corporeality occurs both in the fictional worlds she examines and outside of them.

To explain the range of cognitive and sensorial interactions between film and viewer, Ndalianis argues for spectatorship as an experience of multifaceted dimensions; she describes the act of horror film spectatorship using the analogy of a 'ping-pong match with multiple balls in play at once [where] each ball [represents] a different way of "being touched" by what's onscreen',[72] and she argues that at any moment in time the viewer may be

> picking up on a generic reworking or allusion to other horror films; recognizing the social critique embedded in the narrative; feeling one's skin crawl; laughing at or recoiling from the over-the-top displays of gore and body desecration; empathizing with characters as they deal with abominable horrors; feeling a thrill deep down in that mysterious place called the 'gut'.[73]

While acknowledging the importance of the spectator's cognitive response, Ndalianis contends that horror 'endows the senses with an intelligence of [their] own: in worlds where meaning and culture collapses, the senses become a powerful – and often horrifying – method of communication'.[74] Her model examines how it is that the vivid sensory spaces of horror fiction can '[translate] their sensorial enactments across our bodies'.[75] Ndalianis's work reveals the myriad ways horror not only works on the bodies on screen, but also carries over to the body of the spectator. She writes that

> New Horror Cinema deliberately addresses its spectator through an intense and unforgiving corporeality that demands the attention of the senses. Onscreen, characters suffer graphic violence at the hands of the monsters, and this violence continues to be played out offscreen and across the body of the spectator.[76]

This notion is also of key importance to Xavier Aldana Reyes, who proposes that '[h]orror uses [on-screen] bodies in order to affect ours' and 'corporeal threat lies at the heart of the moment of [h]orror'.[77] While this book's aim of exploring the affective potential of horror coincides with the work of both theorists, the key point of difference is in their shared focus on the presence of on-screen bodies; my approach, by contrast, is to examine how the corporeal aspects of spectatorship can also be emphasised by films like found footage horror, which de-emphasise the bodily presence of the protagonist and use alternative methods to address the sensorium that Ndalianis discusses.

Rethinking the viewing experience of horror through the sensorium enables us to consider how our bodily response to sensory input is capable of producing an experience that may surpass a cognitive disavowal of the authenticity of the image: while we are consciously aware of the fictionality of the film we are watching, our bodies are capable of contradicting this logic in the way they process the sensory components of the sound and image. The affect generated by the film shifts moment to moment in relation to this.

Under most cognitivist frameworks, affect is simply a feeling or sensation that has yet to be channelled into emotion through the activation of certain cognitive processes. This concept of affect is distinct from Massumi's concept, in that it sees content and intensity as concomitant; the purpose of an image is in its content's ability to elicit a particular emotional response from a viewer. If we were to relate this limited conception of affect back to the example posed by the conclusion of *The Blair Witch Project*, in this understanding there would be no unqualifiable intensity a viewer is left with at the film's conclusion: it would be simply a moment of empty signification until it is transformed into an emotional response (of fear or dread) after the viewer has cognitively understood that Heather and Mike were victims of some undisclosed and unseen monster (acting in much the same way Rustin Parr did). This stance in cognitive film theory does not consider the full experience of spectatorship; it simply bypasses or 'brackets' the primacy of affect by considering it as a bodily intensity that only becomes relevant after cognitive appraisal.[78]

In this way, many of the theories advocated by cognitive theorists neglect cinema's capacity for generating intensities that defy or precede cognitive grasp, which is especially pertinent for the horror genre. The fact that it is often difficult to articulate or encapsulate the precise origin or nature of our embodied response should not elide its significance. Neither should it be rearticulated merely as a psychological response – as if the bodily intensity the viewer feels has been brought about because they believe Heather and Mike have been killed by Rustin Parr or the Blair Witch – as doing so negates the complexity of the affective imbrication of viewer and film: that there are varied intensities and flows of affect in the moment of viewing, sometimes concurrent with our cognitive appraisal, yet at other times contradictory to it. Rethinking the experience of spectatorship from this perspective requires not that we overturn the paradigm of cognitive engagement with the film, but that we expand the boundaries of our understanding so that we can consider the full integration of body and mind in the process of viewing.

Notes

1. Mulvey, 'Visual Pleasure and Narrative Cinema', p. 836.
2. The gaze here referring to the relationship between a viewer and that which is viewed, traditionally conceived of in terms of power dynamics.
3. Urbano, '"What's the Matter with Melanie?"', p. 25.
4. Turner, *Found Footage Horror Films*, p. 3.
5. For example, *Them!* (1954) explored the consequences of atomic testing; the ghosts of *Poltergeist* (1982) haunted the family television; and *The Lawnmower Man* (1992) looked at the potential terrors of VR and artificial intelligence.
6. Hart, 'The Searching Camera', p. 75.
7. For a detailed investigation of how various forms of technology have been considered 'haunted', see Jeffrey Sconce's *Haunted Media*. For an explanation of how technology informs the evolution of horror as a genre, see Brian N. Duchaney's *The Spark of Fear*.
8. Sconce, *Haunted Media*, p. 53.
9. Nineteenth-century photographs were believed to contain spectral images. Later technologies, such as the phonograph, the telegraph, the radio and the telephone, were all at some time thought to contain voices from beyond the grave.
10. Blake and Reyes, *Digital Horror*, p. 3.
11. Duchaney, *The Spark of Fear*, p. 5.
12. Benson-Allott, *Killer Tapes and Shattered Screens*, p. 15.
13. Ibid. p. 1.
14. Ibid. p. 3.
15. Ibid. p. 2.
16. McRoy, *Nightmare Japan*, p. 4.
17. Benson-Allott, *Killer Tapes and Shattered Screens*, p. 104.
18. Tirrell, 'Bleeding Through', p. 130.
19. Ibid. p. 140.
20. Jackson, *Technology, Monstrosity, and Reproduction in Twenty-First Century Horror*, p. 35.
21. Ibid. p. 35.
22. Egginton, 'Reality Is Bleeding', p. 208.
23. Ibid. pp. 208–11.
24. Ibid. p. 212.
25. Zimmer, *Surveillance Cinema*, p. 77.
26. Black, *The Reality Effect*.

27. Action/drama (*End of Watch*, 2012), science fiction/superhero film (*Chronicle*, 2012) and comedy (*Project X*, 2012), to name a few. Xavier Aldana Reyes makes the argument that found footage is not technically a subgenre, but a 'framing device' that may be applied to different subgenres such as the monster film, the haunted house film, or the possession film (Reyes, *Horror Film and Affect*, p. 105).
28. Meslow, '12 Years after "Blair Witch"'.
29. With a budget of around $60,000, the film grossed over $140 million on its theatrical release.
30. Heller-Nicholas, *Found Footage Horror Films*, p. 32; Sayad, 'Found-Footage Horror and the Frame's Undoing', p. 44 (among others).
31. Heller-Nicholas, *Found Footage Horror Films*, p. 36.
32. Wetmore, *Post-9/11 Horror in American Cinema*, p. 78.
33. Heller-Nicholas, *Found Footage Horror Films*, p. 22.
34. Briefel and Miller, *Horror after 9/11*, p. 1.
35. Keller, '"Nothing That Is Not There, and the Nothing That Is"', p. 74
36. Ibid. p. 74.
37. Heller-Nicholas, *Found Footage Horror Films*, p. 92.
38. Ivan Milat was a serial killer convicted of the murder of seven backpackers in New South Wales between 1989 and 1993. Peter Falconio and Joanne Lees were British tourists who were confronted and attacked in the remote Australian outback by an assailant named Bradley Murdoch in July 2001. Lees was abducted, but later escaped, and Falconio was believed to have been shot and killed, although his body was never located.
39. Sayad, 'Found-Footage Horror and the Frame's Undoing', p. 45.
40. Dogme 95 was an avant-garde filmmaking community conceived by directors Lars von Trier and Thomas Vinterberg in 1995. It had a strict set of rules that were designed to purify filmmaking by focusing on performance, story and theme over the use of filmmaking technology or special effects. Nagib and Mello point to the new cinemas emerging in Brazil, Argentina, Mexico, Lithuania, Russia and Iran from the mid-90s onwards; see Nagib and Mello, *Realism and Audiovisual Media*, pp. xiv–xxv; see also Hallam and Marshment, *Realism and Popular Cinema*.
41. See Prince, 'True Lies', for a counterpoint to this idea.
42. Ibid. p. 32.
43. Ibid. p. 34.
44. Nichols, *Introduction to Documentary*, p. 34.
45. Ibid. p. 34.
46. Grierson and Hardy, *Grierson on Documentary*, p. 147.
47. Roscoe and Hight, *Faking It*, p. 9. This belief saw the documentary form as intimately tied to the aims of scientific Enlightenment and placed an emphasis on empirical observation.
48. Grant, 'Digital Anxiety and the New Verité Horror and SF Film', p. 153.
49. Ibid. p. 160; Grant's interpretation of affect, it should be noted, differs from that of Massumi, in that it is referring to an emotional response generated by appraisal of the semantic content of the image.

50. Ibid. p. 170.
51. Roscoe and Hight, *Faking It*, pp. 9–20.
52. Heller-Nicholas, *Found Footage Horror Films*, p. 8.
53. Ibid. p. 8.
54. Sobchack, *Carnal Thoughts*, pp. 258–85.
55. Ibid. p. 261.
56. Ibid. p. 284.
57. Ibid. p. 268.
58. Ibid. p. 268.
59. Ibid. p. 284.
60. Radford and Weston, 'How Can We Be Moved?', pp. 67–80.
61. Sinnerbrink, *New Philosophies of Film*, pp. 77–8.
62. Carroll, *The Philosophy of Horror*; Currie, *Image and Mind*.
63. Sinnerbrink, *New Philosophies of Film*, p. 81.
64. Heller-Nicholas, *Found Footage Horror Films*, p. 24.
65. Ndalianis, *The Horror Sensorium*, p. 163.
66. Turner, *Found Footage Horror Films*, p. 3. Turner argues that 'somatics are not as central to viewer engagement as the use of off-screen space and the imagining of off-screen camera operators' (ibid. p. 15).
67. Powell, *Deleuze and Horror Film*, pp. 4–5. Writing on *The Blair Witch Project*, Powell promotes the value of a Deleuzian approach in the concept of 'machinic assemblage', which addresses the composite of viewer body and technology of cinema brought on by the film's 'material movement, force and intensity'; see Powell, 'Kicking the Map Away'.
68. Ndalianis, *The Horror Sensorium*, p. 19.
69. Ibid. p. 16.
70. Ibid. p. 23.
71. Ibid. pp. 40–56.
72. Ibid. p. 30.
73. Ibid. p. 30.
74. Ibid. p. 30; in particular, 'New Horror', the phase of horror Ndalianis identifies as emerging from the mid-2000s that places greater emphasis on 'the sensory impact of graphic depictions of horror, violence and bodily destruction' (ibid. p. 16).
75. Ibid. p. 3.
76. Ibid. p. 5.
77. Reyes, *Horror Film and Affect*, p. 3.
78. Carroll, *Engaging the Moving Image*, p. 60.

CHAPTER THREE

Camera Supernaturalis

THE OUT-OF-FRAME OF FOUND FOOTAGE

Horror film theory that focuses its account on the semantic content of the image reduces the cinematic experience to the effect of structures of representation, further buttressing the hierarchical paradigm of cognition 'making sense' of affect. However, if we examine the ways in which horror film often works against privileging this meaning-making, we can find productive gaps that destabilise this hierarchy. Found footage horror film's common withholding of key information which would allow meaning-making to occur requires that we reassess its imagery for affective resonances that support this reframing of the corporeal interface as the basis for our engagement. In doing so, we find that, within these films, an affective surplus is often generated by that which we specifically cannot see: the out-of-frame.

Horror film, as a genre, has a long history of manipulating the viewer through the unseen (although sometimes heard) presence of that which is out-of-frame. Found footage horror specifically manipulates the intensity of its sounds and images through the freedom it possesses to exploit the out-of-frame more fully, a freedom granted by its realist form: given that it purports to be a document assembled from previously recorded footage, the repeated failures to 'properly' frame the content being recorded can often be ascribed to the exigencies of the horrific situation. Given that they are often fleeing from a monster, the camera operators within the film are largely forgiven for not carefully composing their frame. The out-of-frame of found footage horror highlights the embodied response of the viewer, as it engenders an intense sensory engagement, one that the viewer may less keenly feel when watching content that safely positions the frame within a larger diegetic world that is, in a sense, known.

Cognitivist understandings run counter to this stance. Carroll and Seeley, for instance, recognise framing as the process by which the filmmaker '[enhances] the perceptual salience of elements within depicted scenes'.[1] They claim that the filmmaker does this through editing, camera movements and lens movements, and that its primary purpose is to 'index, bracket, and scale' the information required by the viewer to make sense of the narrative.[2] These techniques, which Carroll and Seeley label 'externally imposed attentional scripts', are utilised with the goal of promoting 'narrative understanding' and are also designed to 'prefocus' a viewer's attention, so that they come to know what they need to know when they need to know it, at the filmmaker's behest: the spectator is 'a passive participant whose attention is entrained to the informational structure of the movie, the communicative intentions of the movie maker'.[3] They argue that the film works best if it mimics the 'visual routines' of the world outside of cinema, where our perception is guided moment to moment by the 'salient' features of our environment.[4] To the degree that cinema replicates this visual routine, it does so, they argue, by being 'paired to the behavior of the characters'.[5]

This is the process of framing as the isolation of territory: the selection of spaces, objects and figures that will be captured by the camera and the mode in which they are presented. Tom Gunning describes this process as 'arranging composition and spatial relations'.[6] Cecilia Sayad, in her treatise on the frame and found footage, acknowledges that this is the normal primary function of the frame: to 'isolate the represented world from the surrounding reality'.[7] However, she argues that, through its absorption of the camera into the diegesis, found footage, in a manner, 'merges the film and the extrafilmic'.[8] For Sayad, a key element of found footage is that this produces a keen awareness of the world outside of what the frame contains. She draws attention to the Bazinian notion of the realist film frame as centrifugal, when she writes that the realist frame '[invites] us to conceive of the off-screen, to imagine what goes on beyond the edges of the image', as opposed to the centripetal frame of a painting, which 'isolates the depicted space from the surrounding real'.[9]

This conception of the frame working against its usual isolating function can be very clearly evidenced in found footage horror. In conventional horror, the frame is strategically deployed as a border that is often transgressed by the intrusion of a figure or a threatening element that aims to startle or shock. In contrast, found footage horror instead employs the out-of-frame in more abstract, enigmatic, and thus more threatening ways. For many films in the subgenre, it is primarily that which is out-of-frame that generates fear, and its eventual capture within the frame is often transient or fleeting, or, on occasion, is never actually achieved (such as in the example of *The Blair Witch Project*'s conclusion, described in the previous chapter). Adam Charles Hart contrasts the conventions of the 'killer POV' – an 'unattributed subjective camera' (point of view) that rose to prominence in 1970s horror – with the diegetic camera of found footage. He argues that while the killer POV signals 'invulnerability and omniscience', the subjective viewpoint of the camera in found footage 'signifies utter vulnerability because neither the viewer nor the camera-person – whose views are here aligned – know what exists beyond the edges of the frame'.[10]

The aural qualities of the found footage works mimic this emphasis on the power of the out-of-frame. Michel Chion deploys the terms 'acousmatic' and 'acousmêtre' to describe how sound and vision are strategically detached from each other.[11] Acousmatic describes an auditory situation in which we hear sounds without seeing their cause or source.[12] Acousmêtre involves a being or character who derives mysterious qualities from the fact that they are either heard off-screen or are on screen but hidden: it is the acousmatic in the form of a disembodied voice. For example, in the opening of Bryan Singer's *The Usual Suspects* (1995), as the character Keaton lights a cigarette, we hear a repeated dripping noise. This acousmatic sound is later revealed to be the dripping of leaking petroleum. An acousmêtric sound, by comparison, is present in the Club Silencio sequence of David Lynch's *Mulholland Drive* (2001): when singer Rebekah Del Rio collapses onstage while performing a Spanish version of Roy Orbison's 'Crying', the vocals enigmatically continue from no known origin, and are thus suddenly psychically relocated to an unknown person or being in the out-of-frame. Chion argues that this out-of-frame position confers certain powers on this unseen character, bestowing on the disembodied voice the powers of 'ubiquity, panopticism, omniscience and omnipotence'.[13] When conferred upon a potential threat, these powers further intensify its threatening properties.

Into the Woods: *Willow Creek* and *The Blair Witch Project*

Willow Creek (2013), considered by many as a contemporary update of *The Blair Witch Project*, presents a valuable site to examine the visual and aural concepts of the out-of-frame and acousmêtre, and elucidate their connections to the embodied experience of the spectator. As A. A. Dowd argues, *Willow Creek* often feels like a spiritual successor to the keystone film of the subgenre, returning the found footage horror film to the woods.[14] The story follows filmmaking couple Jim and Kelly on their journey into the deep forests of Oregon. The couple are young, boisterous, easy-going. Jim is a Bigfoot enthusiast, on a mission to visit the site of the infamous 1967 Patterson–Gimlin footage: the famous shaky, poor-quality images of a bipedal, ape-like man, captured in the Northern Californian forests, that is considered contentious evidence for the existence of Bigfoot. His girlfriend Kelly is an avowed sceptic, and while she wants to make this a fun weekend for her boyfriend, she will not indulge his childhood fantasies of actually coming into contact with Bigfoot. It will simply be a few nights' camping in the magnificent wilderness of the Pacific Northwest.

As the sun sets on a day of laborious but optimistic hiking, the couple establish camp in the depths of the forest. This is the midpoint of the film: the first half is framed as an amateur documentary, staging the often humorous arguments between believer Jim and cynical Kelly, and the apparent gullibility of the locals they interview about the Bigfoot mythology. Documenting every moment on his handycam, Jim carries his love of the Bigfoot mythology with unabashed enthusiasm, gleefully exclaiming, 'That could be Bigfoot scat!' as they stumble upon a large pile of animal excrement. The couple's dynamic is captured in Kelly's dour response: 'Or it could be bear shit.' In spite of the humour, it is at this point that the film shifts dramatically in tone, and the second half becomes an interminable escalation of tension and fear.

Night falls. Inside the tent Jim records an enthusiastic confessional to camera, almost vibrating with excitement about the possibility of finding the elusive Sasquatch. He finally switches off the camera lamp, and he and Kelly try to sleep. Shortly after, Jim stirs. He tells Kelly he heard a knocking sound. As he switches on the camera for both illumination and posterity, the first strains of angst ripple over Jim's face in the dim light. Suddenly, we hear a piece of timber crack, echoing like a gunshot. The couple argue briefly over the source of the sound. Kelly suggests it may be a bear. Jim is not convinced. Kelly admonishes Jim to switch off the camera and go back to sleep, but he can't. The static image of his sleep-stained face against the ripple of the tent wall stretches out like elastic. Minutes pass. It's the sound that fills this moment, like liquid stretching the skin of a water balloon. There's the gentle susurration of a nearby creek, and behind it a vast aural emptiness that is alien to modern city-dwellers.

In this confined moment, weighted with the suspense of Jim's obvious angst, the scene is imbued with a sense of the immensity of the forest and the distant boundaries of roads and trails that tie it to the real world. In the hollow hush, their tension grows. Upon both my first viewing of this scene and subsequent viewings, my eye is drawn from Jim's face to the slight undulation of the tent wall behind him: this delicate border between the frail human body and the only thing keeping the 'out there' from 'us'. Enveloped in the tent, haloed in the lens of the camera and its muted light, the scene presents us with an all-too human tableau of foolish security (Figure 3.1).

A wail pierces the almost-silence and the nylon border of the tent skin. It rattles out into the night, five seconds that feel even longer. The couple huddle together, pushing their bodies as close as physically possible. The near-silence returns.

The eighteen-minute sequence that evolves from this moment is the film's tour de force. The bodily reaction it may provoke for the viewer is predicated on a slow-building dread, but also a strange sense of the material thinness of

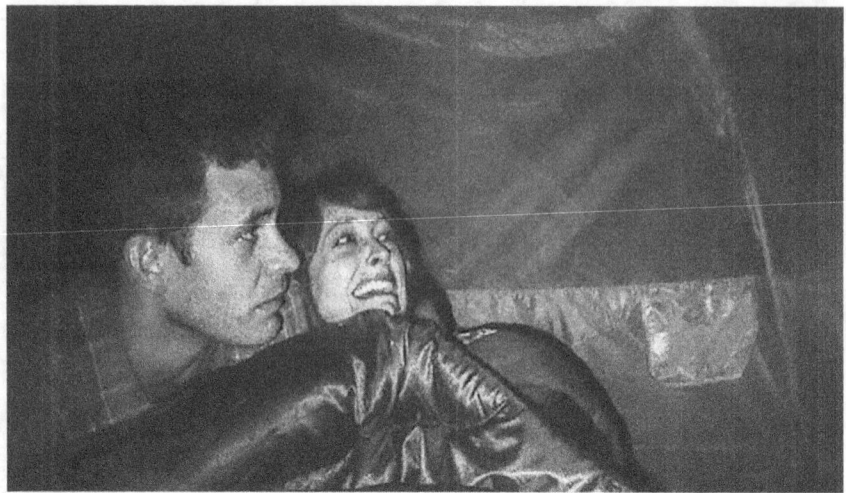

Figure 3.1 Inside the tent in *Willow Creek*.

the tent walls and the awful immensity of the surrounding forest. One could argue that this spectatorial engagement with *Willow Creek* is a consequence of cognitive evaluation: that we identify with Jim and Kelly, and that we imaginatively put ourselves in their place, or that we cognitively engage in 'active horror fantasy', where we pretend that this documented account is authentic. However, this conception does not account for the power of the film to affect us in a bodily way, even when we choose to deny its authenticity, or when our allegiance or identification with the characters is insufficient. One could argue that found footage horror often provides little in the way of conventional character development designed to facilitate identification. Identification does not account for how the viewer may feel the fragility of the tent wall at the end of the sequence, as something predatory pushes against it. It also does not account for the power of the sounds of cracking branches, footsteps, breathing, and finally, the haunting wail, to conjure such fear and dread: not only for the characters, but for the viewer themselves.

Why is it that, in the experience of watching *Willow Creek*, there can be an almost palpable quality to the surrounding woods, and, at the film's conclusion, the pressing darkness? Can it merely be derived from our identification with the characters of the campers, or is there something else occurring? This material quality can be more clearly understood when we rethink how the frame works in found footage. As the in-the-frame is presented as a 'fragment of the real world', the out-of-frame retains a tangible link to the materiality of this 'real' world, one that emerges as an affective surplus to the image. Both the immensity of the forest and the unknown form of the entity stalking around the tent become tangible presences despite never being seen. The force of the acousmêtre in this case is magnified through the combination of this sensory knowledge of the Bigfoot's tangibility and our inherent fear of its tangible form (which is, in our imaginations, charged with the omnipotence and ubiquity that Chion ascribes to the acousmêtre). What is clear is that the sensory aspects of the scene described above far exceed the visual content of the frame.

Explaining this tangibility in our experience of a two-dimensional screen image requires an expanded view of our interaction with images, one that returns to embodiment as central to experience. In 'What My Fingers Knew', Sobchack wrestles with the difficulty of what she sees as a vacillating corporeal response between the 'as-if-real' sensual experience and the direct sensual experience of the spectator.[15] Sobchack observes that much of contemporary film theory has struggled with the comprehension of human bodies being 'touched' or 'moved', not only in the figurative sense, but also in the literal sense. Arguing that 'we see and comprehend and feel films with our entire bodily being, informed by the full history and carnal knowledge of our acculturated sensorium', Sobchack posits a primary engagement with the sensory qualities of the image, with its materiality on a sensible level.[16]

Importantly, this concept does not place the sensuous embodied experience to one side, bracketing it, as Sobchack notes is so often done, as either 'phantasmatic psychic formations, cognitive process, or basic physiological reflexes'.[17] Sobchack's alternative is a conception of spectatorship as consciousness and flesh amalgamated, wherein off-screen and on-screen bodies subversively function 'both literally and figuratively': this she terms the 'cinesthetic subject'. This is a neologism that she has derived from cinema, synaesthesia and coenaesthesia. Here Sobchack is considering the ways in which the dominant senses of sight and hearing in the cinematic experience can be transmuted to the other sensory modalities. In clinical synaesthesia, there is the involuntary stimulation of one sense in the perception of another: for instance, literally seeing the sound of a horn as red. In coenaesthesia, there is a perception of one's whole sensorial being: Sobchack uses the example of the general and diffuse sensual condition of the child at birth, before the hierarchical arrangement of the senses through cultural immersion and practice. The integration of these concepts provides her with a way of commuting seeing and hearing to touching, and back again 'without a thought'. Merleau-Ponty presents the concept of the lived body as 'a ready made system of equivalents and transpositions from one sense to another. The senses translate each other without any need of an interpreter, and they are mutually comprehensible without the intervention of any idea.'[18] What Sobchack does with this foundational phenomenological concept is to apply it to the process of spectatorship in order to argue how the predominantly visual and aural medium of cinema can have a multi-modal array of sensory effects beyond these senses.

Sobchack's conception of an amalgamation between consciousness and flesh transforms spectatorial bodies into 'matter that means' and on-screen images into 'meaning that matters', where each informs the other in the co-creation of experience.[19] While the presence of the literal and the figural vacillates, they are both simultaneously at hand within the spectrum of spectatorial experience, not as separated entities, but as reciprocal and reversible presences. This conception allows us to bridge the gap between the literal body of the spectator and the figural representation of the image. In *Willow Creek*, for example, the camping sequence turns the fluttering tent wall (a two-dimensional image) into a tangible, material presence for the spectator. On the other side of the equation, the spectatorial body, open to a sensory interplay where light and sound are not simply processed by the visual and aural senses, becomes the foundation upon which we make meaning of the sequence: the matter of our bodies – skin, muscles and viscera – is not at the mercy of our cognitive assessment, but instead grounds it.

Drawing on phenomenological understandings of the film–viewer relationship, Elena del Río explains the possibility of a material engagement between body and image through the notion of 'surface'. Del Río expounds on filmmaker Atom Egoyan's description of the affective exchange between a viewer and a screen image; in Egoyan's words,

> a true surface can be developed if the viewer breaks the impassive nature of the screen identification process with a degree of involvement. This involvement may be internalized – the image may trigger a memory of an event or a conversation – or it may find more overt manifestation.[20]

In turn, del Río proposes that viewer and image can be rethought as 'surfaces in contact, engaged in a constant activity of reciprocal realignment and inflection'.[21] Acknowledging that Egoyan's use of the term is somewhat contradictory, given that 'surface' connotes that which is 'flat, immediate, and obvious', del Río explains that the surface-image is in fact quite different from those connotations, in that it represents 'a mobile, subjectively-inflected layer, an individuated form of perception and interaction that exceeds the image's ready-made signifying status'.[22] Rather than thinking of the body and film as 'discrete units', del Río considers the image as having layers of affect that can produce a 'surplus of subjective significance'; however, this surplus resides not in 'mental abstraction', but in a sensory and bodily interface with the image.[23] This conception of 'surfaces in contact' presupposes that there is the potential for an interaction with cinema that goes beyond our identification with the semantic content of the image.

Thinking of film and viewer as 'surfaces in contact' also offers us a way to think about how images such as the tent sequence from *Willow Creek* are necessarily inflected with what the viewer brings to the exchange; as del Río states, 'what becomes apparent in the encounter between body and artefact is the idea that the body is always outside of its visible form, that it constantly extends itself beyond its objective spatial and temporal boundaries'.[24]

This is a more resonant conception than that posed by mere imaginative engagement, because it more fully accounts for why film so powerfully interfaces with our bodies. Anne Rutherford echoes this point when she argues that the power of cinema is in its capacity to create 'an affect, an event, a moment which lodges itself under the skin of the spectator'.[25] Such a moment is facilitated by qualities of sound and image that intensify its affective properties, of which the acousmêtre and the strategic use of the out-of-frame are but two.

Other scholars have also contributed to a clearer understanding of the 'cross-modal flow' theorised by Sobchack above, which provides a foundation for how the affective properties of cinema are amplified. Anna Powell utilises Deleuze and Guattari's concept of the 'body-without-organs' in her claim that the images and sounds of cinema do more than merely produce a sensory response in the corresponding eye or ear of the spectator.[26] Powell claims that the body of the film and the body-without-organs of the viewer are engaged in a mutable 'molecular' assemblage which results in a fusion that allows for sensory experience beyond that occurring in the moment of viewing.[27] She elaborates that 'affects and percepts are not limited to our organic bodies', and that the body-without-organs, engaged with the film, enables the viewer to 'virtually recreate the corresponding [on-screen] corporeal effect and "feel it"'.[28] Powell explains that this results from the way certain perceptions of images of sensation are difficult to process in their 'undiluted affect', but makes clear that the meld between spectator and screen is not mimesis understood as 'a copying of on-screen behaviours', but rather the reverberation that occurs between sense and thought, 'a mental encounter made through the viscera'.[29]

This concept of mimesis as contact is further elaborated in the work of Michael Taussig, who promotes a conception of the cinematic experience that invokes the dynamic transfer of 'mimetic' experience in the 'palpable, sensuous, connection between the very body of the perceiver and the perceived'.[30] Drawing on Walter Benjamin's conception of the mimetic faculty as the human inclination to mimic or to imitate, to recognise and produce similarities to objects in a manner that can transform the relationship between subject and object, Taussig argues for a bi-fold concept of mimetic experience that differs from the traditional understanding of mimesis as copy, or mimetic replication of reality. For Taussig, mimesis is both copy and a form of contact, and mimetic experience in this second understanding allows for the distinction between viewer and image to become porous, generating a unique, sensuous and tactile exchange between the two.[31]

Rutherford develops this potential of mimetic experience as the antithesis of epistephilia in her consideration of documentary affect. Epistephilia, which Bill Nichols describes as the 'desire to know' that is specifically stimulated by the documentary mode, is often posited as an explanation for how documentary-style images work to draw us in.[32] Rutherford points to the limitations of the conventional concept of a purely epistephilic drive behind spectator interest that negates the mimetic capacities of cinema: when we consider documentary only as the meeting point of a 'rational, intact subject' and a 'completed, formed and unchanging' real, we lose the possibility of a cinema in which the image 'brings the material world into play, to life, in the moment of its reception'.[33] In found footage horror, this epistephilic drive is also often frustrated by the manner in which the camera misleads the viewer or denies revelation of the source of the horror: for example, when the single most graphic visual element of *The Blair Witch Project* is a bloody scrap of shirt containing a tooth.

The found footage genre often engages with this capacity to employ images that are in excess of, or even contradictory to, the 'desire to know', and which instead heighten our corporeal and sensory engagement: the out-of-frame offers one such example. In many cases, the out-of-frame becomes a location for the deliberate obfuscation of the source of the terror. We can return to *The Blair Witch Project* to illustrate this. The approach of a third night in the woods has been met with dread by the three reluctant campers. Darkness falls, and with the pronouncement that the lights are potentially drawing attention (from *what*, they do not and cannot say), Heather, Josh and Mike switch off the camera lights and attempt to get some sleep. The screen goes black. Five seconds pass, and then, in a distant murmur, the sound of children's voices. It's interrupted by a rapid shudder of breath: Heather's, as she fumbles with the Hi-8's camera lamp. Now the viewer is presented with a glimpse of the interior of the tent, but seen through a foggy condensation that coats the lens. Panic seeps into the voices of the protagonists as they each react to the approach of the childish murmurs. Little can be seen of any notable detail, just glimpses of bedding material and shapes and, as Heather puts on her jeans, we are visually presented with the edge of the air mattress captured by the temporarily dropped camera. The sonic landscape, however, builds a vivid and disquieting picture: its layers are the hyperventilating breaths of the lost filmmakers, Josh's plaintive, repeated 'Oh Jesus, oh Jesus', and the strangely malevolent giggles of children. Suddenly, there is a new sound – something amorphous violently pushing up against the tent walls. The image suddenly switches to Josh's 16mm camera, and he

Figure 3.2 Heather fleeing the tent in *The Blair Witch Project*.

screams for them to 'Go, fucking go!' as he follows his own advice, tearing into the night. Now we have more detail in the image, although it's densely granular and rapidly undulating, as Josh and Heather flee into the darkness, away from the tent, lit only by the twin lights of their cameras. Heather bobs in and out of the frame as Josh runs, a white figure against obsidian black, there for one moment, lost the next (Figure 3.2). She slows slightly, turning to face something in the out-of-frame. Whatever it is prompts her to scream, her terror captured in her repeated cries of 'What the fuck is that?', and all the while she is still running and, crucially, still filming.

This strategic deployment of the unseen is often vital to the production of horror affect, in that we react just as intensely to the components of the image we are not given. If what we are given is visually insufficient to provide the required narrative information, such as the intense darkness that restricts vision in this sequence, it results in the intensification of other senses (in this example, the acousmêtric property of the noises of the children). While the sound and image may contain very little semantic content, their effects are intensely powerful.

The 'Empty' Frame of Found Footage Horror

The second element related to found footage horror's specific use of the out-of-frame is the employment of negative screen space: the blackness or potentially 'empty' frame, where the narrative content is simultaneously occurring or suggested to be occurring within the out-of-frame. So rarely can this be justified in conventional filmmaking terms that its use in found footage is striking and deeply affective. In examples where darkness is used, such as the sustained moment at the end of the sequence in *The Blair Witch Project* described above, the spectator scans the full frame, searching for the first break in the dark, the glimmer of any light. In examples where there is visual content but it has a lesser semantic role, we are also drawn in. Rather than a passive immersion in the image, these 'empty' frames produce an active spectator response that feeds into the construction of greater terror and suspense.[34] In his assessment of *The Blair Witch Project*, Scott Dixon McDowell writes: 'I can think of no other film that prompts the viewer to anxiously search the periphery of the screen for a glimpse of something that simply is not there.'[35] This opinion would no doubt have been updated with his exposure to the *Paranormal Activity* series, which utilises the 'empty' frame far more frequently and to greater effect: perhaps its most clever application is the constantly panning camera of *Paranormal Activity 3*, created by the central character strapping his video camera to the base of a cooling fan, allowing it to pan across a range of roughly 140 degrees and move from 'empty' frame to 'empty' frame, each pan threatening the viewer with the possibility that the frame will no longer be empty on its return. For Dennis Giles, this 'delayed, blocked or partial vision [. . . is] central to the strategy of horror cinema', a strategy that in this particular subgenre involves actively highlighting the process of visual perception.[36] Horror film, as J. P. Telotte argues, often specifically 'calls attention to the way in which we perceive its horrors and underscores that manner of seeing with specific imagery of a failed or improper vision'.[37] Kjetil Rødje concurs with this, arguing that images 'on the brink of collapsing' are central to found footage.[38] Among the 'trademarks' of the form he identifies are events such as batteries running flat, lenses cracking, cameras being knocked over, garbled or missing sound, and of course, the death or injury of the camera operator.[39]

This 'failed' or 'improper' vision does not jeopardise the power of the found footage film. On the contrary, it further imbricates the body of the viewer. This can be illustrated with a return to *The Blair Witch Project*: in the moments following Josh's disappearance, Heather swings her Hi-8 camera around in a dizzying manner, capturing only the dense thicket of scrub surrounding their campsite and the cage-like trees encircling them. The lens drops at a certain point, focusing on the leaf-strewn soil and the shadows of the trees, and remains at this angle, the camera dangling from Heather's hand as she hyperventilates over Josh's disappearance. The textural properties of the image, accompanied by Heather's ragged breathing, offer us very little in terms of narrative development. Yet something about this scene produces more and not less presence for the spectator: the forest becomes not merely the tableau upon which this drama is being acted out, but as in Sobchack's cinesthetic subject, a location that is in some respects more sensorially present, and thus even more frightening. While the viewer cannot touch the leaves or trees surrounding Heather, there is a sensory transfer from what they see and hear to what they feel on a bodily level.

This emphasis on the experience of the image over its semantic content is further explicated by phenomenological explorations of cinema. Julian Hanich offers one of the most comprehensive phenomenological accounts of horror film in his book, *Cinematic Emotion in Horror Films and Thrillers: The Aesthetic Paradox of Pleasurable Fear*. Hanich examines the dissolution of the boundary between film and viewer as a vacillation of phenomenological distance; contending that proximity shifts are a key feature of horror cinema, Hanich states that horror film engages the viewer directly through the 'vividness and impressiveness of threateningly close cinematic images and sounds'.[40] The 'closeness' he refers to is the distance of our 'intentional relation' to the image and sound, 'intentional relation' being a phenomenological term that refers to the aspect of our mental state towards an object, real or imagined. He argues that, while our physical distance from the images and sounds cannot be bridged, the phenomenological distance fluctuates on a continuum between intensely close and distanced. Hanich builds upon previous phenomenological understandings by stating that there are conscious strategies that we apply after the fact that can work to either intensify or de-intensify the affective quality of the image. There are also semantic and aesthetic techniques that a film can use to manipulate this intensity and therefore our phenomenological distance. Among those that Hanich suggests are the construction of allegiance (to character or actor), the accentuation of somatic empathy (through focus on the on-screen body), and, specific to the field of horror, 'exceptional immorality and brutality' of the image.[41]

This phenomenological distance is also negotiated in other ways. Hanich refers to the aversive experience of temporary avoidance, for example, that audiences use when the phenomenological distance becomes too intensely close: the viewer's closing or covering of eyes and ears, the conscious decision to look *at* the image and consider it as artifice (rather than looking through it, as we do when we are immersed), or cognitively shifting our focus to its fictional status. These are all potential responses that can reset the phenomenological distance, although, should they choose to re-engage, most viewers find it relatively easy to be drawn back into the filmic world.[42]

While Hanich does not discount the cognitivist understanding of why we feel certain ways in the process of viewing, he focuses more specifically on *how* we feel them. He points out that cognitivist film scholarship 'emphasize[s] the thinking part of an emotion – the evaluation or judgment about the object of the emotion – and often treat[s] the emotional experience as epiphenomenal', and that, as a result, this type of analysis is less dimensional than that which explores what these emotional experiences *feel* like.[43]

While hermeneutic approaches (like those offered by Benson-Allott and Tirrell in the previous chapter) can reveal certain ways that horror and technology have been integrated, to understand horror as an experiential mode we need to look beyond representations of technology to the lived-body experience in its negotiations with the varying forms that horror takes. One manner of demonstrating this is to utilise Hanich's phenomenological framework in a consideration of how *Paranormal Activity* (2007) employs the camera and the out-of-frame to intensify cinematic dread.

CINEMATIC DREAD AND THE CAMERA OF *PARANORMAL ACTIVITY*

To explore the fluctuation of phenomenological distance that Hanich proposes, we can specifically examine how his concepts of cinematic dread, cinematic shock and suggested horror emerge in the experience of found footage horror film *Paranormal Activity*, directed by Oren Peli. *Paranormal Activity* demonstrates how found footage horror capitalises on the spatial and temporal foundations of these types of experience. The film involves the domestic haunting of the home of Southern Californian couple Micah and Katie, and Micah's attempts to capture the demon responsible on camera. Almost the entire film takes place inside the confines of the couple's home, and it is captured entirely on a high-end consumer camera purchased by Micah at the film's beginning.

Scholars have analysed the film from a variety of perspectives: psychoanalytic interpretations, feminist conceptions, even consumerism and consumption as a site of abjection.[44] Examining the *Paranormal Activity* franchise as a site where the domestic take-up of security cameras is problematised, for example, Janani Subramanian argues that the destruction of the protagonists occurs 'despite their increased *visual* security' and that this 're-emphasizes the connection the franchise consistently makes between domestic (in)security and technology, as increasing the amount and sophistication of the cameras fails to protect domestic space from outside threats'.[45] At the same time, scholars such as Therese Grisham, Julia Leyda, Nicholas Rombes and Steven Shaviro have examined the film from the perspective of theories of the post-cinematic.[46] Leyda, for example, makes the cogent observation that the cameras of *Paranormal Activity* operate with an omniscience that borders on 'torture'. She writes that 'the cameras are superior, all-seeing witnesses that cannot intervene, and force us also to witness helplessly'.[47] Shaviro, in a discussion in the same collection of works, points out how the cameras appear to function as 'conductors, or facilitators of demonic possession', ironically amplifying the forces they are there to simply make record of.[48] Alternatively, Shane Denson's approach is to argue that these films act as exemplars of post-cinematic horror in the way their cameras produce images that are 'discorrelated' from the phenomenological framework of human embodiment and subjective perception (I will further unpack Denson's argument, and its relevance to the project of this book, in Chapter 6).[49]

My focus in this chapter is on the experiential aspects of watching the film: how the film draws the viewer into an entanglement with the uncanny in a way that conventional horror rarely achieves (or aspires to). *Paranormal Activity* does not feel, as so much of cinema does, like a *representation* of events carried out by actors. Instead, it seems to harness the verisimilitude of *presentation* – achieved, in part, by mimicking what we accept as the presentational elements of documentary or surveillance-style footage. It also engages the viewer through its use of the techniques of obfuscation and negative space. The feeling of authenticity produced by this presentational mode translates into an affective tremor, one that starts as small as the rumble which announces the presence of the film's demonic haunting, but which gradually swells like incoming waves on a rising tide, building to the seismic fissure at the film's jarring and dramatic conclusion.

Found footage's reliance upon the diegetic presence of the camera can be either the engine which successfully drives the narrative, or alternatively the source of a viewer's extrication from immersion, as they are forced to interrogate the authenticity of the presence of the camera: the common 'why is Character X still filming this?' question. *Paranormal Activity* leans more towards the former, as the camera becomes a proxy for character Micah's obsessive mission to rid his home of its haunting. As Micah says in one early scene, 'Once we get it on camera, we can figure out what's going on.' Because each scene is underscored by this determination to capture the 'paranormal activity' on camera, the viewer is less inclined to question the credibility of the narrative. Ironically, it is the camera that appears to fuel the manifestation of the demon Toby, as noted by its victim Katie multiple times throughout the film.

The camera of *Paranormal Activity* is particularly productive of Hanich's 'cinematic dread'. With the bold claim that dread 'enables the strongest form of immersion in all cinema', Hanich refers to the way in which dread makes the viewer 'advance' into the filmic world.[50] He argues that there are several cinematic qualities of dread that generate this 'undertow': spatial immersion, temporal immersion, and visual restriction.[51] What separates dread from direct horror is that dread resides in the future, in the possibility of what may be seen or heard. Drawing on the phenomenological theory of

Hermann Schmitz, Hanich isolates dread as generated by a particular split kind of intentionality.[52] Schmitz extends the notion of intentionality into two parts, a 'concentration section' (*Verdichtungsbereich*) and an 'anchoring point' (*Verankerungspunkt*).[53] This concept can be demonstrated by imagining a patient with a fear of needles visiting a doctor. For the patient, their fear appears to be directed at the needle but it is commonly actually the blood-letting which is the real source of their concern. In this example, the needle itself becomes the concentration point, at which attention condenses, while the loss of blood is the anchoring point, as this is where the patient's emotion is principally 'anchored'. Hanich points out that, in direct horror, concentration and anchoring point are synchronised, whereas dread splits the two aspects of intentionality: the film *The Texas Chainsaw Massacre* works as direct horror, for example, when Pam is chased and caught by the macabre Leatherface, because the anchoring point of Pam's inability to escape is also the point at which our concentration is focused.[54] It works as dread, however, in the sequence where another of the teenagers, Kirk, first investigates Leatherface's house, because our concentration is on his passage through the home, but our anchoring point is our concern that he is walking directly into mortal danger.

Scenes of dread appear to eschew what Hanich identifies as two vital principles of conventional storytelling: 'maximum visibility and temporal economy'.[55] Instead of giving us vital information and removing wasted screen time, scenes of dread revel in their lack of spatial information and delay of outcome, which again returns us to the importance of the out-of-frame, which is where much of this lack or delay resides. Despite the deficiency of information, there is, for the viewer, an intensity and increased proximity to the world of the image. It is in the anticipation that dread fully grasps the viewer. In the words of Dennis Giles, 'the viewer senses a terrible presence in the articulation of imagery, but the images themselves display only an absence of the terrible object, or the possibility that it may become visible'.[56]

Paranormal Activity illustrates this concept within the repetitive nightly recordings Micah makes of the couple's darkened bedroom. The narrative falls into a routine in which the couple record themselves sleeping each night, as many of the supernatural incidents have occurred in the early hours of the morning. The viewer's dread coalesces around these long, repetitive, static takes of the murky bedroom. It is intensified by a low, ominous, diegetic sonic rumble which accompanies each of the demon's manifestations, and which gradually comes to cue the viewer's attention. When I watch the film, my concentration point shifts continuously, from the doorway, to the external hallway, to the interior of the room, to the sleeping couple; however,

Hanich would identify my anchoring point as the fearful anticipation of the demon's inescapable violence towards the couple and the effect of the shock or horror that results from this, not only for the characters, but *for me as viewer*. This can account for the intensity of the experience when there is insufficient sympathy or empathy for characters to justify our response: we can simply be fearful *for ourselves*.

The intensity of these sequences is also fuelled by the three elements mentioned above: the first of these, spatial immersion, is pivotal in horror. Hanich refers to how the moving camera can create a sense of spatial immersion, such as that which occurs when the camera follows a character into a dimly lit basement. While *Paranormal Activity* does utilise this technique (when Micah operates the camera after fleeing the bedroom for the living room, for one example), it builds its spatial immersion in a different way: through the containment of the locked-off camera.

In the repeated bedroom sequences, the limitations of the low-resolution consumer-level camera's clarity in darkened environments, combined with the specific composition which accentuates the darkened areas of frame such as the hallway, works to draw us in as viewers. I find myself, in watching these scenes, rapidly shifting between trying to look for specifics (movement in the frame or a shifting shadow) and trying to take in the whole of the image. When the demon is visibly evidenced, through movement or interaction with the bodies of the protagonists, the shift in my attentional directedness brings about an increased proximity to the image, at the level of my own body. Hanich describes this operation in the following way:

> We feel the field of consciousness reorganized and flexibly shifting emphasis; our bodily experience instantly becomes more complex; a gradual, sometimes abrupt sensual metamorphosis takes place. Suddenly, the hitherto occluded, absent body comes to the fore and tacit corporeal dimensions are brought into awareness.[57]

Hanich's claims are staked on the cinema auditorium as the locale par excellence for immersion. He argues that the merging of the darkness of the filmic space with the darkness of the auditorium makes the boundary between filmic world and reality more tenuous. Found footage horror is partly able to transcend this limitation as a result of its aforementioned realist tendencies. Unlike the conventional horror film, in which engagement more fully coincides with emotional immersion, and is more readily achieved in the darkened environment of the theatre, found footage can work differently. As the previous chapter stresses, we instead participate with the found footage image as a 'fragment of the real', and respond to it as such.

Figure 3.3 Katie sleepwalks in *Paranormal Activity*.

Limitations to visibility only partially explain how *Paranormal Activity* utilises Hanich's cinematic dread. Hanich complements this concept with a discussion of temporal immersion, which he also identifies as a key component. The passage of time is key in found footage horror film, and especially so in *Paranormal Activity*: the bedroom sequences discussed above have a rhythm that intensifies our attentional directedness, in that they present a time-lapse from when the couple go to bed through to the moment just prior to when the demon becomes present. The sudden return to 'real time' in the deceleration of the speeding time-lapse image establishes an expectation that something horrifying is coming, and yet the specifics of how it will manifest remain inchoate (Figure 3.3). Sound becomes a potent harbinger in these sequences, the silence of the time-lapse gradually replaced by the low bass rumble. The intensity of these occurrences builds with each night of footage, to the point where our dread coalesces with the slowing of the clock. We become suddenly aware of each second as it ticks by, and, in these moments, the tacit presence of the spectatorial body emerges. Hanich labels this a temporal 'thickening'.[58]

Fear is amplified by the emerging presence of our spectatorial bodies, but crucially it is less of a response to our vicarious fear for the characters Micah and Katie than it is a fear for ourselves. Returning to Schmitz's split intentionality, the anchoring point for this fear can reside just as much in the out-of-frame or the acousmêtre as it does in identification with the characters. The intensification of foreboding can be cued not only by a slowly approaching threat, like that skilfully utilised in *It Follows* (2014), where the supernatural entity pursuing the protagonists can only approach at a walking pace, but also by the very possibility that the threat exists, unseen, outside of the limited view we have been provided within the frame. This kind of cinematic fear can enable both the centrifugal movement of the viewer towards the collective (in the case of viewing with other spectators in a theatre) that Hanich describes, and the centripetal intensification of the lived-body experience of the individual.

The Monster as Visual and Aural Intensification

From a survey of the films presented in this chapter, a common thread emerges: the aesthetics of found footage horror film, and in particular its use of the out-of-frame or the 'empty' frame, accentuate the manner in which cinema can have transformative effects on a spectator that go beyond our identification with character or engagement with narrative. The pursuit or capture of the supernatural on camera, in its various forms, taps into our pre-existing relationships with modern image recording technology and, through found footage horror's similarity to the documentary form, intensifies its presence. Within this subgenre, the affective potential of the out-of-frame and the threatening omnipotence of the acousmêtre imbue the image with increased sensory resonance. These heightened sensual properties bring our corporeal presence to the fore in ways that can transcend the limits of an emotional engagement (or disengagement) with the narrative or characters. Found footage horror works counter to much of the 'monstrous' imagery of conventional horror film: the 'monster' is often not so much a creature or thing as it is the intensification of the sound and image, an intensification that can be produced by what is not seen (the out-of-frame), as much as by what is.

The various conceptions of embodied perception that underpin the work of scholars such as Sobchack and Hanich unite around the belief that seeing is a form of touching at a distance. By shifting our attention as film theorists to the manner in which we are drawn into the image in a bodily way, as well as cognitively and perceptually, found footage horror films reveal a new paradigm of the relationship between technologies of perception and expression, and our bodily interaction with them. Rather than interpreting found footage horror through a purely hermeneutic frame, we can reframe our interaction with the image as one that is predicated on the sensory-affective dimensions of corporeality that are at the basis of embodied perception. In doing so, we can understand how these films produce a new experience of horror spectatorship, one that relies less on the presence of a 'monster' than on our bodies' inherent responsiveness to images that are denuded of their narrative content.

Transformations of existing technologies and the emergence of new technologies invariably manifest themselves within the genre of horror. The ubiquity of cameras and screens in contemporary life has been synthesised in horror through the genre of found footage horror. This synthesis allows us to examine how it is not necessarily the iterations of monsters and their various terrifying forms that underpin the complex relationship between horror and technology in cinema: it is instead the way in which the developments and revolutions of technology alter the aesthetic dynamics of the form of the horror film, imbuing the film itself with the monstrous dimensions of sensory intensification.

Notes

1. Carroll and Seeley, 'Cognitivism, Psychology, and Neuroscience', p. 62.
2. Ibid. p. 62.
3. Ibid. p. 65.
4. Ibid. p. 65.
5. Ibid. p. 65.
6. Gunning, *D. W. Griffith*, p. 19.
7. Sayad, 'Found-Footage Horror and the Frame's Undoing', p. 56.
8. Ibid. p. 58.
9. Ibid. p. 57.
10. Hart, 'Killer POV', p. 82.
11. Chion, *Film, a Sound Art*, pp. 465–6.
12. Ibid. p. 466.
13. Ibid. p. 466.
14. Dowd, 'Bobcat Goldthwait's *Willow Creek*'.
15. Sobchack, 'What My Fingers Knew: The Cinesthetic Subject, or Vision in the Flesh', in *Carnal Thoughts*, pp. 53–84, p. 73.
16. Ibid. p. 63.
17. Ibid. p. 60.
18. Merleau-Ponty, *Phenomenology of Perception*, p. 273.
19. Sobchack, 'What My Fingers Knew: The Cinesthetic Subject, or Vision in the Flesh', in *Carnal Thoughts*, pp. 53–84, p. 75.
20. Egoyan, 'Surface Tension', p. 28, cited in del Río, 'The Body as Foundation of the Screen', p. 101.
21. Del Río, 'The Body as Foundation of the Screen', p. 101.
22. Ibid. p. 102.
23. Ibid. p. 102.
24. Ibid. p. 102.
25. Rutherford, 'Cinema and Embodied Affect'.
26. Powell, *Deleuze, Altered States and Film*, p. 100.
27. Ibid. p. 100.
28. Ibid. p. 100.
29. Ibid. p. 100.
30. Taussig, *Mimesis and Alterity*, p. 21.
31. Ibid. p. 21.

32. Nichols, *Introduction to Documentary*, p. 40.
33. Rutherford, 'The Poetics of a Potato', p. 236.
34. The convention of the audience being trained to scan the frame for the presence of visual evidence of the ghost is common to reality TV 'ghost-hunting' shows.
35. McDowell and Myrick, 'Method Filmmaking', p. 141.
36. Giles, 'Conditions of Pleasure in Horror Cinema', p. 39.
37. Telotte, 'Faith and Idolatry in the Horror Film', p. 25.
38. Rødje, 'Intra-Diegetic Cameras as Cinematic Actor Assemblages', p. 218.
39. Ibid. p. 218.
40. Hanich, *Cinematic Emotion in Horror Films and Thrillers*, p. 98.
41. Ibid. p. 158.
42. Ibid. pp. 100–1.
43. Ibid. p. 21.
44. See for example Hahner et al., '*Paranormal Activity* and the Horror of Abject Consumption'; Leyda, 'Demon Debt'; Joy, 'The Patriarchal Construction of Hysteria'.
45. Subramanian, 'Candid Cameras'.
46. Grisham et al., 'The Post-Cinematic in *Paranormal Activity* and *Paranormal Activity 2*'.
47. Leyda, 'Demon Debt', p. 420.
48. Shaviro, cited in Grisham et al., 'The Post-Cinematic in *Paranormal Activity* and *Paranormal Activity 2*', p. 863.
49. Denson, 'Crazy Cameras', p. 205.
50. Hanich, *Cinematic Emotion in Horror Films and Thrillers*, p. 160.
51. Ibid. p. 160.
52. Intentionality, a central concept of phenomenology, refers to the 'directedness' or 'aboutness' of experience. It is the way we are 'in touch with' the world.
53. Schmitz, *Der Gefühlsraum*, cited in Hanich, *Cinematic Emotion in Horror Films and Thrillers*, p. 157.
54. Hanich, *Cinematic Emotion in Horror Films and Thrillers*, p. 158.
55. Ibid. p. 163.
56. Giles, 'Conditions of Pleasure in Horror Cinema', p. 40.
57. Hanich, *Cinematic Emotion in Horror Films and Thrillers*, p. 232.
58. Ibid. p. 23.

CHAPTER FOUR

Perception and Point of View in the Found Footage Horror Film: New Understandings via Deleuze's Perception-Image

For just a moment, it feels like we're getting to the truth. Caught on camera in the glare of the spotlight, Josef appears to be about to break. Then suddenly he shoves past us, darting back into the house and down the main stairwell – towards the only viable exit.

We are witnessing this scene through the lens of a camera, somewhat reluctantly operated by Patrick, a modest and docile man in his thirties. We hear the anxiety in Patrick's breathing.

This odd man, Josef, alternately charming and unsettling, has lured us to the house and conned us with his lies, and now stands between us and escape. We enter the house from the porch, furtively. We creep forward, past the dining table to the head of the stairs. Then we descend, slowly, tentatively, down the stairwell. We turn each corner with great trepidation, until finally – the doorway. The exit.

Blockading the door, wearing the cartoonish yet somehow terrifying visage of a hungry wolf, is the man. The wolf is called Peachfuzz. We know this because Josef has told us of how his father created the 'friendly wolf' when he was a child.

Patrick says: 'Josef. Please let me go. Are you going to let me go?'

Josef (or is it Peachfuzz?) shakes his head.

Patrick says: 'Why are you doing this to me? Are you just trying to scare me, or . . . ?'

Josef/Peachfuzz nods vigorously, his arms and legs spread out to barricade our point of escape.

Patrick says: 'Well, I'm terrified, okay. You won. Now will you just step aside and let me go.'

Josef/Peachfuzz begins to growl, a repetitive low moan. We watch as he begins to rub himself against the door, gyrating his hips. The performance of his movements is a mélange of three disparate tendencies: they are somehow all-at-once threatening, comical and erotic.

With repetitive cries to stop, each cry becoming more plaintive, Patrick reaches a breaking point. Escape is the only option – and so we charge forward with him, the camera slamming into Josef/Peachfuzz. The sound cuts, and the image degrades before it evaporates, leaving us only in the black.

How Do We Get 'Inside' a Movie?

The above scene from the 2014 film *Creep*, directed by Patrick Brice, is quintessential found footage horror, in that it is, like the rest of the film, entirely composed of the video record of the chilling and bizarre meeting between Aaron, a videographer, and his employer and subject, Josef, who transforms into Peachfuzz by donning a wolf mask in the above sequence. My choice to narrate the sequence in the first-person plural is a deliberate one, in that it is designed to elicit a more subjective involvement with the reader's memory of, or imagining of, the sequence. By writing 'we', I am borrowing a stylistic device used by some Hollywood screenwriters to place the reader 'inside the movie': the 'we' in both uses is not simply a conjunction of the viewer and the protagonist. In a screenplay, its purpose is to descriptively facilitate an imaginative integration of sorts between the viewer/reader and the fictional world. The central argument of this chapter is that the form of found footage horror not only produces a similar subjective involvement, but that it is also uniquely capable of producing an experience that is immersive in a manner that extends beyond identification with either the camera or the protagonist wielding it. There is something more here: a deeper, embodied connection with the image that is specifically facilitated by the found footage form. That is not to say that the experience of conventional horror film is somehow less rich, only that it operates on different levels, with an approach to generating audience immersion that focuses more on compelling narrative and characterisation.

As the previous chapters have argued, found footage horror, like all cinema, generates an embodied spectatorial experience. Extending from this understanding, this chapter continues to explore the spectatorial experience as an encounter and exchange between the film and the viewer that occurs on this bodily level. Because the traditional notions of how film elicits an empathic connection with its protagonists are complicated by the found footage horror form, we need to examine more productive ways to approach this question, methods that are less reliant on these traditional models.

The use of the subjective voice of first-person plural in the description of the sequence from *Creep* that opens this chapter is an attempt to express how it is that the spectator is integrated differently into the found footage film. These films operate in a manner that is less reliant on the traditional process of imaginative intervention, or simulation as Currie would describe it, where the viewer projects themselves imaginatively into the situation of the acts and events of the fiction, and these imaginative processes run 'off-line', 'disconnected from their normal sensory inputs and behavioural outputs'.[1] In found footage, we commonly experience the world *with* the protagonist, through a shared perceptual verisimilitude: we literally see the world as they are seeing it/recording it. Kjetil Rødje extends this concept to argue that the cameras of found footage are more than simple recording devices: they are 'actors' that partake in the film's events and become 'the most central characters' in terms of how they structure the narrative for the viewer.[2]

Because the genre of found footage deliberately implements a marked point of view, typically requiring the film to be a record of events captured by someone (or some object, in the case of an unoperated camera, as in certain sequences of the *Paranormal Activity* series), found footage horror presents a location to investigate both the boundaries and the opportunities to horror presented by the form. Examining *Creep* as an exemplar film opens questions about subjectivity and spectatorship that are universal to found footage films, yet differentiated from conventional cinema; questions such as how the subjective camera of found footage alters the subjectivity of cinematic spectators, and how specifically these films may produce an oscillation between subjective and objective vision.

In the sequence described above, Aaron, played by Patrick Brice, has found himself a reluctant visitor to Josef's remote cabin. Josef, played by Mark Duplass, has hired Aaron to record a documentary of his life in the late stages of his terminal illness, to give to his unborn child at a later date. What begins as a somewhat benign film project gradually devolves into horror, as Josef's entreaties become more sinister and bizarre throughout the day. The film is presented almost entirely as the camera record of Aaron's experience of that day and subsequent days, and later as Josef's continued monologue direct to camera. The sequence above, like much of the film, is presented as Aaron's recording of an attempted escape from Josef's house, in the long takes of documentary style. Like much of found footage horror, it manifests as Aaron's perceptual experience of the horrific moment, mediated only by the camera.

This optical perceptual verisimilitude, rarely utilised in genres outside of the found footage or documentary mode, is, however, only one of the two common forms of found footage images. The second is the so-called objective camera: operating much like a surveillance camera, this is the static or automatic record of the scene. Like a surveillance camera, it implies impartiality: the image is no one's point of view but the camera's own. Often this is the only time we see the protagonist on screen.

Together, these two different ways of *capturing* the image create an experience of *watching* the image that differs from that of conventional horror: as proposed in the previous chapter, there can be an intensification of the lived-body experience in relation to the aesthetic techniques deployed, such as the strategic use of the out-of-frame. However, there is also in found footage horror an empathic engagement that differs from conventional horror, due to the limitations of the documentary-style aesthetic: because found footage is the record of a camera operator who is usually the central protagonist, we have little to no visual access to the emotional experience of that character through their facial expressions, which challenges some of the traditional notions posited to explain our empathic engagement with cinema. For, where conventional horror cinema can use the face of the protagonist to relay his or her emotional reaction and thus elicit an appropriate response, found footage commonly has to transmute this into the experience as it is recorded by the protagonist's camera – a view that comes to be generally equated with their 'point of view'.[3] There are, of course, occasions when the subgenre does make use of the face of the camera operator: most famously, the sequence in *The Blair Witch Project* in which a crying Heather confronts her predicament is an apt example, as are the moments when Josef turns the camera on Aaron in *Creep*. However, moments such as this are outliers within the form.

The conventions of classical Hollywood cinema create a space in which an intelligible logic of cause and effect can unfold: camera and editing techniques are used to construct an internally coherent diegesis, including, for example, the 180-degree rule and various techniques of montage, such as the shot-reverse shot. Vitally, this process also aids in the formation of a privileged space for the spectator to watch the events unfold: a place inside the diegetic world with a clearly demarcated perspective that is supported by the filmmaking techniques above, but also where he/she who is viewing is mysteriously 'invisible' to the other participants of this diegetic world. This production of a space for the viewer to occupy, more fully explicated in the concept of 'suture' by theorists such as Christian Metz, provides the foundation for a deeper involvement with the filmic world. Suture promotes a convergence between the 'I' of the spectator and the all-seeing 'eye' of the camera. According to its proponents, suture collapses diverse subjectivities into a singular subject through the mental construction of a unified space where, for example, through the process of shot-reverse shot, a sense of subject-hood is established for the spectator in *both* shots, a process which continues throughout the viewing: as Robert Stam puts it, suture gives 'the all-seeing spectator the illusion of being omniscient and omnipresent'.[4] For theorists such as Metz, the primary identification of the viewer in classical cinema is with the camera itself, but this is predicated on the camera's facility for voyeuristic omnipotence and omniscience. Identification with character is, for Metz, a secondary form of identification. The concept of suture is difficult to apply to the found footage genre, given that suture relies on the invisibility of its process, its illusory qualities. Suture is problematised in found footage horror due to the explicit foregrounding of the camera's presence. The camera of found footage is also the opposite of all-seeing, given its firm grounding in the diegetic world as the point of view of a particular character or a literal camera.

Because found footage horror film deliberately foregrounds the diegetic act of recording, and its presentation of a marked point of view, further examining traditional film theories of point of view isolates how these theories may be complicated by found footage's distinctive form. Questions of point of view invariably lead into the interrelations between a cinematic subject and subjectivity. A common analogy ties subjectivity to the subjective camera, which takes the position of a particular character, either corporeally or mentally. Kristin Thompson asserts that cinema's subjective qualities are generally demonstrated within a film by sound and/or image which shares either the character's eyes and ears or both, or those moments in film in which we enter the character's mind.[5] The subjective camera in this understanding presents us with a specific point of view, whereas the 'objective' camera is understood to be from an omniscient position, independent of the characters. This demonstrates the reduction in cognitive interpretations of film-watching experience: the shot is reduced to its function in constructing a viewer's understanding of the diegetic world, its capacity to communicate information from either an 'objective' or 'subjective' position. The viewer 'objectively' sees Character A look, and we then cut to a shot equivalent to the optical perceptual experience of a viewer in the spatial location of Character A, and thus, we are then thought to be 'subjectively experiencing' her world through her gaze.

Point of view shots are often identified as a key element in the production of an image which has subjective qualities. Edward Branigan uses the term 'internally focalized (surface) shot' to describe point of view shots, and argues that this type of image provides access to a character's subjective experience within the diegetic world.[6] Bordwell and Thompson similarly claim that 'optical' point of view shots largely equate to perceptual subjectivity.[7] Robert Montgomery's 1947 film, *Lady in the Lake*, epitomises one of the most comprehensive uses of point of view in conventional Hollywood cinema. Shot entirely from the perspective of a diegetic character, *Lady in the Lake* attempts to entirely replicate the optical perceptual experience of a character within a cinematic narrative, although as Branigan notes, many critics considered it 'a mere trick, a curiosity or a failure'.[8] He points to the limitations of equating optical point of view with the experience of being a character and contends that, for a film to be 'genuinely' subjective, it requires something more than the formal act of reproducing a consistent point of view shot.[9] Branigan argues instead for broader conceptions of a subjective view that may allow for a more multifaceted interface between what we see and our way of experiencing it, considering, for example, that 'we may see through one character's eyes while our sympathy is for another'.[10]

Found footage is clearly operating with the paradigm of replicating the optical perceptual experience of diegetic characters as they record it. However, it challenges the notions of primary identification as Metz proposes it, by explicitly drawing attention to the equivalence between the spectator's optical perceptual experience and that of a diegetic camera being wielded by a character. Even so, it still forges a powerful interface between spectator and the filmic world, drawing the viewer into the image in a way that is difficult to ascribe to the traditional notions of primary or secondary identification.

'BECOMING-WITH' THE FILM

If we turn here to the cinema theory of Gilles Deleuze, we can find a productive alternative way to think about the creation of this interface. Deleuzian (and Deleuzo-Guattarian) theory enables us to more expansively address the capacities of cinematic spectatorship, by examining spectatorship as a process of flux.

Central to Deleuze's work on cinema was his insistence on challenging the dominant image of thought. Deleuze posits that artistic domains like cinema are inherently capable of initiating this challenge and are often the first site to respond to dramatic social change; it is then philosophy's role to investigate these shifts. Gregory Flaxman sees Deleuze's cinematic theories as a means of processing and understanding how, in today's hyper-visual modern world, we feel we have become 'unwilling repositories of and accomplices in a plan to populate the world with mindless images'.[11] Flaxman asks:

> How can we understand, evaluate, and finally value images when the entire culture seems to have gone visual? Are there differences among images or has their propagation flattened out all distinctions? Is there still a reason to esteem cinematographic images apart from those we see on television or in tabloids?[12]

Given that found footage horror films are, in some senses, repositories of mindless images in the way Flaxman describes, in that they are sometimes presented as recordings of events that are apparently unmediated (like the surveillance recordings of the *Paranormal Activity* films), how are they still capable of generating affective intensities? One way of rethinking our engagement with the image is the notion, proposed by Deleuze and Guattari, of assemblages: 'complex constellations of objects, bodies, expressions, qualities, and territories that come together for varying periods of time to ideally create new ways of functioning'.[13]

Deleuze rethinks our engagement with images beyond the concept of a viewer–image binary, and the concept of 'assemblage' offers more productive ways to think of the relationship between spectator and film. Powell develops this thought and demonstrates how a Deleuzian model opens up understandings to a wider continuum of assemblages. She argues for the co-relation of 'molar' and 'molecular' frameworks in the experience of spectatorship.[14] The terms 'molar' and 'molecular' are derived from Deleuze and Guattari's notion of all bodies existing simultaneously on two planes of existence: the molar corresponds to the rigid segmentation found in hierarchical or bureaucratic institutions; the molecular corresponds to the fluid, intersecting characteristic of 'unconscious micropercepts, unconscious affects, rarefied divisions'.[15] This notion sees the intensive vibrations that are brought about by visual, aural and other stimuli of film, and its material force on the sensorium, as able to stimulate a kind of thought that moves towards a Bergsonian 'intuition': much like existence on the molecular plane, this intuition is a mode through which one would receive access to the undifferentiated flow of life, its indivisible affect, as opposed to that which is produced by the sensory-motor schema, which operates on the molar plane. This concept of sensory-motor schema emerges from Bergson's understanding of human perception and action. For Bergson, in order to act upon its environment, a body must separate from the undifferentiated flow of perception only that which interests it, upon which it can then choose to act.[16] This reduces multifaceted and intricate relations between objects and images to causal and spatial links, leading to a linear cause-and-effect logic.[17]

Deleuze, however, examines the limits of Bergson's concept, and argues that the transformative power of cinema specifically arises from an ability to dislocate or subvert the sensory-motor schema, which in turn produces non-cognitive affective intensities that can persist beyond the conscious consideration of narrative or identification.[18] While cognitivism sees cinema as naturally conducive to human systems of meaning-making, in turn naturalising how these systems work, Deleuze instead proposes an acentred and nonhuman perspective that interrogates the deterministic, analogous link between our schemata of thought and the classical patterns of narrative cinema. He argues that cinema is capable of destabilising the normative flow of time, and thus the sensory-motor schema of human thought where perception leads to action, which in turn destabilises what we consider the 'natural' order of events presented by this image relay.[19]

The concept of 'becoming-with', drawn from Deleuze and Guattari, is an alternative to fixed categories or subjectivities. It involves the dynamic process of change, flight, or movement within any assemblage: in this case, the assemblage between film and viewer. This allows for the film and viewer to be considered as a dynamic and ongoing assemblage of forces as opposed to isolated entities. As Elizabeth Grosz posits:

> In Deleuze and Guattari's work, the subject is not an 'entity' or thing, or relation between mind (interior) and body (exterior). Instead, it must be understood as a series of flows, energies, movements and capacities, a series of fragments of segments capable of being linked together in ways other than those that congeal it into an identity.[20]

While the dynamic exchange between film object and viewing subject has been examined from various perspectives in this book, Deleuze presents a way of interrogating the concept by challenging the proposed distinction between subjective and objective images, which is especially relevant in relation to found footage horror cinema. Although point of view shots have traditionally been presented as providing a viewing subject 'subjective' access to the so-called objective world of the film, Deleuze's concept of the perception-image offers another way of rethinking the differences between them.

Deleuzian 'Spectatorship'

Any attempt to draw Deleuze into the fray of spectatorship theory requires that we reconcile the common assertion that Deleuze's *Cinema* books have little interest in the notion of spectatorship with this expanded understanding of Deleuze's perception-image. Scholars such as Ronald Bogue and Felicity Colman rightly argue that much of Deleuze's focus in the *Cinema* books is on film content, as opposed to the viewing experience, while Laura Marks explicitly contends that Deleuzian cinematic theory is not a theory of spectatorship.[21] Similarly, Mark B. N. Hansen posits that Deleuze's blurring of the boundary between film and spectator is problematic for spectatorship theory in any Deleuzian context. He claims that a Deleuzian spectator is one who is entirely *subjected to* the cinema, in which the spectator loses the characteristics that would define subjecthood.[22] Richard Rushton, however, takes issue with this characterisation, arguing that Hansen misidentifies cinema's 'affectivities' as 'entirely within the films themselves' rather than also in the spectatorial body.[23]

Acknowledging that Deleuze's approach to cinema does challenge the established notions of unified subjectivity that were foundational for the film theory of the 1970s and 1980s, Rushton asserts that there is a dearth of scholarship that examines a Deleuzian alternative in terms of the actual experience of film spectatorship. As previously explained, for Deleuze, the problematic of subjectivity is considered as 'a process of becoming': manifesting as a qualitative multiplicity, subjectivity in a Deleuzo-Guattarian sense is not a presupposed identity but something produced in a process of individuation which is always collective.[24] Del Río clarifies the distinction between the phenomenological mode and what Deleuze proposes:

> While for Merleau-Ponty movement and affect are subjective phenomena arising out of an intentional and individuated rapport with the world, Deleuze regards the kinetic and the affective as material flows whose individuation and exchange do not rest upon subjectified intentions, but rather upon the workings of a non-organic, anonymous vitality.[25]

Deleuze's concept challenges the Kantian understandings of the foundations of subjectivity. Colebrook explains the distinction between a Kantian and Deleuzian notion of subjectivity thus:

> For Kant, our experienced world of time and space is possible only because there is a subject who experiences and who connects (or synthesises) received impressions into a coherent order. For Deleuze, by contrast, there is not a subject who synthesises. Rather, there are syntheses from which subjects are formed; these subjects are not persons but points of relative stability resulting from connection, what Deleuze refers to as 'larval subjects'.[26]

The quandary posed by this Deleuzian notion of subjectivity in relation to cinema becomes thus: if there is not a unified subject who encounters the film, who or what does?

THE PERCEPTION-IMAGE

Found footage horror films offer a constructive site to examine Deleuze's concept of the perception-image, given their interplay of subjective and objective camera. To investigate this claim, it will help to lay out the foundations of how previous scholars, drawing on Deleuze, have used the perception-image as a pathway to consider alternative answers to the question of who or what encounters the film in the act of spectatorship. Richard Rushton, Teresa Rizzo and Louis-Georges Schwartz have each attempted to reconcile Deleuzian theory with the presence of a spectator through the concept of the perception-image: in Rizzo's terms, 'the possibility that the perception-image produces a cinematic subject or specific cinematic consciousness that invites the viewer to connect with it'.[27] The concept of the perception-image, developed in *Cinema 1*, is drawn primarily from Deleuze's consideration of the theoretical work of Pier Paolo Pasolini and Jean Mitry, and their attempts to explicate cinema's unique capacity for the expression of a subjective and objective perspective within a single shot.[28] Deleuze, in attempting to isolate the 'felt-quality' of these particular types of images, utilises two distinct terms from Pasolini and Mitry: Pasolini's definition of the phenomenon of 'free indirect image' or 'free indirect camera', and Mitry's terminology of a 'semi-subjective shot'.[29]

In Pasolini's conception, 'free indirect camera' draws from the linguistic style of free indirect discourse, which oscillates between subjective voice of character and objective voice of narrator. Deleuze describes free indirect discourse as 'carrying out two inseparable acts of subjectivation simultaneously': these acts are a bi-fold constitution of the character in the first person combined indivisibly with the constitution of the narrator.[30] This can be illustrated cinematically in the ambiguity of film shots that are presented as neither completely originating from the point of view of the character, nor from an omniscient position that appears external to the character. Instead, we are presented with images wherein the subjective and objective perspectives are revealed to be merely provisional, or where perspective can shift almost effortlessly within a shot. What this produces, Rushton argues, is the capacity for a complex *interaction* between spectator and screen. Rushton chooses the word interaction specifically to highlight his contention that 'cinema *is* interactive. It is a composite of subject and object in which each determines, interrogates and investigates the other.'[31] Rizzo posits that the 'felt-quality' of the perception-image 'implies a film-viewer'. Quoting Deleuze – 'the perception-image is endowed with a felt quality that gives the impression of 'being-with' characters' – Rizzo argues that this 'felt quality' necessitates the generation of a kind of embodied consciousness.[32] She also points out that, unlike the inscribed positioning of the transcendental subject proposed by Baudry and Metz, where the subject is an idealised bodiless entity pre-existing at the centre of a world of vision, the 'act of differentiation central to the perception-image implies a subject that is in a state of becoming'.[33]

Schwartz describes Deleuze's extension of Pasolini's 'free indirect cinematographic discourse' as a technique which enables a director to reproduce a variety of voices and perspectives, in a manner that taps into the essential qualities of cinema, producing a kind of cinematic consciousness: '[b]y making Pasolini identify free indirect images with the essence of cinema, Deleuze forges an ontological link between cinema and subjectivity.'[34] This conception of a cinematic consciousness arises from the potential for fluctuation between subjective and objective perspectives within a shot. Rushton, in his critique of Mark B. N. Hansen, expands on this concept of cinematic consciousness to elucidate the specifics of how this idea integrates with the experiential spectator. For Rushton, Deleuze's work 'effectively draws a map of the way the spectator works with cinematic images and sounds'.[35] Rushton proposes this cinematic consciousness as the meeting point of the 'empirical-bodily' aspects of the spectator and the transcendental aspects of spectatorship.[36] It should be noted that this is a different conception of transcendental than that offered by Metz's apparatus theory.[37] Instead, the transcendental aspect of film viewing, for Rushton, is the Deleuzian potential for objective perception in the cinema: Deleuze defines this through negation, by simply differentiating it from subjective shots that are implied as a particular character's point of view. Deleuze writes: 'We should be able to say, in fact, that the image is objective when the thing or the set are seen from the viewpoint of someone who remains external to that set', although he does assert that this definition is provisional (a shot may be later revealed to be internal to the set).[38]

Rushton draws his frame of the transcendental aspects of spectatorship from Deleuze's concept of the Cogito. In *Cinema 1*, in a rumination on the free indirect image, Deleuze writes:

> Can we not find this dividing-in-two, or this differentiation of the subject in language, in thought and in art? It is the *Cogito*: an empirical subject cannot be born into the world without simultaneously being reflected in a transcendental subject which thinks it and in which it thinks itself. And the *Cogito* of art: there is no subject which acts without another which watches it act, and which grasps it as acted, itself assuming the freedom of which it deprives the former.[39]

Rushton proposes that this bifurcation corresponds to a concept of spectatorship. Importantly, this bifurcation is more specifically an *integration*. It is, in Deleuzian terms, the Cogito, which recognises that there are objective and subjective dimensions of experience. Rushton uses the term 'empirical-bodily aspects' of the spectator as a way of describing the body's response to the affects and intensities of cinema, although he defines this as an 'automatic' and 'mechanical' response, in order to separate it from the transcendental aspect, which is more circumspect. The transcendental aspect of the spectator, for Rushton, works in the same manner as Deleuze's transcendental subject, which '"sits back" and observes, monitors or watches the automatic, empirical aspect of the subject'.[40]

Rushton's interpretation of the Deleuzian perception-image proposes that spectatorship, for Deleuze, is always doubled in this way: 'one part of the spectator receives and responds to images automatically, while another aspect of the spectator monitors these automatic responses'.[41] In the cinema of the movement-image, sensation and thought are always intertwined. Rushton argues that the experience of an image should always be considered as an integration of the bodily-empirical and transcendental aspects of the spectator.

Crucially, while certain images appear to be subjective, as though from a subjective point of view, this subjectivity is completely determined by the camera. We can return here to the character of Aaron approaching Peachfuzz in the scene in *Creep*; our feelings of subjectivity emerge from the way the scene is composed, with the camera mimicking Aaron's gradual descent down the stairs. As Rushton goes on to explain:

> Any subjectivity that I may experience in respect of what I see on the screen is imposed on me by the camera – all I can do is receive it. In this way, so-called subjective shots in the cinema are wholly determined by the cinematic object: they are *objective images imposed on a spectator-subject*.[42]

Moreover, in Rushton's conception, objective images, despite their apparent objectivity, still require that the spectator bring something to the table. He utilises Edward Branigan's argument that spectators repeatedly make theoretical leaps in understanding narrative or constructing hypotheses about potential or past occurrences, as they place the filmic material into a structure, a consequence of the fact that there are parts of the film's world that they are unable to view.[43] Rushton, drawing on Branigan, describes this act as the construction of a 'potentially objective diegetic world'.[44] While this objective filmic world is composed of all of the elements that are captured by the camera and presented to the spectator, it is the transcendental spectator-subject's *subjective* capacities that manifest the conceptual contents of films that are, in Branigan's terms, 'independent of certain angles of view'.[45] Rushton writes:

> These are the images or concepts of a film that simply would not exist were it not for the fact that there is someone to watch, listen to and make sense of them. It is nothing less than what the spectator, at any point during the viewing of a film, *adds to* that film. This is manifestly a transcendental level of understanding: what a subject adds to the viewing experience in order to grant that experience a potential objectivity.[46]

It is not just the past events of the film itself that contribute to this transcendental level of understanding, but, as Rushton claims, 'the whole of one's past', meaning all the wealth of our experiences of an objective world outside of the film, including our experiences watching other films.[47] He draws on Deleuze's understanding of this transcendental processing of images as wholly passive, and not the result of the subject's conscious effort. Rushton writes: '[transcendental processes] emerge *without the active or conscious provocation of the subject*. In other words, these transcendental conditions *happen to* the subject, rather than being *caused by* the subject.'[48] This is part of Deleuze's larger challenge to the way representational structures construct a subject.

Rushton's interpretation of Deleuze's perception-image offers an expanded way of interpreting how found footage horror's so-called subjective images do not simply encourage a form of 'perspective taking': they are affective moments of sense data that are corporeally experienced and yet they are also reliant on the 'transcendental' aspects of the spectator to fill out this 'objective' presence with their subjective capacities. However, this is not achieved solely through deliberate appraisal, as cognitivist models may argue.

The following example of two shots from the contemporary classic, *No Country for Old Men* (2007), further illustrates this concept. Towards the film's conclusion, remorseless killer Anton Chigurh (played by Javier Bardem) visits

Carla Jean (Kelly Macdonald), the wife of slain protagonist Llewelyn Moss (Josh Brolin). Early in the film, Chigurh promises Moss he will kill Carla Jean if Moss refuses to hand himself over to the killer. The implication of the visit to Carla Jean is that Chigurh has come to fulfil his promise, yet, as he has done previously in the film, he gives Carla Jean the opportunity to win the flip of a coin to extricate herself from the situation. 'The coin don't have no say, it's just you,' she proffers. The scene cuts to a shadowy, almost subjective shot (from Carla Jean's perspective) of Chigurh as he responds: 'I got here the same way the coin did.' The scene then cuts to an idyllic exterior long-shot of Carla Jean's house as two young boys pass by on bicycles. Chigurh steps out of the front door, checks the soles of his shoes, and proceeds down the front path.

Branigan's argument implies that the spectator will infer or intimate what has occurred in the cut between the two shots on the basis of the diegetic world being an *objective* place. We do not infer that in an instant Chigurh was transported from Carla Jean's couch to the front door – we instead gather that something occurred in the space in-between, and based on the previous actions of Chigurh, the strong likelihood that Carla Jean is dead. To unpack how this demonstrates the difference between the empirical and transcendental aspects of the Deleuzian spectator, we can say that our ability to realise that the second shot occurs chronologically after the first is an 'empirical' process.[49] This ability to position events in time occurs due to what Deleuze calls the 'passive synthesis of habit'. This is the first of three syntheses of time, a concept developed from the Kantian notion of intuition, which explains how we intuit the passage of time between the two moments automatically.[50]

There is also another element at play here: the whole coherence of the objective world that constitutes the diegetic space of the film. Knowing what we know about Chigurh's actions in the world of the film, the previous outcomes of his coin-flips, and his implacability, the temporal elision between the two shots is imbued with this knowledge. Also contributing is our experience or memory of previous similar narratives, and our experience or memory of the world outside of the film. This is a function, in Deleuzian terms, of the 'second passive synthesis of memory', in which, as Rushton points out, 'the present can only function as "present" on the basis of a past which conditions it *as* present'.[51]

Taking these as *transcendental* conditions, as Deleuze proposes, in that they establish a relation between the two shots, leads to an acknowledgement that the relation is not objective, in the sense of being an element of the film that is actualised *without* the input of a viewer. Branigan asserts as much, when he argues: 'the spectator completes the action; or rather, the spectator constructs a virtual time in which the action is realised'.[52]

Returning to the film *Creep*, there are some different nuances of this process in action. As Aaron gradually becomes aware of Josef's deception, each of the scenes begins to have a different resonance in the present. What may have been innocuous in the previous context becomes shaded with sinister potential. At the end of their day together, Josef reveals that he had been surreptitiously watching Aaron and taking photos of him when Aaron had first arrived, before they had even met. This revelation is the first glimpse into how disturbed Josef is, and while it is not a particularly menacing reveal, its consequences carry over into the following scene.

It is night, and the duo return to Josef's cabin. Climbing the precipitous stairs, the camera halts one flight below Josef, and he is haloed by the yellow light but his face remains in darkness (Figure 4.1).[53] While this is clearly a subjective shot, in that it is designed to place us in the exact position of Aaron's optical perceptual experience, it is also clearly not our body as spectator that is present recording it. This is what Mitry defined as the 'semi-subjective': subjective in style, but with a manner of objectivity, in that the spectator cannot change it or interact with it. This does not negate our embodied experience of the image, only our capacities for interaction. The transcendental aspect of our experience of this moment, however, is everything that we already bring to the moment that grants it possible objectivity: our understanding of 'human nature', our memories, our unique or collective fears. To reiterate, this is not a conscious decision to activate thought in response to the image, but simply the conditions that allow an experience to be *experienced*. To return to Deleuze, 'an empirical subject cannot be born

Figure 4.1 Aaron's point of view in *Creep*.

into the world without simultaneously being reflected in a transcendental subject'.[54]

Whereas Mark B. N. Hansen proposes that Deleuze's understanding of cinema elides the body of the spectator, Rushton instead recapitulates Deleuze's Cogito of art, where this division between the empirical and the transcendental aspects of the subject 'never goes to the limit. It is rather an oscillation of the person between two points of view on himself, a hither-and-thither of the spirit . . . a being-with.'[55] As Rushton states, Deleuzian cinematic subjectivities are 'composites of subject and object in states of deformation and reformation which respond to and act upon the fluctuations of empirical reception and transcendental structuration'.[56] In this way, Deleuze's perception-image does return the body to experience, as it sees no fundamental schism between sensation and thought in the cinematic experience.

FOUND FOOTAGE HORROR AND 'CAMERA-CONSCIOUSNESS'

Where does this bring us to in a consideration of the genre of found footage horror? What becomes abundantly evident is that the concept of the subjective camera is not quite so black-and-white as may be assumed. Where the camera often stands in for the optical perceptual experience of a character, and, thus, is designed to reproduce the subjective aspects of that character's experience, often it is a character in itself, often it simply *feels* like a character itself, and at other times it can be seemingly external to the subjective world of the characters. *Creep* exemplifies this capacity for the camera to become character, in the scenes in which the camera is recording but is not operated by Aaron, such as the sequence in which Aaron confesses to camera that Josef's masked alter ego, Peachfuzz, is haunting his nightmares. The third capacity, of seeming objectivity, is more evident when the diegetic camera is used for surveillance in a manner which is seemingly neutral and unmediated by the characters, such as the examples previously described in the *Paranormal Activity* series, and the 'grave-digging' sequence in *Creep*. This sequence cleverly takes advantage of the supposition that we are watching an objective record of the events: after the seemingly violent confrontation between Aaron and Josef described in this chapter's opening, and the ominous cut to black, we then cut to a static shot of Josef moving through frame, lugging what appears to be a body in garbage bags, and digging what appears to be a grave. It is only after a few drawn-out moments that Aaron reveals that it is *he* who is recording himself watching *this* footage on his home TV – and that it is the contents of a video that had been mailed to him several days later by Josef (leaving the unresolved question of what – or who – was in the bags) (Figure 4.2). The ambivalent nature of the

Figure 4.2 Josef takes out the trash in *Creep*.

identity of the viewer/recorder in this sequence illustrates how found footage often 'plays' with notions of subjective and objective vision.

What this 'play' achieves, in a sense, is a further variation on the perception-image's capacities: Rizzo describes this as a movement 'away from a centred universal form of human subjectivity to a cinematic experience based on interaction, variation and change'.[57] The effect of this dynamic oscillation between points of view further highlights the question of whether empathic engagement can be solely established through our access to a character's subjectivity or through the immersive properties of the physiological response. Instead, a consideration of how we experience found footage adds nuance to each of these accounts, through the way the shifts in point of view promote a coexistence of perspectives.

Regarding Pasolini's free indirect camera, Deleuze writes:

> A character acts on the screen, and is assumed to see the world in a certain way. But simultaneously the camera sees him, and sees his world, from another point of view which thinks, reflects and transforms the viewpoint of the character [. . .] the camera does not simply give us the vision of the character and of his world; it imposes another vision in which the first is transformed and reflected.[58]

However, found footage horror film necessarily works differently to this. The camera *does*, in a sense, give us the vision of the character and his world as they record it; they literally 'see' the world in a certain way, which we are often privy to. But in doing so, it does not abrogate the possibility for this vision to be transformed or reflected in another vision, as it is never fully the 'subjective' experience of the observer – it is always mediated by the diegetic presence of the camera. Although there is no 'second camera' (in the Deleuzian sense), no other point of view seeing the world, there is the presence of the camera, as so-called objective recording device within the diegetic world of the film, independent of the character's consciousness, which becomes in a sense the second vision which can still transform and reflect the first. It does so in the way Mitry describes, by not 'mingl[ing]' with the character, but also not being 'outside'.[59]

This dual operation can be seen in the way the diegetic camera is often employed in found footage horror films. Deleuze refers to the following as one of 'stylistic procedures' analysed by Pasolini which reveal the cinematographic Cogito:

> 'insistent' or 'obsessive' framing, which makes the camera await the entry of a character into the frame, wait for him to do and say something then exit, while it continues to frame the space which has once again become empty, once more leaving the scene to its pure and absolute signification as scene.[60]

This feature can still be considered an indicator of an 'independent aesthetic consciousness', even if it can be attributed to the diegetic presence of a camera, including one that is not being operated by one of the protagonists. This 'obsessive' framing is often present in the found footage horror subgenre and largely occurs without the presence of a diegetic camera operator. For instance, in *Creep*, we are presented with the generic convention of the horror film villain watching his potential victim, seen by the audience, but unseen by his prey. However, this moment is felt differently in found footage than in conventional horror film. The running camera, deposited on the bed by Aaron as he searches his house for intrusion, captures Josef's appearance at the entrance to the house, and his subsequent malevolent disappearance. This is not a subjective image, nor a wholly objective image. The camera is not, as Deleuze defines objective, 'external to the set'. This type of framing is also demonstrated in the continually recording surveillance cameras of *Paranormal Activity*, as discussed in previous chapters.

It is arguable that this conception is not entirely equivalent to Deleuze's argument, wherein 'the perception image finds it status [...] from the moment that it reflects its content in a camera-consciousness which has become autonomous'.[61] While the camera-consciousness of found footage horror is not completely autonomous, it repeatedly infiltrates the image in subtle ways, as described above.

Camera-consciousness, for Deleuze, is a concept that encompasses in part, but not in full, the consciousness of any viewer, the viewpoint of a centred subjectivity, *and* the transcendental expression of truth apprehended by technological means. It is perhaps better described, as Spencer Shaw does, as 'a consciousness expressed through the flux and transformation of an ever evolving temporal artwork that assimilates all centers and incorporates them into an indivisible flow'.[62] Deleuzian philosophy may appear, in this conception, to be in opposition to an embodied human spectator, particularly when Deleuze writes: 'The sole cinematographic consciousness is not us, the spectator, nor the hero. It is the camera – sometimes human, sometimes inhuman or superhuman.'[63] However, what the idea of 'camera-consciousness' allows for is the existence of different perspectives and different voices, be they human or inhuman. Reflecting on the perception-image in *Cinema 2*, Deleuze labels this process a 'circuit', where 'objective and subjective images lose their distinction' and 'contaminate' each other.[64] The result, he contends, is a cinematographic *Mitsein* (being-with), a concept which draws on the Heideggerian term for how others are always implicated in our existence.[65] This 'being-with', in Rizzo's interpretation of Deleuze, is produced by the 'oscillation of different perspectives' and 'points to a subjectivity that is always in motion, always becoming, and always differing from itself'.[66] This Deleuzian circuit contests the logic of a cinematic apparatus that generates a universal subject, in favour of a form of subjectivity that is always in flux, and therefore opens cinema to have radical potential in terms of challenging the politics inherent in such a limited conception of the subject. In this understanding, cinema can be a difference-making machine, and the perception-image, Deleuze contends, as a component of the movement-image, produces this 'universal variation'.[67]

While cognitivism understands cinema through the implicit division between viewer and film, Deleuze instead proposes that cinema is capable of destabilising the normative division between objective and subjective perception, and thus any hierarchical conception of film as object and viewer as subject. This concept has particular political relevance, as the intensities brought about by this 'molecular' thought bring into question the notion of a presupposed fixed identity, allowing for mutability in what are perceived as rigid hierarchies of the identity of the filmic subject (such as gender and race). It also allows us to further develop conceptions of spectatorship that consider our affective and intellectual experiences of the image as more closely intertwined.

DELEUZE AND REPRESENTATION

An expanded understanding of spectatorship emerges from this consideration of found footage horror films as exemplars containing a perception-image that allows for the interplay of subjectivity and objectivity. Found footage horror films complicate the process of identification and empathy and question representational models. They present a clear challenge to a unitary identification with any character or with the recording camera as an objective 'eye' on the filmic world, instead allowing for a mutability in our experience of the image.

In *Difference and Repetition*, Deleuze critiques representational thinking for its capacity to limit difference. For Deleuze, representation is characterised by four aspects: identity, opposition, analogy and resemblance. Within such a narrow band of definable aspects, potential for difference is abrogated, as difference becomes determined only by the manner in which the object of representation is related to its conceived identity, a conjured opposition, a decided analogy or a perceived similarity.[68] This is especially important in relation to representational models that have been applied to cinema, which are, as del Río observes,

> [e]ither unwilling or insufficient to address the way in which the experience of the moving image can at times escape binary determinations and established signifying codes. Driven by notions of representation, semiotic, psychoanalytic, and ideological analyses unwittingly furthered oppositional binaries that the cinema itself has consistently proven quite capable of undoing, binaries such as reality/illusion, subject/object, thought/emotion, activity/passivity, and so on. The imposition of a totalizing picture of reality as structured meaning carried out by the representational approach left little, if anything, to the unstructured sensations that are likewise set in motion in the film-viewing experience.[69]

Similarly, Pisters locates the importance of Deleuze's 'rhizomatic' challenge to representation in how it contests the model of the eye as the most important factor for perceiving and judging difference. She notes how traditional film theory 'conceives [of] the image as a representation that can function as a (distorted or illusionary) mirror for identity construction and subjectivity'.[70] In this model, representation is seen as a process that is intimately linked to a valorisation of the 'I' behind the 'eye'.[71] Pisters points to how sight has been esteemed above all other sensory aspects of experience within the representational model, in which 'I see' necessarily leads on to 'I think', 'I judge', 'I compare'. The alternative conception, proposed by Deleuze, is that of the brain as the screen. This is cinema, in the words of Powell, as something which both 'expresses' and 'induces' thought.[72]

This concept of the 'brain-screen' is particularly relevant to the specific cinematic engagement with diegetic screens and cameras. As Robert Pepperell argues, the screen of the mind and the screens of the world are neither distinct nor unified. The dominant traditions of internalism, which locates the screen entirely in the mind, and externalism, which sees screens as only in the world outside the mind, are insufficient when considered as independent of each other. Pepperell proposes instead a 'dialethic' state, which acknowledges the simultaneous distinction and unity of the two.[73] The brain, in this model, is the membrane between the inside screen and the outside screen.

The intertwined intellectual and affective responses of the embodied brain present a more feasible model for how we perceive ourselves as subjects. In this model, images bring about a complex interaction between body and brain, perception and memory: images have the capacity to be directly affective without being subsumed by our cognitive drive to construct meaning from their relations. Pisters agrees, contending that, under this Deleuzian reconfiguration, the distinction between subjective and objective becomes blurred. She argues that 'we have entered an age [in which] a new camera consciousness makes clear distinction between the subjective and the objective impossible; the past and the present, the virtual and the actual have become indistinguishable'.[74]

Through an analysis of the Kathryn Bigelow film, *Strange Days* (1995; itself not a found footage horror film, although still pertinent to this philosophical consideration), Pisters examines the subjective use of camera in relation to Deleuze's cinematic theory.[75] *Strange Days* features several sequences that are presented as recorded versions of first-person perceptual experience: everything that the character visually perceived was recorded by a headset device known in the movies as a SQUID (a creation of science fiction, but not out of the question considering the recent advances in recording technologies). From her analysis, Pisters identifies the inherent weakness of an equivalence between purely subjective camera (such as that of *Lady in the Lake*) and how spectatorial identification occurs, even if such a system was considered a legitimate means to understand the subjective camera in the way Bordwell and Thompson claim that 'optical' point of view shots generally equate to perceptual subjectivity.[76] Pisters argues for an expanded account of self, according to which

> spectators no longer can confirm their identity by identifying with subjects on screen but have to negotiate between the images presented to their minds and the memories induced by their own bodies. Body, brain and perception work together to establish a sense of self in each point of time, which differs according to the demands of the specific situation.[77]

Pisters attributes this direct challenge to the notion of the transcendental subject of apparatus theory to the shifting contemporary image culture, and in particular the volatility of camera-consciousness. The reconfigured camera-consciousness she identifies in *Strange Days*, much like found footage horror, produces an encounter that is defined by the 'diminished distance between who is seeing and what is seen, through the physical and intensive implication of the spectator'; what emerges from this encounter between viewer and image is a type of thought that differs from representational thinking, one that resonates intensively and extensively.[78]

Rethinking Deleuze's perception-image in relation to found footage horror provides a new framework for considering how we are drawn into a film, in ways that may challenge the theoretical orthodoxy of primary or secondary identification. Found footage horror film often works against the bases of these forms of identification, by reducing the presence of the on-screen body of the protagonist and foregrounding the presence of the diegetic camera. The 'becoming-with' that this model conceives of is an integration between viewer and image that exceeds the limits of concepts such as identification or the type of 'affective alignment' that Adam Charles Hart proposes.[79]

When exposed to a found footage horror film, the modern spectator immediately identifies the generic markers of 'subjective' footage, but the effects of these films go beyond the capacities of what should then be considered a 'fake documentary'. While a viewer watches the film *Creep* unfold as Aaron records it, specifically through his act of recording it, their perception never fully correlates with either his perception or that of the recording camera. The spectator is presented with a somewhat subjective view of this world, but they bring to their experience of it an interoceptive response *and* a transcendental understanding, in the Deleuzian sense, which is crucially integrated with their empirical-bodily affectivity.[80] This transcendental aspect does not remain at a distance, but is what the viewer adds to the experience to grant it potential objectivity. The combination of the two aspects allows for a more holistic understanding of potential subjectivity and objectivity as components of any image. In doing so, it prompts us to reconceive notions of film-object and spectator-subject as Rushton does, as ever-evolving 'composites', always in 'states of deformation and reformation'.[81]

Notes

1. Currie, *Image and Mind*, p. 144.
2. Rødje, 'Intra-Diegetic Cameras as Cinematic Actor Assemblages', pp. 207–8.
3. Turner argues that the viewer may read the bodily cues of the character through the dynamics of the cinematography; see Turner, *Found Footage Horror Films*, p. 16.
4. Stam, *Film Theory*, p. 137.
5. Thompson, 'Categorical Coherence'.
6. Branigan, *Narrative Comprehension and Film*, p. 112.
7. Bordwell and Thompson, *Film Art*, p. 91.
8. Branigan, *Point of View in the Cinema*, p. 7.
9. Ibid. p. 7.
10. Ibid. p. 23.
11. Flaxman, *The Brain Is the Screen*, p. 9.
12. Ibid. p. 9.
13. Livesey, 'Assemblage', p. 18.
14. Powell, *Deleuze and Horror Film*, p. 66.

15. Deleuze and Guattari, *A Thousand Plateaus*, p. 220.
16. Bergson, *Matter and Memory*, p. 27, cited in Deleuze, *Cinema 1*, p. 63.
17. Deleuze, *Cinema 1*, pp. 56–66.
18. Ibid. p. 58.
19. Deleuze, *Cinema 2*, p. 169.
20. Grosz, 'A Thousand Tiny Sexes', p. 173.
21. Bogue, *Deleuze on Cinema*; Colman, *Deleuze and Cinema*; Marks, *The Skin of the Film*, p. 150.
22. Hansen, *New Philosophy for New Media*, pp. 6–7.
23. Rushton, 'Passions and Actions', p. 125.
24. Deleuze and Guattari, *A Thousand Plateaus*, p. 9.
25. Del Río, *Deleuze and the Cinemas of Performance*, p. 115.
26. Colebrook, 'Disjunctive Synthesis', p. 80.
27. Rizzo, *Deleuze and Film*, p. 28.
28. Mitry, *Esthétique et Psychologie du Cinema*, II, p. 61, cited in Deleuze, *Cinema 1*, pp. 71–6; Pasolini, *L'Expérience Hérétique*, pp. 139–55, cited in Deleuze, *Cinema 1*, pp. 71–6.
29. Deleuze, *Cinema 1*, p. 72.
30. Ibid. p. 73.
31. Rushton, 'Passions and Actions', p. 126.
32. Rizzo, *Deleuze and Film*, p. 29.
33. Ibid. p. 32.
34. Schwartz, 'Typewriter', p. 122.
35. Rushton, 'Passions and Actions', p. 127.
36. 'Empirical-bodily' is a Kantian term Rushton uses to describe the production of knowledge primarily from sensory experience in the interaction between the body and world (as opposed to transcendental knowledge, which is purely conceptual); ibid. p. 128.
37. Metz proposes the spectator's identification with the camera as the formation of a 'transcendental subject'; Metz, *The Imaginary Signifier*, p. 50.
38. Deleuze, *Cinema 1*, p. 71.
39. Ibid. p. 73.
40. Rushton, 'Passions and Actions', p. 127
41. Ibid. p. 127.
42. Ibid. p. 129.
43. Branigan, *Narrative Comprehension and Film*, p. 165.
44. Rushton, 'Passions and Actions', pp. 130–1.
45. Branigan, *Narrative Comprehension and Film*, p. 165.
46. Rushton, 'Passions and Actions', p. 133; original emphasis.
47. Ibid. p. 133.
48. Ibid. p. 130; original emphasis.
49. Deleuze, *Difference and Repetition*, p. 81.
50. Ibid. p. 79.
51. Rushton, 'Passions and Actions', p. 132.

52. Branigan, *Narrative Comprehension and Film*, p. 182.
53. It is worth noting that this was a primary image used in the marketing of the film.
54. Deleuze, *Cinema 1*, p. 73.
55. Ibid. p. 74.
56. Rushton, 'Passions and Actions', p. 136.
57. Rizzo, *Deleuze and Film*, p. 34.
58. Deleuze, *Cinema 1*, p. 74.
59. Mitry, *Esthétique et Psychologie du Cinema*, cited in Deleuze, *Cinema 1*, p. 74.
60. Pasolini, *L'Expérience Hérétique*, cited in Deleuze, *Cinema 1*, p. 74.
61. Deleuze, *Cinema 1*, p. 74.
62. Shaw, *Film Consciousness*, p. 165.
63. Deleuze, *Cinema 1*, p. 20.
64. Deleuze, *Cinema 2*, p. 149.
65. *Mitsein* is human existence in so far as it is constituted by relationship or community with others; a being-with.
66. Rizzo, *Deleuze and Film*, pp. 33–4.
67. Deleuze, *Cinema 1*, p. 64.
68. Deleuze, *Difference and Repetition*.
69. Del Río, *Deleuze and the Cinemas of Performance*, p. 2.
70. Pisters, *The Matrix of Visual Culture*, p. 4.
71. Ibid. p. 7.
72. Powell, *Deleuze, Altered States and Film*, p. 4.
73. Pepperell, 'Where's the Screen?', p. 192.
74. Pisters, *The Matrix of Visual Culture*, pp. 43–4.
75. Ibid. pp. 23–44.
76. Bordwell and Thompson, *Film Art*, p. 91.
77. Pisters, *The Matrix of Visual Culture*, p. 43.
78. Ibid. p. 26.
79. Hart, 'The Searching Camera', p. 77.
80. Interoceptive refers to stimuli or somatic sensation produced by the body.
81. Rushton, 'Passions and Actions', p. 136.

CHAPTER FIVE

Horrific Entwinement: Affective Neuroscience and the Body of the Horror Spectator

As distant thunder rumbles, it is Becca's ragged breath that dominates the soundtrack. The young girl's camera lamp cuts a swathe through the darkness of the bedroom where she is trapped. It is her footage that we are watching, her record of the event. In the torchlight, an old woman's hand appears from underneath the bed, an image from the primal fears of every sleepless child. It grabs a handful of the bedcovers and pulls them down.

Searching for an exit, Becca swings the camera wildly – we see a candle holder, and a mirror, but nothing else distinct. She turns the thin blade of light back to the bed.

From behind the bed, the moaning old woman slithers up onto the mattress, her body obscured by the bedsheet, which she crawls under. She rises up, shrouded, a caricature of a ghost – but nonetheless frightening, especially for Becca, who turns away, eyes closed, refusing to meet the veiled form with her gaze. Both the camera and her terrified face are reflected in the mirror, but she does not see the shrouded woman approaching, slowly creeping into the light.

Becca's eyes open, and then widen, now sharing our view of the woman's approach – until the woman drives her face forward, into the glass, shattering our mirrored perspectives.

The Question of Empathy

This moment from M. Night Shyamalan's film *The Visit* (2015) (Figure 5.1) draws us into the focus of this chapter: alternative conceptions of empathic engagement with the image, that may build upon our identification with the film's protagonists, but that are not predicated upon it. This chapter seeks to expand on the previous chapter's investigation of the bond between viewer and image. To this end, I will examine new ways of conceiving of this spectatorial interface by exploring the role of the body in emotional and 'empathic' engagement. In doing so, I will ask the following questions: does found footage produce a different experience of spectatorial empathy? And can the subjective camera and marked point of view, like that discussed in the previous chapter, reconfigure our engagement beyond traditional notions of empathy?

Figure 5.1 Becca's filmed reflection.

For those who are unfamiliar with *The Visit*, the film tells the story of two adolescents, Becca (Olivia DeJonge) and Tyler (Ed Oxenbould), who choose to visit and spend a week with their grandparents, whom they have never met, while their single mom goes on a vacation with her boyfriend. Becca is an aspiring documentarian and decides to make a film about her grandparents in an effort to reconcile the estrangement between them and her mother. She enlists her younger brother as a second camera operator, and while they film the events of the week, they are both disturbed by the strange and ominous behaviour of their elderly hosts. The film is largely presented as found footage, comprised of Becca and Tyler's documentary footage (although clearly edited and condensed by an unspecified entity, complete with title cards for each day of the five-day visit).

Like the films discussed in previous chapters, many of the scenes in *The Visit* mimic the processes of human perception in the way they are shot: the camera's record of events is equivalent to Becca's or Tyler's vision through the viewfinder. The connections between this act of perception and the spectator's typical processing of the cinematic image are part of the focus of this chapter.

As discussed in Chapter 1, cognitivist theorists typically look to a spectator's natural perceptual processes as the foundations for their interaction with the filmic image. Noël Carroll, for example, argues that one of the key drivers for a viewer's engagement can be found in the way spectators subconsciously raise questions throughout the viewing experience; according to him, '[spectators] frame narrative questions tacitly and they subconsciously expect answers to them'.[1] These answers are then actualised by later scenes. This process is a return to the erotetic model and is based, according to Carroll, on an instinctual human urge to forage for information in our environment that will assist in our survival: when viewing a film, we are unaware that we continually repeat this process on behalf of the characters.[2] The distinction in Carroll's concept is one of sympathy over empathy. To clarify, Alex Neill describes sympathy as a feeling *for* someone while empathy is feeling *with* them.[3] In Carroll's conception, the feelings of care or understanding towards the character are a feeling *for* them, distanced and reflective. Sinnerbrink offers this further distinction between empathy and sympathy in relation to film spectatorship:

> From a phenomenological perspective, empathy and sympathy can be described as poles between which we are 'moved' perceptually and affectively: poles marking two distinct yet related kinds of subjective perspective-taking having different but related emotional dynamics and evaluative valences (more immediate, immersive, and affective in the case of empathy, more mediated, reflective, and normative in the case of sympathy).[4]

Murray Smith also addresses the problematic elements of the concept of secondary identification with his proposal of three different levels of engagement between audience and character: recognition, alignment and allegiance. Recognition, for Smith, is the 'spectator's construction of character: the perception of a set of textual elements, in film typically cohering around the image of a body, as an individuated and continuous human agent'.[5] Alignment is the process by which 'spectators are placed in relation to characters in terms of their access to their actions, and to what they know and feel'.[6] Smith proposes two interlocking functions that underpin alignment: 'spatio-temporal attachment' and 'subjective access'.[7] These functions determine how we are given access to the mind of the character or their relationship to the space they inhabit. The third term, allegiance, relates to our moral evaluation of the character: how we judge their actions by imaginative access to their state of mind. Importantly, Smith also makes the distinction between sympathy and empathy, and sees the relation between recognition, allegiance and alignment as constituent components of 'structures of sympathy'.[8] Empathic engagement, he proposes, occurs differently to sympathetic concern. In his account, empathy is 'other-focussed personal imagining' combined with additional low-level pre-reflective responses, such as affective mimicry and emotional contagion.[9] Smith describes this concept of other-focused personal imagining thus: 'Person A [. . .] imagines perceiving, cognizing, or feeling, partially or globally, the perceiving, cognizing, and feeling of [person] B, where such imagining involves conscious, qualitative awareness of the state imagined.'[10]

Found footage horror films arguably draw most strongly on Smith's notion of 'alignment', given that they work specifically to provide the 'spatio-temporal attachment' and 'subjective access' Smith proposes. Empathic engagement, however, as Smith sees it, may be more problematic, given the viewer's scarce access to the stimuli that typically allow for affective mimicry and emotional contagion: the body and face of the protagonist.

A more expansive model of empathy's relation to art can be drawn from Robin Curtis, who examines the origins of the concept of empathy in the work of theorist Theodore Lipps. For Lipps, the act of *einfühlen* (which translates as 'to feel into') explains the human inclination to empathise not only with other creatures, but with other objects, be they animate or inanimate. This extensive account allows for an empathic engagement with phenomena such as colour, sound and atmosphere, and goes beyond the rudimentary processes of empathy that occur between real and/or fictional persons. Curtis argues that this broader engagement with the world (described by the term *Einfühlung*) is evidenced by the way people viewing dance will themselves 'begin to sway or rock', or the 'sympathetic tension' felt by someone observing a tightrope walk.[11] This concept could certainly hold relevance for the lack of visual access to the central characters in found footage horror.

This limitation of the viewer's visual access to the protagonist also requires alternative perspectives on the generation of engagement. Joseph D. Anderson's notion of 'affordances' provides one such approach. Derived from Anderson's development of an 'ecological film theory', the concept of affordances draws on our hardwired biological responses to new environments.[12] An affordance is how the viewer processes each shot of a film based on its 'action possibilities', or what is potentially useful for their needs, a response that directors can use to craft our attention and engagement.[13] Anderson's approach would suggest that when we watch Becca's captivity in the sequence from *The Visit* described in the introduction to this chapter, our interest moves to the potential use-value of her possibilities of escape or harm (the potential that she may successfully confront the old woman, or alternatively, the potential that she may, at worst, be killed).

Anderson identifies 'perspective-taking' as a key function of our engagement with film. He writes:

> To evaluate the affordances in a narrative context (that is, in a diegetic world), one must perceive them in relationship to a character in that world; one must, in other words, perceive them from that character's perspective. The protagonist usually has a problem to solve or a goal to achieve. Whether we are able to share that protagonist's definition of the problem or understand his motivation for pursuing a particular goal, that is, share his perspective, is a factor in our experience of the movie.[14]

While the perspective-taking Anderson refers to is a psychological process, found footage horror offers a literal translation of perspective-taking in the way shots can be composed to mimic the optical perspective of the protagonist and replicate their processing of the affordances of an environment. For example, in *The Visit*, when Becca's younger brother surreptitiously stalks his Pop Pop (Peter McRobbie) with a recording camera, we share the goal of watching Pop Pop's movement and actions, because doing so will assuage our curiosity. Anderson's model and the other models examined above offer alternative ways of thinking about how found footage horror film problematises the conventional notions of primary and secondary identification, given that these films are often attempting to replicate the optical perceptual experience of diegetic characters. This also requires rethinking the conventional theories of empathic or emotional engagement and advancing new models to address these limitations.

Empathic Identification and 'Embodied Simulation Theory'

As discussed in Chapter 2, there have been two common approaches within film theory towards attempting to understand our empathic or emotional engagement with the image and why we react to the filmic image 'as if' it were real: theories that propose that cognitive processes are at the root of this connection, and theories that propose more phenomenological methodologies which explore the implications of embodied experience as the basis for how we interface with the image. The most prominent cognitive methodology to explain this engagement, 'theory of mind', holds that we use our real-world ability to understand the behaviour and actions of others in terms of their mental states – intentions, beliefs and desires – and that we employ this same technique when experiencing a filmic narrative, through identification with the character's behaviour and actions: this is Grodal's conception of empathy as 'a viewer-activation of affects and emotions in identification with the interests of a fictive being'.[15] Ultimately, under the cognitivist conception, we are empathically engaged because the film-viewing experience mimics our experience of the world outside of the theatre.[16] In Jeffrey Zacks's description: 'Our brains didn't evolve to watch movies: Movies evolved to take advantage of the brains we have.'[17]

Recent neuroscientific models have confirmed that a viewer's engagement with cinema is to some degree an extension of their perceptual system's grasp of the real world. One specific field that has captured the attention of film theorists is that of the research into mirror neurons, discovered by Giacomo Rizzolatti and his colleagues at the University of Parma in 1996.[18] Studying macaque monkeys, this research into motor-neural activity discovered that particular neurons were triggered not only when the monkeys performed an action, but also when the monkeys saw an action demonstrated to them. This discovery, and its expansion into theories of empathy, saw the positing of mirror neurons as a key element to the emotional engagement that can occur between a spectator and the cinematic image. Theorists such as Smith, however, have pointed to the insufficiency of mirror neurons as a complete explanation, acknowledging that, while the system of mirror neurons 'does suggest how simulation of higher-order states can work from the platform of motor and affective mimicry', it should be best considered as a 'scaffold' for imagination, especially empathic imagination.[19] This conceptual stance appears to revert to a hierarchical approach to understanding the construction of empathy, where motor and affective mimicry are simply a 'platform' and 'higher order' empathy is produced through imaginative engagement with narrative. However, horror cinema often intentionally frustrates these 'higher order' processes by restricting our access to the narrative content that underpins it, which in turn accentuates the motor and affective mimicry that remain at the fundamental basis of our ongoing interaction with the image.

The positing of mirror neurons as the fundamental substratum of our empathic or emotional engagement with the image has some limitations. While the action of mirror neurons may address the special quality of 'realness' that the filmic world contains, despite its 'unreal' quality, they do not completely account for the particulars of the experience of film spectatorship. For example, they do not fully explain the 'something more' in the experience of viewing that qualitatively differs from our real perceptual experience. And, importantly in relation to found footage horror, they rely on the explicit visual presence of a motor action or expression of emotion by an actor, which found footage often hinders by placing the protagonist behind the camera.

Informed by the phenomenological approach, the recent neuroscientific research into 'embodied simulation theory' (EST) expands upon the concept of the mirror neuron mechanism and develops new insights into how the body may figure more prominently in understanding our empathic engagement with cinema and how we may overcome the 'paradox of fiction'. Embodied simulation theory belongs within the paradigm of embodied cognition scholarship, a field that has sparked much interest in the last decade and has become increasingly important within the domain of cognitive film studies.[20] Theories of embodied cognition arose in response to a movement away from the accepted models of early mainstream cognitive science, which asserted a computational view of the mind as 'abstract information processor'.[21] Under the models advanced by embodied cognition, sensory and motor functions play a crucial role in how the body shapes the mind. Coëgnarts and Kravanja note the shift to these models in the cognitive sciences more broadly, asserting that 'cognition is no longer conceived as the product of a disembodied abstract information processor, but the product of our ongoing interactions with our changing environments (or "enactions" as Varela, Thompson and Rosch have labelled them)'.[22]

Accordingly, most branches of cognitive film studies have reacted to this shift, although with varying degrees of emphasis on the primacy of the body. Nannicelli and Taberham identify a second wave within cognitive film studies which has seen the focus shift from '"cold cognition" (information-driven mental processes described in terms of inferential and computational models)' to '"hot cognition" (affect-driven mental processes)' and contend that cognitive film theory is a largely pluralist field in terms of theoretical commitments.[23] However, the question of how affect 'drives' these mental processes is one that finds a myriad of responses, and one that is crucially determined by the particular understanding of affect involved, as discussed in Chapter 2.

If we return here to embodied simulation theory, we can further unpack how this conceptual model offers new ways of understanding empathic engagement. Originating in the work of Vittorio Gallese, embodied simulation theory argues that the 'actions, emotions and sensations' of others, both in the real world and on the fictional screen, are translated onto an observer's own sensory-motor and viscero-motor neural pathways, producing corresponding physiological responses simply through the act of perception.[24] The mechanism behind EST is universal, involuntary and non-conscious, and '[grounds] our identification with and connectedness to others'.[25] Gallese and Guerra write:

> According to [embodied simulation theory] our brain-body system re-uses parts of its neural resources to map others' behavior. When witnessing actions performed by others, we simulate them by activating our own motor system. Similarly, by activating other cortical regions we re-use our affective and sensory-motor neural circuits to map the emotional and somato-sensory experiences of others. By means of [embodied simulation] we have a direct access to the world of others.[26]

EST further fleshes out the argument that the perceptual processes of watching film are directly analogous to our perceptual interactions with the real world. Advocates of EST contend that the theory more pertinently explains the intensity of our empathic engagement with cinema, in that EST offers a way of understanding how this interface often exceeds the effects of a purely imaginative engagement with narrative. Gallese, reflecting on our processing of fictional narratives, rejects 'suspension of disbelief' as that which allows for intensity of immersion, proposing instead that cinema can allow for 'liberated embodied simulation', an 'immersive state' in which we 'fully deploy our simulative resources'.[27] This 'liberated' embodied simulation allows us to temporarily forego embodied simulation in the real world, which in turn magnifies our receptivity to the cinema screen. Gallese and Wojciehowski describe this as the way we '[leave] the world behind' when we appreciate art, placing ourselves instead in 'an immersive state in which our attention is focused on the narrated virtual world' almost entirely.[28]

EST can also help explain the authenticity of our response to horror films despite our incredulity towards their narrative content. For Gallese and Guerra, EST offers an answer to the question of how, being aware that we are spectators to a film, we can still be gripped by 'suspense', and more importantly, why we feel the same or similar feelings on second or third viewings: they label this aura of authenticity film's 'reality effect'. They also acknowledge Bordwell's interesting contribution to this debate, when Bordwell writes: 'a great deal of what contributes to suspense in films derives from low-level, modular processes. They are cognitively impenetrable, and that creates a firewall between them and what we remember from previous viewings.'[29] EST accounts for some of the 'low-level' processes of Bordwell's proposed 'firewall', in that the observer is unable to limit the sensory-motor and viscero-motor pathways that are activated by the image, regardless of their ability to exercise an intellectual rationale over the reality of what they are observing.

As useful as EST's understanding of the mirror mechanism can be, it cannot fully explain immersion in found footage horror films in which the viewer's visual access to the actions or expressions of emotion of an on-screen other are restricted. Many films in the found footage horror genre constrain identification with character due to the limitations of the visual form: while we may have 'alignment' with many of the characters in found footage horror, in terms of 'spatio-temporal attachment' and 'subjective access' to their optical perceptual experience, we typically have less access as viewers to the other dimensions that more commonly foster identification, such as the bodily presence of the protagonist, their voice, and importantly, their face. A viewer is given less access to the conventional aspects of a film that, according to theory of mind, enable the fullest form of identification and therefore empathic engagement. Concurrently, we also have less access to some of the visual aspects that the mirror mechanism draws on.

The neuroscientific foundations of EST are, however, not entirely reliant on the input of the mirror neuron mechanism. Gallese and Guerra note that the mirror mechanism is only one process of embodied simulation, and that other processes contribute to a more expansive understanding of the viewer–image relationship. The two that are most relevant in relation to found footage horror are those that have emerged from studies into canonical neurons – neurons located in the premotor and posterior parietal cortex.

Canonical neurons are activated in the observation of an object: according to Gallese and Guerra, '[s]eeing a manipulable object selectively recruits the same motor resources typically employed during the planning and execution of actions targeting the same object.'[30] They use the term 'peri-personal space' to describe the 'space surrounding our body'. Importantly, they define peri-personal space as multisensory (visual, tactile, auditory and proprioceptive), somatically centred (not encoded purely by visual processing) and concerned with our potential for movement (perhaps best understood as both an attitude towards a potential motor task, and how the potentiality of that task shapes our perception).[31] When an object is observed, canonical neurons 'integrate visual and auditory information' about those objects by 'mapping it onto the motor programs required to interact with those objects within that space'.[32]

This process offers an alternative conception of empathic connection in our relation to found footage horror. Though these films may be largely devoid of the bodily presence of the one recording the events, the objects and spaces presented are nonetheless somatically simulated by the viewer, corporeally imbricating us with the unseen operator of the camera. This is perspective-taking not limited to that of a psychological process, but perspective-taking that imbricates the corporeal response to the objects and spaces presented in the image.

Guerra, in his analysis of film style from an embodied perspective, draws attention to how the moving camera modulates the presence of the viewer in the shot. Referring to an experiment he conducted with Gallese on the 'feeling of movement' which used EEGs to study the activation of the mirror mechanism in relation to four types of shots – still, zoom, dolly and Steadicam – Guerra observes that the Steadicam produced the strongest activation.[33] He attributes to the Steadicam a kind of 'biological' movement, given it is mounted on the operator's body, and refers to how operators of the camera rig such as Garrett Brown and Larry McConkey each contend that this movement produces a 'more empathetic, more involved' audience.[34] While found footage horror does not often engage a Steadicam, the moving camera of found footage shares motor resonances with our own 'biological' movements through space and thus helps to accentuate relations between the film's body and the viewer's body.

From the examples discussed above, we can see how EST posits an entirely different basis for the generation of empathy than that argued for in concepts which solely utilise 'theory of mind'. However, in the distinction between empathy generated by embodied simulation (traditionally seen as a bottom-up approach) or empathy generated by perspective-sharing of the emotions of the other (alternatively, a top-down approach), it is valuable to examine the interrelation between the two. Patricia Pisters suggests that 'two camps' have emerged in the understanding of empathy and emotional engagement, each drawing respectively from the phenomenological and cognitive schools of thought; Pisters, however, attempts to reconcile the two. Drawing on the empirical studies of neuronal activity in the work of Gal Raz et al., Pisters proposes that the top-down and bottom-up neuronal processes used to explain empathic engagement are best considered as reciprocal networked circuits, and that more value can be gained by asking 'when and why one networked circuit is more dominant than the other, and how these networks might influence one another'.[35] According to Pisters's approach, while the close up of the face may more fully activate the empathic structures that underlie EST, there may also be simultaneously a cognitive consideration of the character's potential future based on their actions, which would involve activation of the prefrontal-temporo-parietal circuit of the brain, an area identified with the kind of cognitive processes that underpin 'theory of mind' in cinema.

The close-up of the face and its expressive capabilities are vital to both processes. Deleuze recognised this, arguing that 'the close-up makes the face the pure building material of the affect'.[36] Plantinga contends that the close-up of the actor's face not only *reveals* emotion, but has the 'capacity to elicit emotion through processes such as facial feedback, affective mimicry, and emotional contagion', processes that embodied simulation theory also attempts to address.[37] However, it is difficult to reconcile the intensity of experience of the found footage horror film with these traditional notions of empathic connection being primarily fostered by the affective qualities of the facial close-up, particularly given our often limited access to the face of the character wielding the camera.[38] While *The Visit* uses its mock documentary format to provide ample access to the faces of its protagonists, the logic of many found footage horror films prevents the camera operator from recording themselves. In *Creep*, for example, Aaron's presence in front of the camera is restricted to roughly twenty minutes of its eighty-five-minute running time; similarly, in *Cloverfield*, the camera operator Hud is seen on screen for only a fraction of the runtime. What is it about the particularities of the form of *Creep*, *Cloverfield* and other found footage horror films that may allow them to overcome this apparent limitation?

Mimetic Innervation

While EST acknowledges the somatic basis of our engagement with the image and reconceptualises empathy, thinking of cinema as a dynamic exchange between the film object and viewing subject provides a framework that allows us to explain the intensity of spectatorial experience in a way that addresses potential insufficiencies in access to narrative information or aspects of the character that aid in audience identification. Barker, for example, claims that limiting our emotional response to character-centric forms of 'mimicry' removes the possibility of the resonance of 'textural, spatial and temporal' cinematic structures with the 'textural, spatial and temporal' structures of the viewer's experience.[39] While Barker looks to mimesis in terms of a copy or mirroring between cinematic world and viewer as a method of explaining how these resonances come about, it is perhaps more productive to examine Miriam Hansen's concept of mimetic innervation, a concept she draws from Walter Benjamin. Mimetic innervation is, Hansen emphasises, a two-way process: 'a decentering and extension of the human sensorium [. . .] into the world [. . .] and an introjection, ingestion or incorporation' of the film into the body.[40] This notion of mimetic innervation also presents another way to understand the 'diminished distance between who is seeing and what is seen, through the physical and intensive implication of the spectator' that Pisters refers to in her discussion of *Strange Days* (see Chapter 4).[41]

Engaging with both Hansen's and Michael Taussig's interpretations of Walter Benjamin's concept of mimetic experience, Anne Rutherford further elaborates on how this mimetic innervation comes about, arguing that it is the '"elements" of mise-en-scène' that are the sites for mimetic innervation, sites that produce a 'porous interface' between the spectator and the material world of the film.[42] Rutherford places emphasis on how these sites of contact are the 'glue that holds narrative together',[43] and how it is an

> accumulation of sensory-affective intensity, that builds up layer upon layer, that carries the viewer through the narrative on the level that matters – on the level that activates the embodied self in an experience of mimetic engagement in the film in all its dimensions.[44]

We can attempt to apply some of these conceptual models to a scene from *The Visit*. Midway through the film, Becca recruits her younger brother Tyler to be a second camera operator on her film. Her lecture to him on the principles of documentary cinematography could serve well as a blueprint for any horror filmmaker: 'we're looking for visual tension. Things that pull the frame. Things that force us to imagine what is beyond the frame.'

The scene in question occurs shortly after. While playing a prank on Becca, Tyler surprises her by emerging from a crawl space underneath the house. He notes the heightened quality of the area beneath the house, hinting at the scene to come: 'You can play hide and seek down here. There's, um, there's lots of visual tension.' In the sequence that follows, both Tyler and Becca operate their cameras as they crawl under the house in what begins as a playful game of hide and seek. As Tyler moves to hide, he clambers through the claustrophobic rows of shadowy concrete foundations, hands and knees in the dirt. The movement on screen is familiar to anyone who has ever scrambled in a crouched position, uneven and bumpy.

Becca seeks Tyler out with her camera, making her own way into the dimly lit maze of columns. What we gain as spectators is little knowledge of the geographical space in relation to Becca and Tyler's game. Instead, our understanding is primarily informed by the textures of the space: the interplay of light and dark, the rough edges of the foundations, the feeling of dirt underneath hands, the enclosure of the narrow headspace.

Pausing to describe to camera her need to use 'strategy', Becca (and the audience by proxy) is surprised when she turns the camera back to the space and is confronted by the lunging, animalistic form of Nanna, bounding towards her in an unnaturally fast gait. Becca, not surprisingly, flees.

We cut to Tyler, who doesn't know there is now another participant in their game. When Nanna shocks him by also emerging out of nowhere, his flight is a jumbled array of images: light and darkness, soil, the textures of his clothing, and Nanna's figure in glimpses, upside down.

The sequence ends with a shot of Becca in the foreground, catching her breath, while the out-of-focus figure of Nanna crawls towards her ominously (Figure 5.2). It is another moment, like that described in the opening of this chapter, of Becca's refusal to look, while we the spectators are made to. Before Nanna can reach her, Becca again retreats, sprawling out of the crawl space into the safety of sunlight.

Figure 5.2 Hide and seek in *The Visit*.

The scene itself ends innocuously with Nanna emerging, laughing at what she sees as a joke and dusting off her dirty knees. 'I'm making chicken pot pie!' she announces, and then walks out-of-frame, her loose-fitting skirt revealing a disturbing lack of underwear. 'What the hell was that?' Tyler demands, and an audience member may likely ask the same.

While this sequence does little to progress the narrative, it does demonstrate how the elements of mise-en-scène work in concert to forge a heightened connection between the spectator and the image: the composition of the image, the actors, the lighting, the set, the costumes and the sound, all work to draw the viewer into an embodied connection with the material aspects of the scene. The distinctive movement of the two cameras, operated by the crawling protagonists, also works to produce comparable motor resonances with the spectatorial body.

Foraging through Found Footage: Panksepp's SEEKING Instinct

The literal game of hide and seek in the scene described above repeats some common tropes of horror film: the push/pull of the desire to see and the fear to do so. Hide and seek as a metaphor can also aptly describe the operation of many horror films, which rely on both a hidden source of tension and the viewer's compulsion to seek answers. The work of neuroscientist Jaak Panksepp may provide us with a more productive insight into this process of seeking by a spectator. Panksepp, who coined the term 'affective neuroscience', worked primarily in the field of human and animal emotion. His major contribution to the field is a challenge to the idea that emotions come from the cerebral cortex, which is the part of the brain considered principally responsible for thinking, perceiving, producing and understanding language. Instead, Panksepp contends that emotion originates in more primitive areas of the brain, such as the amygdala and the hypothalamus.

The process of vision, in Panksepp's understanding, occurs before the formation of language or the symbolic and relies on what he terms the SEEKING instinct. The SEEKING system (insistently capitalised, to indicate it has been evolutionarily 'built' into the nervous system at a fundamental level) is the 'emotional instinct' to seek resources that Panksepp has identified across all mammalian species.[45] Importantly, according to Panksepp, this instinct is located in the primordial area of the brain and is a 'primary' response to environment, in that it is not an outcome or somato-sensorial symptom of perception. Rather, it is an element of the 'core' self as an emotional self, where emotion drives cognition; as Panksepp writes, '[a]ll sustained cognition is *affectively* directed and motivated, often invisibly in a fashion that promotes the illusion of cognitive autonomy from emotion.'[46] These affects are not equivalent to emotions in the way that cognitivist film theorists would classify them: they are instead core drivers, equivalent to instincts, that are later codified by the neo-cortex as more determined emotional responses. Panksepp argues that this process occurs on several levels: the primary level is the emotional, sub-cortical level (originating in the most ancient parts of our evolutionary neurobiology), while at the tertiary level cognition is also engaged by this instinct, and these affects become classified as emotions in the way most cognitivists would understand them. It is at the tertiary level that Panksepp argues that SEEKING is at its highest intensity, becoming 'obsessive' and 'question-asking'.[47]

To further clarify, the SEEKING-EXPECTANCY system is the most important of what Panksepp terms the 'ancient social-emotional systems' (which include ANGER, FEAR, PANIC/GRIEF, MATERNAL CARE, PLEASURE/LUST and PLAY), because it impels all mammals to enter their environment and hunt for resources or information that will enable them to survive. Promoted by the neurochemical deployment of dopamine, this instinct drives foraging, investigation, curiosity and expectation.

Film theorists have previously examined Panksepp's contentions: Grodal, for instance, identifies the SEEKING system as intrinsic to the spectator's 'prime fascination' with detective fiction or the excitement viewers have in watching characters overcome adversity.[48] This instinct to learn 'what happens next' in the example Grodal gives is certainly tied to SEEKING, but only at the tertiary level; it is a deliberate cognitive process. Karin Luisa Badt further expands this hypothesis beyond the boundaries of puzzle films or narrative tales of adversity, arguing that 'the SEEKING system is engaged when a human being watches *any* film', and that 'SEEKING may explain our emotionally charged attention to the screen at *a pre-story* primary' process level (the emotional, sub-cortical level, as Panksepp defines emotion), as well as at the tertiary level.'[49] In doing so, she attempts to overturn the dichotomy between emotional reading of the image and cognitive reading of the image, or what Panksepp labels 'the illusion of cognitive autonomy from emotion'.[50]

Badt writes: 'Our eyes and bodies are primed to take emotional excitement from a plethora of new environmental cues as our "survival" instinct sets in gear, at its most basic level: to seek and scan what is around us.'[51] She contends that, because cinema is an 'accelerated and moving representation of environments', it intensifies this seeking and scanning experience, not only at the level of narrative, but also in relation to 'shapes, lights, colours and movement'.[52] Thus, in Badt's assessment, Panksepp's SEEKING system allows us to understand how both levels are concurrently engaged with the image.

Badt's concept of a cinematic application of SEEKING offers a valuable new way to consider the experience of found footage horror films, with their constantly searching and scanning cameras. On one level, the activity of the cameras in these films could be interpreted as a diegetic extension of how our instincts guide us to interact with an environment. The cameras simulate the tertiary level of foraging for new information that will enable survival, and they do so very specifically under the threat of potential doom; for example, Becca's continued operation of her camera at *The Visit*'s conclusion is, at the macro level of narrative, tapping into an instinctual response to the environment.[53] However, at the primary level, in relation to affect and attention, SEEKING can entrance or engage us with aspects of the image that have little to no relation to narrative. This is especially relevant to horror, where the fearful potential for the out-of-frame to intrude remains with us, often unconsciously so, and leads us to apprehensively assess the borders of the image. This is a fear that may never be catalysed by the narrative.

It should be noted that Panksepp's theoretical framework does not undermine the Deleuzian concepts of the Cogito discussed in the previous chapter: to reiterate, that 'an empirical subject cannot be born into the world without simultaneously being reflected in a transcendental subject which thinks it and in which it thinks itself', while the Cogito of art contends that 'there is no subject which acts without another which watches it act, and which grasps it as acted, itself assuming the freedom of which it deprives the former'.[54] Panksepp's theory may help to explain that, at a neurobiological level, the 'empirical subject' is distinct from the 'transcendental subject'. In this understanding, the 'fluctuations of empirical reception and transcendental structuration' that Rushton proposes in the previous chapter could be considered the outcome of tertiary cognitive processes redefining or codifying primary affect.[55] SEEKING is also, in Deleuzian terms, an aspect of 'molecular' thought, in the way in which it is grounded in the affective and intensive qualities of experience.

It could be argued that the cognitive processes of 'theory of mind' and the corporeal responsiveness of embodied simulation are also recognised in Panksepp's differentiation of emotion-affective processing: embodied simulation would be a process that arguably has been learnt through instrumental or operant conditioning to the point where it is an 'emotional habit', in Panksepp's terms, while 'theory of mind' could be considered a tertiary process, a cognitive executive function that is still guided by affect.

Redefining the viewer's engagement with the audio-visual image at a pre-cognitive level illustrates the fruits of Panksepp's theory in relation to cinema. The SEEKING instinct, as Panksepp defines it, is particularly relevant to the found footage horror film, as both its form and content replicate the perceptual process of foraging. Under this conception, the function of the first-person camera is no longer equated purely with a type of subjective identification; it goes beyond this, implicating instinctive perceptual processes, which then become integrated with a cognitive appraisal of the narrative. For, while a viewer may empathically engage with narrative and character, these are tertiary processes of 'meaning-making' that are retroactively fashioned after the primary affective response. It is the primary affective response that is most fully informed by exteroceptive multi-sensory stimuli, such as movement, colour, light and sound, and it is this response that more comprehensively accounts for the spectator's intensely immersive engagement with the audio-visual image of found footage horror.

Returning briefly to *The Visit* allows an examination of this point. Watching the game of hide and seek between Nanna, Becca and Tyler, the spectator's reception of the image and sound is operating on multiple levels. At what Panksepp defines as the primary level, they are scanning the screen in a manner that accords with the foraging instinct in non-filmic perception: all of their sensory inputs are not only working in concert, but are, as proposed by Sobchack's 'cinesthetic subject', cooperative and commutable.

Aurally, they process the atmospheric noises of the crawl space: the rough noise of the characters' clothes scraping along the ground, a low hum, and the panting breath of Nanna. The spectator is also pre-cognitively processing the acoustics of the voices of both Tyler and Becca, in terms of pitch, timbre and amplitude. Visually, there is a destabilisation of the framing that denotes panicked optical perceptual movement. There is also a visual engagement with the white light from outside the crawl space and the opacity of the spaces this light cannot reach. Nanna's face in this sequence is one of these opaque on-screen spaces, obscured by either the darkness or her hair, yet the viewer is visually compelled to scan the space where her facial features would usually be, seeking to determine if the normal affectively charged contents of the facial register are present (which would indicate that Nanna is playing a game and nothing more sinister).

At another level, the viewer's perceptual resources are prompting an embodied simulation of our presence within the space of the diegetic environment and an interaction with its objects: their perception of the image is being translated onto their sensory-motor and viscero-motor neural pathways, producing corresponding physiological responses. At yet another level, they are drawn into the moment through how Carroll's erotetic model posits that we process narrative, by posing questions that require answers: what does Nanna want from the children? How can they extricate themselves from this situation? Finally, there is the specific manner in which this is presented as a record of an objectively existing situation through its documentary-like form, combined with the subjective nature of the recording (the viewer is in some shots perceiving the scene in an almost identical way to Becca and Tyler as they operate the camera).

Crucially, it is the formal properties of found footage which are most productive of the process of SEEKING. As the subjective camera itself echoes the instinctive foraging process, it produces a doubling of sorts for the spectator. Indeed, when Becca searches out the room for escape, as described in this chapter's opening, this doubling comes to the fore. While her operation of the camera reproduces her perceptual experience of new environmental cues, moment by moment, so too does the viewer capitulate to the images presented: more than just cognitively asking, 'what happens next?', we interface with the sensory-affective aspects of the film at a core level of experiential processing, moment to moment.

Both embodied simulation theory and Panksepp's SEEKING system offer alternative but complementary frameworks for considering how we are drawn into a film, in ways that challenge the theoretical orthodoxy of primary or secondary identification. Found footage horror film often works against the bases of these forms of identification, by reducing the presence of the on-screen body and foregrounding the 'foraging' camera. By examining the operation of these films in light of EST and the SEEKING system, this chapter offers a more expansive model to account for how a spectator becomes entangled with the image.

Notes

1. Carroll, *Theorizing the Moving Image*, p. 98.
2. Ibid. p. 97.
3. Neill, 'Empathy and (Film) Fiction'.
4. Sinnerbrink, *Cinematic Ethics*, p. 92.
5. Smith, *Engaging Characters*, p. 82.
6. Ibid. p. 83.
7. Ibid. p. 144.
8. Ibid. p. 86.
9. Smith, 'Empathy, Expansionism, and the Extended Mind', p. 103.
10. Ibid. p. 103.
11. Curtis, '*Einfühlung* and Abstraction in the Moving Image', p. 429.
12. Anderson, *The Reality of Illusion*, p. 41. These responses are biological in the sense that they are predicated upon our natural processes of perception in the act of watching a film.
13. Ibid. p. 137.
14. Ibid. p. 138.

15. Grodal, *Moving Pictures*, p. 93.
16. Zacks, *Flicker*, pp. 3–23.
17. Ibid. p. 4.
18. Rizzolatti and Sinigaglia, *Mirrors in the Brain*.
19. Smith, 'Empathy, Expansionism, and the Extended Mind', p. 102.
20. For an overview, see *Embodied Cognition and Cinema*, edited by Maarten Coëgnarts and Peter Kravanja.
21. Wilson, 'Six Views of Embodied Cognition', p. 625.
22. Coëgnarts and Kravanja, 'Film as an Exemplar of Bodily Meaning-Making', p. 20.
23. Nannicelli and Taberham, *Cognitive Media Theory*, p. 5.
24. Gallese and Guerra, 'Embodying Movies', p. 184; see also Ebisch et al., 'The Sense of Touch'.
25. Gallese, 'Mirror Neurons, Embodied Simulation, and the Neural Basis of Social Identification', p. 524.
26. Gallese and Guerra, 'Embodying Movies', p. 185.
27. Gallese, 'Embodied Simulation Theory', p. 199.
28. Gallese and Wojciehowski, 'How Stories Make Us Feel'.
29. Bordwell and Thompson, *Minding Movies*, p. 100, cited in Gallese and Guerra, 'Embodying Movies', p. 194.
30. Gallese and Guerra, 'Embodying Movies', p. 185.
31. Ibid. p. 186.
32. Ibid. p. 186.
33. Guerra, 'Modes of Action at the Movies', pp. 152–3.
34. Ibid. p. 153.
35. Raz et al., 'Cry for Her or Cry with Her', cited in Pisters, 'Dexter's Plastic Brain', p. 61.
36. Deleuze, *Cinema 1*, p. 103.
37. Plantinga, 'The Affective Power of Movies', p. 101.
38. It is also worth noting the critique that the performances given in found footage horror films, like the performances in many horror films, are at times somewhat lacking, which raises further questions about how 'facial feedback, affective mimicry, and emotional contagion' can be at the foundations of an intense engagement.
39. Barker, *The Tactile Eye*, p. 74.
40. Hansen, 'Benjamin and Cinema', p. 332.
41. Pisters, *The Matrix of Visual Culture*, p. 26.
42. Rutherford, *What Makes a Film Tick?*, pp. 61–3
43. Ibid. p. 72.
44. Ibid. p. 72.
45. Panksepp, 'Affective Consciousness', pp. 30–80; Panksepp, 'Cross-Species Affective Neuroscience Decoding', pp. 1–16.
46. Panksepp, 'Damasio's Error?', p. 115; original emphasis.
47. Panksepp, cited in Badt, 'A Dialogue with Neuroscientist Jaak Panksepp', p. 67.
48. Grodal, *Embodied Visions*, p. 125.

49. Badt, 'A Dialogue with Neuroscientist Jaak Panksepp', p. 67; original emphasis.
50. Panksepp, 'Damasio's Error?', p. 115.
51. Badt, 'A Dialogue with Neuroscientist Jaak Panksepp', p. 75.
52. Ibid. p. 75.
53. There is fertile ground here for future research into Panksepp's FEAR instinct and its potential relation to horror cinema.
54. Deleuze, *Cinema 1*, p. 73.
55. Rushton, 'Passions and Actions', p. 136.

CHAPTER SIX

What Hides behind the Stream: Post-Cinematic Hauntings of the Digital

There's something there, beneath the surface. It's like an itch I can't quite reach, tormenting me. The grand lure of a puzzle.

The YouTube video is of a masked figure in a black cloak standing inside a derelict building. With the bird-like shape of its mask, it looks similar to the plague doctors of the seventeenth century. The figure raises its hand, and then its fingers in a pattern: 3, 1, 2.

A discordant electronic rumble plays under the image, occasionally changing in tone. The image constantly jump cuts, and the surface of the image often shifts, only slightly and only for a moment, hinting at the notion that there is something under the image that is veiled to me.

I pause the video for a moment, hoping to catch a glimpse of the letters and numbers that sometimes flit across the screen. The Birdman's stare is a silent challenge.

In the two chapters that follow I will build on an understanding of the primacy of the sensory-affective components of the image, examining how horror's continued evolution within the media form of online streaming video emphasises these properties in an attempt to intensify the spectatorial experience. As previously discussed, horror has an almost parasitic relationship to developing technologies, inevitably 'bleeding through' into new media artefacts in ways that fearfully question the speed of change and subsequent societal and cultural consequences that new technologies bring. These artefacts are often employed as a location for new forms of fictional storytelling, but they also often utilise the ambiguous truth status of the image in a similar manner to the found footage horror films examined in previous chapters.

This chapter looks at several new media artefacts as exemplars for this interface between horror and digital media: a selection of 'non-fiction' YouTube videos I label as 'post-cinematic horror shorts'. From this examination, the following questions arise: does the digital aesthetic and delivery modality of new media generate a unique bodily intensity? Do these newer forms employ an 'aesthetic of distortion' at both a visual and an aural level that may be more productive of fear than conventional horror film, and if so, why? Is it perhaps the specific sensory-affective attributes of destabilised sounds and images, and the synaesthetic and haptic qualities that accompany them, that are key to this shifting audio-visual experience for the spectator? Or is it the 'discorrelation' of post-cinematic images from human phenomenological frameworks that is foundational for the kind of horrific affect examined?

While the earlier chapters discussed in detail the affective visual and aural properties of the out-of-frame, and the potential of a subjective/objective interplay in the way found footage utilises point of view, this chapter will focus on several non-narrative or non-semantic constituents of the new media image that may also bring about an intensification of the viewing experience. These elements include the hapticity of the image, its peripheral or background elements, and the unintended or intended distortion or breakdown of the audio-visual image.

The Affect of Apocrypha: *Suicidemouse* and *11bx1371*

As previously noted, the inescapable presence of the Internet in almost all aspects of our daily lives and its concurrent torrential stream of information have served to exacerbate modern concerns for the truth status of the image. It is therefore unsurprising that YouTube and other video streaming sites have become locations where the status of the supernatural is brought into question, and where it is granted a provisional form of existence through its presence in the visual archive. These manifestations, often catalysed through an interface with the medium itself, are historically connected with the emergence of information technologies, wherein the presence of the paranormal in media often articulates our evolving relationship to media technologies. Importantly, as digital videos are freed from their indexical link to real objects, they become, in Steven Shaviro's terms, less about bodies and images as semantic content and more about 'the articulation and composition of forces'.[1] As such, they become perfect sites for the emergence of inhuman and incorporeal paranormal phenomena. However, our experience of these videos is exquisitely human, in that we are affectively imbricated with these images at a corporeal level, which further complicates our relationship with their content and its believed authenticity or inauthenticity. These videos manifest the liminal state of the meeting point between incredulity and the affective force of the audio-visual image.

Two particular 'non-fiction' YouTube horror videos provide us with a location to examine this contention. The first came to light not in video form, but as a story posted to the website 4Chan in October 2009. The apocryphal tale detailed an unreleased Mickey Mouse cartoon produced by Disney in the 1930s, found by a reviewer who was compiling a complete collection of Disney's work.² The cartoon was composed of a continuous loop of Mickey walking on a footpath. What was odd about the animation, the post suggested, was that Mickey's demeanour was so morose. It got stranger still: after the loop supposedly ended, there were several minutes of black screen and then Mickey returned unexpectedly. No one had realised there was additional footage until the original had been digitised.

However, there was something odd about this new footage. The author of the post described what it was they found so shocking about it:

> The sound was different [. . .] It wasn't a language, but more like a gurgled cry. As the noise got more indistinguishable and loud over the next minute, the picture began to get weird. The sidewalk started to go in directions that seemed impossible based on the physics of Mickey's walking. And the dismal face of the mouse was slowly curling into a smirk. [. . .] [T]he murmur turned into a bloodcurdling scream [. . .] Colours were happening that shouldn't have been possible at the time. Mickey's face began to fall apart.³

It was not only Mickey's face that disintegrated: the entire image degenerated into indefinable visual noise. The story continues with the outlandish claim that, after the final Mickey Mouse logo appeared on screen, there was an additional thirty seconds of footage, and that, after seeing this content, the only viewer immediately stole a security guard's firearm and shot and killed himself. The storyteller of the original post labelled the clip 'Suicidemouse' and demanded that '[i]f you ever find a copy of the film, I want you to never view it. [. . .] When a Disney death is covered up as well as this, it means this has to be something huge.'

In November 2009 a video was uploaded to YouTube by a user called Nec1. It was accompanied by the same text in the description, and seemed to be an accurate account of the first section of the video described.⁴ In the video, Mickey does indeed walk morosely in front of a repetitive background, and, after a pause of several minutes of black, the video concludes with the degeneration of the image, accompanied by hellish screaming and a final eerie piece of music (Figure 6.1).

Discordant and unsettling, it is, however, indeterminate if Nec1's video is the authentic *Suicidemouse*, as detailed on 4Chan. This would be further complicated by later uploads, claiming to be the real *Suicidemouse*, which present similar imagery with varying visual corruption, and an altogether new demoniacal soundscape of terrified wailing.⁵

While there may be some value in unveiling the true origin or identity of the *Suicidemouse* video, there is also much to be learned by interrogating

What Hides behind the Stream 119

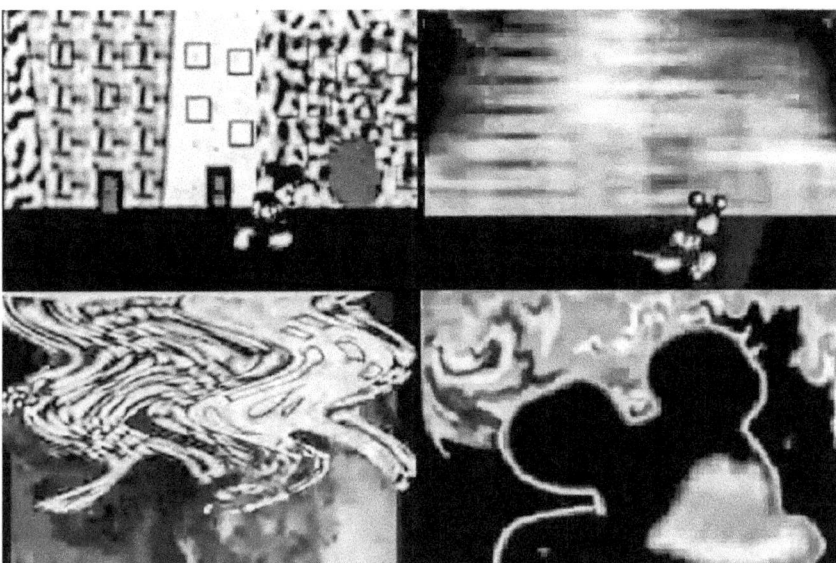

Figure 6.1 *Suicidemouse* by Nec1.

just what is so hellish about Mickey Mouse's 'descent to hell', as it has been described by some commentators. By examining this video, and the other exemplars presented in this chapter that engage with the tropes of non-fiction, it becomes clear that the horrific resonance of these videos emerges from the way they are intensely charged with a particular affective force that resides in their unique capacities as unconventional audio-visual horror artefacts that are only tangentially connected to narrative, or divorced from it almost entirely.

The second such video, briefly described in the opening of this chapter, is that known as *11bx1371*.[6] Uploaded to YouTube in May 2015, this mysterious and disconcerting short sparked immediate conversation about its origins and meanings, a conversation that was only heightened by the unusual circumstances surrounding it: after it was uploaded it was also posted to a Swedish tech blogger, who published an article about its sinister contents and enigmatic origins. Running just under two minutes, it is a black and white video featuring a caped figure wearing a gas mask that has a distinctly beak-like shape. The video is accompanied by a garbled, swirling cacophony of aural noise. In the video, the Birdman (as he came to be labelled by commentators) stands in front of a window inside what appears to be a dilapidated building. Through jump cuts and flashes of on-screen numbers and codes, the Birdman appears to be sending a cryptic message. At one point, he holds up his gloved hand and inside his palm a circular object appears to blink out its own message (Figure 6.2). The video experiments with unconventional

Figure 6.2 *11bx1371*'s 'Birdman'.

shot duration, intercutting long takes and the Birdman's static presence with jump cuts, digital noise, glitches and overlays, while an atonal digital growl continues throughout.

From the moment of the video's upload, its apocryphal origins have been widely debated online, until revelations appeared to unveil it as a deliberately provocative art project by a filmmaker named Parker Wright.[7] Wright had crafted *11bx1371* as an enigma that was no doubt designed to hook the curiosity of the denizens of websites like Reddit – an online space where participants take great pleasure in deconstructing such puzzles and debating the meaning behind the sinister and inscrutable sound and imagery. In the case of *11bx1371*, the challenge was quickly accepted and, over the weeks and months that followed its posting, much was uncovered: the location was identified as an abandoned asylum near Otwock in Poland and certain cryptographic codes were found embedded in the image and in the movements of the so-called Birdman.

Perhaps the most breathtaking revelation was what was excavated from the video's audio files by the process of spectrogrammetry and uploaded to YouTube: in the dissonant noise of the audio track was visual data that had obviously been converted to audio waves (Figure 6.3).[8] This data was far from innocuous. Accompanying the written message, 'You are already dead', were several graphic images of bodies and faces, later revealed to be stills sourced from various existing horror films.[9]

The web of intrigue and investigation that surrounded *11bx1371*, and the revelations it unveiled, is not uncommon for the types of YouTube videos

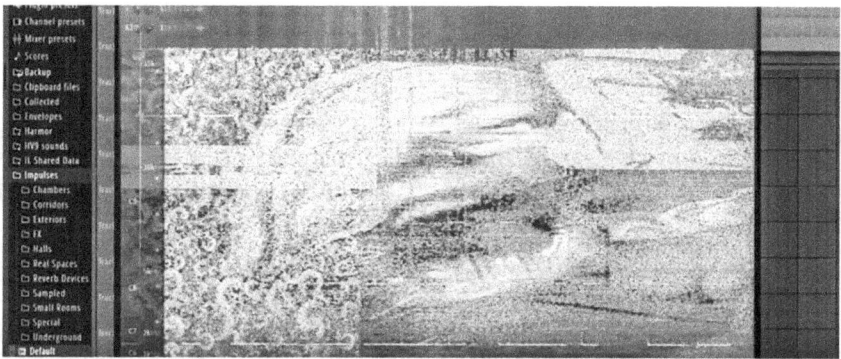

Figure 6.3 Spectrogrammetric analysis of *11bx1371*.

examined in this chapter, which I am labelling 'post-cinematic horror shorts'. This terminology is drawing on recent scholarship in the field of new media that has seen the term 'post-cinematic' begin to take hold as a way of describing the particular qualities or characteristics of hybrid media artefacts that have metamorphosed from cinematic origins.[10] Returning to the qualities Denson and Leyda identify of post-cinematic work – that they are 'digital, interactive, networked, ludic, miniaturized, mobile, social, processual, algorithmic, aggregative, environmental, or convergent, among other things'[11] – we find in many of these terms adequate descriptions for the specific qualities of the post-cinematic horror shorts examined here, and *Suicidemouse* and *11bx1371* as exemplars of this category.

Short horror videos abound on internet video streaming sites. These range from excellent and notable fictional short horror narratives through to videos that are implicitly or explicitly presented as non-fiction.[12] This chapter focuses on the latter, for several reasons. These videos are a potent site to examine the shifting experiences of spectatorship, in that they are presented as oppositional artefacts to horror shorts that present themselves as entertainment narratives. These videos instead revel in the uncertainty behind their authenticity and origins, and are diverse and heterogeneous in their foundations, content and locations. They can often be found in curated collections or playlists, with descriptions like 'The Most Mysterious Unexplained Videos on YouTube', or 'Top 15 Scariest YouTube Videos'. They range from those that explicitly reference the supernatural or the occult, to those that are oblique and inscrutable in their subject, yet irrefutably horrifying in their affect. These videos generally fall into the following categories: found footage in the cinematic style of *The Blair Witch Project* or *Paranormal Activity*; puzzle videos (such as *11bx1371*, and similar videos such as *Webdriver Torso* and *Unfavourable Semicircle*);

lost episodes (such as *Suicidemouse*); re-edits of existing footage; 'haunted' forms of existing media; or abstract art projects.[13]

A common question that emerges from examining these videos, in a sociocultural sense, is their truth value. Bombarded as we are with an ever-rising flood of information in the social media environment, these horror shorts often become lightning rods for debate about the validity of their purported contents. The debate itself is a form of provisional existence: presented in many cases as a documentary record, these short films at least raise the question of the existence of the supernatural they purport to capture, from ghosts, to aliens, to Bigfoot, to the truly indefinable and unexplainable. Similarly, puzzle films like *11bx1371* often provoke a similar pursuit, although in this case it is of the underlying meaning of the video, with competing explanations attempting to codify its purpose: *11bx1371*, for example, was at times labelled a recruitment puzzle, a viral marketing campaign, part of an alternate reality game, an abstract work designed to 'troll' (to generate a response), and even the work of a genuinely deranged mind.

The paranormal activity in these videos is often imbricated with the technology of the internet itself, such as in the example of *Username: 666*, a screen recording in which the repeated attempts to open a YouTube user page specifically named with that staple of occult numeric mysticism leads to the website eventually devolving into grotesque and hellish imagery.[14] Perhaps more frightening than the images themselves is that they cannot be escaped, with the page refusing to shut down, despite the repeated attempts of the on-screen operator.

Other examples have integrated existing mythologies of supernatural manifestations with the technological. One such illustration of this is the *Cursed Kleenex Commercial*.[15] Clearly drawing on the folkloric tale of Bloody Mary, in which the apparition of a woman can be summoned by calling her name three times before a mirror, this haunting manifests as a digital distortion that occurs when the video is played at exactly midnight.[16] In the YouTube horror short that captures this manifestation, a user films their computer screen as they watch the video, once at 11:59 p.m. and then immediately after, as their clock ticks over to 0:00. In the second play through, the video and audio begin to disintegrate, black distortion corrupting the image and jump cuts altering the edit. The face and body of the commercial actress become spectral and ghoulish, her eyes reduced to black orbs. The image becomes locked at the final stage, another set of eyes appearing to emerge from the screen to stare back at the viewer, before the recorded YouTube video displays: 'An error occurred. Please try again later' (a message that does not occur on the first play) (Figure 6.4). What is already a peculiar and somewhat disquieting commercial becomes, through this apparent 'haunting' and the specificities

Figure 6.4 *Cursed Kleenex Commercial.*

of its effects on the sound and image, something that affects the viewer in a different way. Disquiet gives way to bodily discomfort. Dread rises to the surface, in much the same way that the corruption appears to emerge from underneath the image and overlay it.

Why does it feel that, for ordinary users, the more contemporary the technology, the more vivid the experience of its haunting? For Sconce, the ineffable 'presence' that new forms of communications technology appear to have to their earliest operators becomes a potent catalyst for fantastic or supernatural narratives to be constructed around them.[17] In this understanding, YouTube becomes just one station in the long line of our mutual embrace of and superstitious distrust of new technology. Horror scholar Steffen Hantke furthers this understanding, describing how techno-horror performs 'the cultural labour of articulating, illustrating and dramatizing [. . .] anxieties and feeding the larger debate on the uses and benefits of digital technologies'.[18]

Rather than examining in greater detail the way technologies become infused with paranormal presences, it is more productive to turn our attention to how one of the effects of these videos, despite their variations, is to destabilise the viewer's incredulity, opening the possibility for a deeper connection to the sound and image. Chapters 2 and 3 argued that the experience of found footage horror cannot be constrained to 'imaginative' spectatorial identification with its participants or narrative. In a similar way, the disparate audio-visual artefacts of non-fiction YouTube horror share common features that question the imposed 'black and white' binary of fiction and non-fiction (or the related authenticity values of fake and real), relocating the viewing experience to a more grey state of uneasy ambiguity. This returns to an examination of what else may constitute Bordwell's proposed 'firewall' between our cognitive processes and the lower-level sensory-affective processes that can overwhelm this intellectual distance from the image (discussed in the previous chapter).

The verisimilitude of the manifestation of the supernatural in media artefacts has often been central to an examination of these artefacts, with proponents arguing that film or audio records are key sources of evidence, while sceptics rightfully question the assumption that a mediated image can offer any guarantee of the authenticity of its source. These questions have been famously explored in public life many times over the last fifty years, with the debate over the Patterson–Gimlin Bigfoot footage and the Loch Ness Monster being two notable examples. Yet with the evolution of digital image technology, the indexical link between image and referent has been further weakened – in a world where each pixel can be manipulated and where entire images can be constructed with no referent in the real world, the veracity of any image can be questioned.

If, however, the authenticity of all digital audio-visual content is always in question, how is it that the short horror videos of YouTube can still be so disturbing? Should not our contemporary scepticism of the image overpower its capacity to affect us? Certainly, if a modern equivalent to the Patterson–Gimlin footage were released today, much of the analysis would involve parsing its footage for digital manipulation, and the default stance, regardless of how real it appeared, would be that it was a hoax. Yet there are certain aesthetic qualities that many of these videos hold that have the potential to complicate this sceptical response.

The question of how digital media has problematised our understanding of the truth status of the image has been considered by a variety of scholars. Richard Grusin, riffing on Tom Gunning's scholarship on early cinema, coined the term 'cinema of interactions' for how the modern digital media aesthetic encourages viewers to 'feel or act as if the inanimate is animate', despite our understanding that the mediated or programmed image is most definitely 'inanimate'.[19] Grusin argues that not only is this change one of aesthetic properties, but also that, from the perspective of how we interact with technologies, we 'customarily act in ways that suggest [digital media artefacts] are real'.[20] This, he contends, emerges from the manner in which the cinema is no longer solely the experience of watching a film in a darkened theatre, but a continuum of remediated interactive experiences that extends out onto televisions, computers, smartphones and the web.[21] As discussed in Chapter 2, the act of treating media artefacts as 'real' has also been examined specifically within horror studies, with some scholars positing that there is a certain level of 'active fantasy' in the viewer's consideration of most horror texts.

Both of these positions, while cogent and well argued, speak more broadly to the ways in which digital media aesthetics and practices have altered our socio-cultural relationships to the works. What they fail to delve into, however, is the specific qualities of the sound and image that sustain this 'seeming-real': intensities whose affective charge offers us a way to understand how these horror shorts can work despite paucity of narrative and limited duration. By repositioning our analysis so that it goes further than just examining these shorts in their socio-cultural context, and instead, examining what else might carry this affective charge, we can extend and develop our understanding of the shifting experience of contemporary spectatorship.

One quality of audio-visual media that has shifted in works such as the exemplars presented here is what Steven Shaviro labels the 'post-continuity' aspect of post-cinematic works. Shaviro defines this as a 'preoccupation with immediate effects [that] trumps any concern for broader continuity—whether on the immediate shot-by-shot level, or on that of the overall narrative'.[22] Here Shaviro draws attention to how the 'spatiotemporal matrix' of any audio-visual experience is composed of *both* narrative *and* its sensorial and affective dimensions.[23] This is as true of classical cinema as it is of the new media artefacts, but what is different about these short videos is their emphasis on heightening the sensory at the potential cost of narrative cohesion. To borrow Shaviro's term, the 'spatiotemporal matrix' is far more fluid and unfettered by the demands of narrative. Scenes can be composed of indiscernible geography, and the temporal flow can appear to halt, judder, reverse or speed up.

This movement away from a focus on the representational aspects of the horror film or video towards an understanding that accounts for the experiential depth of an embodied interaction with the sound and image is an essential foundation for this book. This conception affords an opportunity to interrogate the capacities of horror across a disparate range of narratives and narrative depths, and to extend beyond the limitations of hermeneutic approaches that may dismiss the relatively abstract content of some of these YouTube horror shorts as meaningless.

Returning to *Suicidemouse*, this can be demonstrated in the manner in which the clip is almost entirely composed of a simplistic animation of Mickey Mouse walking. As the clip continues, it emphasises the elements that obscure the visual content: the images become jittery, blurred, unstable, the image at times seeming to contain a double exposure that is indeterminable. Correspondingly, the audio also becomes almost completely divorced from the images. What begins as an unusual but not anachronous score devolves into an almost suffocating loop of a scream, the effect of which seems to grow rather than dissipate with each loop.

Similarly, *11bx1371* also accentuates aspects that fit the criteria of Shaviro's 'post-continuity' terminology: while there is apparently a coded message, the emphasis of the video is on elements that obscure the message, such as the correspondingly oppressive audio, jittery images, and the relative stasis of the Birdman. The video communicates to us on a visceral level far more than any coded message that can be unpacked from it.

This visceral response arises from the intensified sensory aspects of videos like *11bx1371* and *Suicidemouse*. This is especially evident in the aural component of videos like these. As previously mentioned, the unveiling of the horror imagery that was encoded inside *11bx1371*'s audio track was a dramatic revelation: on one level, purely for the shock that there was a hidden stream of information behind the images. One another level, if we extend this concept in a metaphorical sense, we can ask what else is there that resides 'unseen' in these videos that can only be examined by moving away from conceptions that see the affective capacity of these videos residing in their imagery. For, while there is something undeniably eerie and sinister in the corruption of the image, like that demonstrated in the *Cursed Kleenex Commercial*, these videos also contain a decay or contamination of the audio files which has its own macabre resonance. While there is a unifying element to this quality of decay across both the visual and aural components of many of these videos, there is more to be gained in going beyond a focus on the ways in which the aural and visual properties of the videos are analogous. One such vital extended consideration is how the aural components of these post-cinematic horror shorts intensify their affective power through their untethered relationship to the images. This is a return to Chion's concepts of the 'acousmatic' and 'acousmêtre', where sound and vision are strategically detached from each other. In the case of a disembodied voice, such as the scream of *Suicidemouse*, its location out-of-frame bestows on it an intensification of threat or dread.

To recapitulate, this affective power is constituted by the asubjective, non-conscious and intensive qualities of experience: what has not been quantified and encapsulated as emotional response, but what is instead present as an excess, an overflow, that which cannot be codified. This distinction is important to consider because it may in part explain the residue of unease that remains after watching these videos, even for sceptical viewers. For, while we can easily articulate and categorise our belief in the image, on a scale from complete disbelief to conviction, and our concomitant emotional response, from boredom to fascination, there is a surplus that remains, and that surplus resides in our bodily response. This surplus also feeds into our sense of realism. To return to the argument of Ndalianis discussed in Chapter 2, the realism of 'incredible' horror emerges from sensory rather than intellectual knowledge: this sensory knowledge forges the (often unwilling) link between incredulity and a feeling of authenticity.

THE SOUNDSCAPES OF POST-CINEMATIC HORROR

The soundscapes of these works also operate differently to classical horror cinema soundscapes, by undermining the primacy of the image and intentionally destabilising our habituated sensory-motor schema – the circuit of perception–affection–action which Deleuze identified as pivotal to the classical Hollywood narrative style. Marshall McLuhan argues that all new inventions and technologies invariably demand 'new ratios' among our sense organs.[24] One such altered new sense ratio in post-cinematic works is that of sound to vision. McLuhan goes so far as to argue that new media works promote a sensory shift that is 'audile-tactile': because the visual components of new media artefacts are multiplied and fragmented, our sensory response is no longer centred on the eye, and our hearing and sense of touch are heightened.[25]

Considering film images primarily as symbolic visual representations enables a hierarchy of the senses, according to which vision is privileged above all. These works subvert this understanding; the post-cinematic horror short could arguably belong to what Shaviro identifies as the new 'economy of the senses' that has arisen from the evolution in technology from analogue to digital modes of production.[26] Within the continuum upon which this new economy exists, the role of sound has dramatically shifted – from classical cinema's subordination of sound to image, we have shifted to a realm where the sonic intensities of post-cinematic works are often intentionally dissonant with the image.

In classical narrative cinema, sound provides what Chion labels 'added value' to the image: its purpose is to support the image, so that the sound '"naturally" comes from what is seen, and is already contained in the image itself'.[27] Chion points out that, in this situation, a scene's meaning is thought to be derived from its imagery, and sound is merely additive.[28] For post-cinematic media, this handling of sound is no longer the default operation. Whereas the operation of sound was once covert, it now can operate overtly. Its dissonance, contradiction or disunity to the image is allowed for in the process Chion describes as synchresis: the immediate establishment of a tight relation of interdependence between images and sounds that occur simultaneously, even when in reality they may have scarcely any relationship.[29] This new relation can be especially affectively charged when the sounds are what biological scientists label non-linear sounds: sounds that are physiologically extreme, discomforting or jarring, due to our genetically hardwired fear response. The characteristics of these sounds include non-harmonics, irregular volume shifts, static, sudden pitch change, or frequency-based effects: all aural qualities that are engaged in a concentrated form in post-cinematic horror shorts.[30]

The soundscapes of the post-cinematic horror short are notable for how oppressive and inexorable they feel. Anthony Storr contends that sound has a greater capacity than images to elicit physical responses, in that it is far more difficult to dispel sound as easily as the closing of one's eyes can deny an image.[31] The sounds in these videos are, however, not the conventional sounds of classical horror narrative, where score is more commonly used to establish slow-building tension, and 'stings' of volume or frequency can be used to produce a physiological shock response. They are not limited by an attempt to be complementary to the image; instead, they are but one element of a heterogeneous ensemble. Chion goes so far as to insist that, with the embrace of multilayered audio tracks (or polyphony), 'the visual image is just one more layer and not necessarily the primary one'.[32] He chooses the term 'rendering' to describe how, in the complex intertwining of all of the senses in the articulation of a film's auditory *and* visual texture, sensations are conveyed that are effective regardless of their fidelity to an actual reproduction of the scene's reality. For Chion, this explains how the interrelation of sound and image can 'give us a vast array of luminous, spatial, thermal and tactile sensations that extend far beyond realist reproduction'.[33] This understanding offers us a way of accounting for the added sensory dimensions of the sounds in *Suicidemouse* or *11bx1371*, and how these may produce a sense of bodily heaviness, or of suffocation.

Denson and the 'Horror of Discorrelation'

Denson, as one of the foremost scholars of 'post-cinematic' media, posits a compelling argument for the origins of the affective excess that I assert arises from these YouTube videos and other forms of new media horror, which he labels the 'Horror of Discorrelation'. The discorrelation he refers to emerges in post-cinema's '[radical] nonhuman ontology of the image'; there is, for Denson, a schism between the operation of these images and embodied human subjectivities and phenomenological perspective.[34] Denson asserts that post-cinematic horror films, such as *Paranormal Activity* and *Unfriended*, mediate the 'upheaval and anxiety' of the ontological instability of the digital media landscape.[35]

Denson identifies 'digital production processes, compression algorithms, network protocols and streaming delivery systems, among others' as technologies that 'sever' contemporary moving images from a fundamental subjectivity that was granted by the photographic media regime.[36] He writes: 'the new processuality of images unmoors viewing subjects, assaulting our sensorium with stimuli that exceed our perceptual capacities and fall outside the temporal window of conscious cognition'.[37]

Denson's argument accords strongly with my own, in that we both identify how a 'slippage' between diegesis and medium has become central to modern horror's operation. Denson extends this to argue that the 'pervasive cameras and surveillance apparatuses, digital glitches, online networks, and [use of] social media' in post-cinematic horror work specifically to 'channel the shock of discorrelation' into the generic framework of horror itself.[38]

In my understanding, the affect that emerges from this 'assault on our sensorium', and the incapacities of 'conscious cognition' to account for the microtemporalities of the digital media regime, contributes to the destabilisation of a foundational subjectivity for the viewer, one that operated within the photographic regime, and one which undoubtedly contributes to the successful operation of conventional horror narratives. The post-cinematic horror shorts analysed in this chapter function very differently to these older conventions of horror cinema. Relying less on their narrative content, these shorts are more characteristic of the affective web that traverses the process of digital information production, circulation and distribution, in that they both rearticulate the tensions that underscore our complex relationship with technological change and also actively work to exploit the dynamic affective responses of the viewer – a viewer whose body may be failing to 'make sense' of the discorrelation Denson postulates.

Notes

1. Shaviro, *Post Cinematic Affect*, p. 17.
2. The original post has been removed from the 4Chan archive.
3. The entire content of the original post: 'So do any of you remember those Mickey Mouse cartoons from the 1930s? The ones that were just put out on DVD a few years ago? Well, I hear there is one that was unreleased to even the most avid classic Disney fans. According to sources, it's nothing special. It's just a continuous loop (like The Flinstones [sic]) of Mickey walking past 6 buildings that goes on for two or three minutes before fading out. Unlike the cutesy tunes put in though, the song on this cartoon was not a song at all, just a constant banging on a piano as if the keys [sic] for a minute and a half before going to white noise for the remainder of the film. It wasn't the jolly old Mickey we've come to love either, Mickey wasn't dancing, not even smiling, just kind of walking as if you or I were walking, with a normal facial expression, but for some reason his head tilted side to side as he kept this dismal look. Up until a year or two ago, everyone believed that after [the loop had ended] it cut to black and that was it. When Leonard Maltin was reviewing the cartoon to be put in the complete series, he decided it was too junk to be on the DVD, but wanted to have a digital copy due to the fact that it was a creation of Walt's. When he had a digitized version up on his computer to look at the file, he noticed something. The cartoon was

actually 9 minutes and 4 seconds long. This is what my source emailed to me, in full (he is a personal assistant of one of the higher executives at Disney, and acquaintance of Mr. Maltin himself). After it cut to black, it stayed like that until the 6th minute, before going back into Mickey walking. The sound was different this time. It was a murmur. It wasn't a language, but more like a gurgled cry. As the noise got more indistinguishable and loud over the next minute, the picture began to get weird. The sidewalk started to go in directions that seemed impossible based on the physics of Mickey's walking. And the dismal face of the mouse was slowly curling into a smirk. On the 7th minute, the murmur turned into a bloodcurdling scream (the kind of scream painful to hear) and the picture was getting more obscure. Colours were happening that shouldn't have been possible at the time. Mickey face began to fall apart. his [sic] eyes rolled on the bottom of his chin like two marbles in a fishbowl, and his curled smile was pointing upward on the left side of his face. The buildings became rubble floating in mid-air and the sidewalk was still impossibly navigating in warped directions, a few seeming inconceivable with what we, as humans, know about direction. Mr. Maltin got disturbed and left the room, sending an employee to finish the video and take notes of everything happening up until the last second, and afterward immediately store the disc of the cartoon into the vault. This distorted screaming lasted until 8 minutes and a few seconds in, and then it abruptly cuts to the Mickey Mouse face at the credits of the end of every video with what sounded like a broken music box playing in the background. This happened for about 30 seconds, and whatever was in that remaining 30 seconds I haven't been able to get a sliver of information. From a security guard working under me who was making rounds outside of that room, I was told that after the last frame, the employee stumbled out of the room with pale skin, saying 'real suffering is not known' seven times, before speedily taking the guards [sic] pistol and offing himself on the spot. The thing I could get out of Leonard Maltin was that the last frame was a piece of Russian text that roughly said 'the sights of hell bring its viewers back in.' As far as I know, no one else has seen it, but there have been dozens of attempts at getting the file on Rapidshare by employees inside the studios, all of whom have been promptly terminated from their jobs. Whether it got online or not is up for debate, but if rumours serve me right, it's online somewhere under "suicidemouse.avi." If you ever find a copy of the film, I want you to never view it, and to contact me by phone immediately, regardless of the time. When a Disney Death is covered up as well as this, it means this has to be something huge.'

4. To view the Nec1 video, go to <bit.ly/thesuicidemouse> (last accessed 9 September 2019).
5. To view another variation, go to <bit.ly/theothersuicidemouse> (last accessed 9 September 2019).
6. To view, go to <bit.ly/11bx1371> (last accessed 9 September 2019).
7. For some discussion of the hunt for the creator of *11bx1371*, and a discussion with Parker Wright, see Wehner, 'The Most Disturbing Viral Video Now Has a Sequel'.

8. To view, go to <bit.ly/11bx1371spectrog> (last accessed 9 September 2019). A spectrogram is a visual representation of the spectrum of frequencies of sound.
9. It must be acknowledged here that there is a possibility that this spectrammetric analysis is simply another part of the larger 'myth-building' that occurs around these types of videos; it is not only the authenticity of these videos themselves that is ambiguous, but also the para-factual material that surrounds them.
10. See the collection *Post-Cinema: Theorizing 21st-Century Film*, edited by Shane Denson and Julia Leyda.
11. Denson and Leyda, 'Perspectives on Post-Cinema', p. 1.
12. For a YouTube playlist of fictional horror narratives, go to <bit.ly/thefearfactory> (last accessed 9 September 2019). For an example YouTube playlist of 'non-fiction' horror, go to <bit.ly/nonfictionhorror> (last accessed 9 September 2019).
13. 'Lost episodes' is a term used to describe the 'recovery' of previously unseen versions of existing properties, often with new supernatural resonance.
14. To view, go to <bit.ly/666vid> (last accessed 9 September 2019).
15. To view, go to <bit.ly/kleenexcurse> (last accessed 9 September 2019).
16. Like Bloody Mary, the haunting is able to be 'summoned' through a specific process of actions; the action in this case is playing the video at exactly midnight.
17. Sconce, *Haunted Media*.
18. Hantke, 'Network Anxiety', p. 19.
19. Grusin, 'DVD, Video Games and the Cinema of Interactions', p. 68.
20. Ibid. p. 68.
21. Ibid. p. 68.
22. Shaviro, 'Post-Continuity', p. 51.
23. Ibid. p. 57.
24. McLuhan, *Understanding Media*, p. 66.
25. Ibid. p. 67.
26. Shaviro, 'Splitting the Atom', p. 367.
27. Chion, *Audio-Vision*, p. 5
28. Ibid. p. 5.
29. Chion, *Film, a Sound Art*, p. 492.
30. Blumstein et al., 'Do Film Soundtracks Contain Nonlinear Analogues to Influence Emotion?'
31. Storr, *Music and the Mind*, pp. 100–1.
32. Chion, *Film, a Sound Art*, p. 119.
33. Ibid. p. 240.
34. Denson, 'Crazy Cameras', p. 194.
35. Denson, 'The Horror of Discorrelation'.
36. Ibid.
37. Ibid.
38. Ibid.

CHAPTER SEVEN

The Evolving Screen Forms of New Media Horror

In a darkened office I sit alone at my desk. Lit only by the wan flicker of the computer monitor, I'm searching for answers through the byzantine labyrinth of an online video library. Some are archival records of what happened, some are messages in response. With no way to identify the authenticity of each video, I am left to piece the puzzle together for myself. I press play on the next video, titled Conversion.

This one is a video response. A message. On screen, accompanied by a familiar electronic hum, the flicker of black and white bars reminds me of analogue static. In the noise, as though drifting to the surface, an anthropomorphic shape appears. Suddenly both are gone, replaced on screen with a code – one of many – among coloured geometric shapes. The code too is soon replaced by a new image: an array of coloured digital vectors and a crudely animated spectral white face in the corner of the frame. The audio sounds like the whimper of a dying carnival, and a mutter of indistinguishable voices washes in and out like ocean waves. Behind the image appears the face of a familiar man, someone who is key to solving the puzzle but equally inscrutable in his actions and behaviour. His voice has been muted. On screen, amid the digital hiss of an image saturated with ruptures and static, a new message:

WHO ARE THE LIARS?

Despite knowing this query is directed to someone other than me, the question speaks to my own growing distrust of the people who have created and uploaded the videos, yet also of the images themselves. On screen, other recognisable figures appear, snatches from previous videos that have been compressed, garbled, digitally disfigured.

The video asks: ARE YOU ONE OF THEM. And then threatens: REMEMBER TO LOOK BEHIND YOU (Figure 7.1).

A ghost-like body of static recedes into the darkness on screen. The soundtrack becomes a plangent growl that shifts in pitch as the image continues to break down. The growl recedes, replaced by a deep hum as more perplexing batches of numbers flash onto the screen. While I struggle to comprehend, my body is already offering its own inchoate answer to the question posed by the unnerving sounds and images.

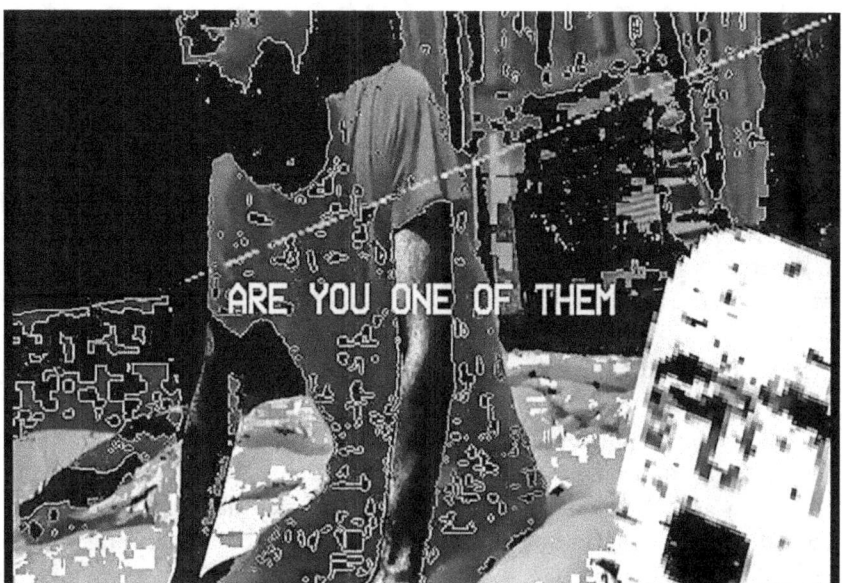

Figure 7.1 ARE YOU ONE OF THEM, in *Conversion*.

The video finishes. YouTube cues the next link: Entry #75. Sitting in the dark, I consider, just for a moment, looking behind me – but I remain still, body tensed, nerves jangling, eyes riveted to the screen as the next video begins to play.

ALWAYS WATCHING: THE EVOLVING SCREEN FORM OF HORROR AND *MARBLE HORNETS*

The introduction to this chapter begins with an experiential description of watching a YouTube video titled *Conversion*.[1] Although it is but one of the 131 videos that comprise the web horror series *Marble Hornets*, my description of this particular video and its spectatorial affect attempts to capture the distinct tenor and atmosphere of the series as a whole. This chapter offers an examination of *Marble Hornets* as an exemplar of the integration of found footage horror and the medium of internet streaming video, and the film *Unfriended* as an exemplar of 'screenlife' horror, asking the following questions: what are the particular effects of the distinctive camera–body and screen–body relation of these new media artefacts? How does their distinctive forms contribute to embodiment relations? And how does each of these series employ an 'aesthetics of distortion' to channel affect?

Made by a core group of three amateur filmmakers, the videos that comprise the series *Marble Hornets* were sporadically uploaded to a YouTube account of the same name between 2009 and 2014.[2] The series explicitly engaged with the tropes of found footage horror, in that it claimed to be the product of twenty-something Jay's investigation into his filmmaker friend Alex Kralie's discarded tapes: an unfinished student film project named *Marble Hornets*. When Alex suddenly and inexplicably ceased working on the project, Jay convinced Alex to allow him to have the tapes, agreeing in return to never mention the tapes again. Subsequently, Alex mysteriously transferred schools and severed contact with Jay. The main gambit of the series is that each video uploaded is a discovery from Jay's exploration of the archive that may shed light on Alex's disappearance. Gradually it becomes clear that Alex's filmmaking endeavour is 'haunted' by a possibly malevolent entity – an unnaturally tall, thin, faceless man in a black suit, who is only ever referred to as The Operator. Those familiar with horror figures will identify him as a version of The Slender Man, a relatively new mythological figure created by artist Eric Knudsen in 2009.[3] The Slender Man mythology germinated in internet forums but soon took on a life of its own, spreading to short stories, films and video games.[4] Within *Marble Hornets*, this enigmatic and frightening figure, in the form of The Operator, first appears only in glimpses but soon begins to have definite and damaging effects on all of those involved in the film (Figure 7.2).

As the *Marble Hornets* videos were gradually released to YouTube, the creators added an innovative twist to the storytelling, in the form of response videos posted from an enigmatic and unknown second 'narrator' called ToTheArk.[5] These occasional reply videos were less interested in unveiling the mystery than in fostering questions that required compulsive

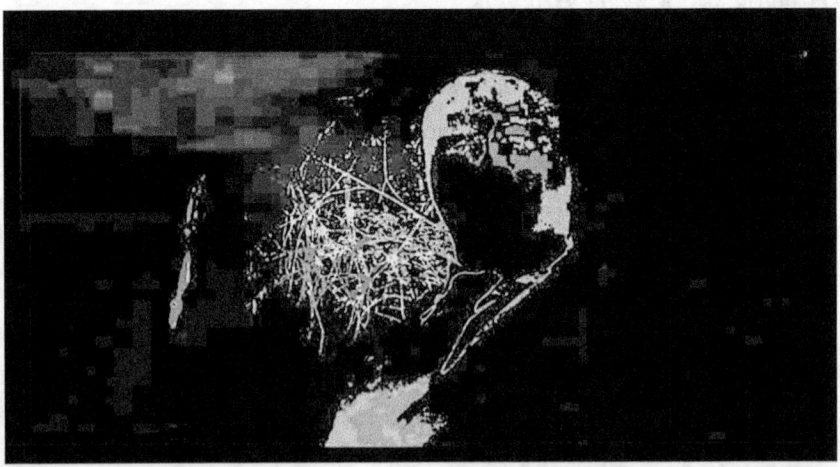

Figure 7.2 A glimpse of The Operator.

further investigation: the video *Conversion*, described in the prologue to this chapter, is a quintessential example. Composed mainly of elaborate visual codes and puzzles, the ToTheArk videos are the most viscerally affective and at times the most terrifying aspect of the series. It comes as no surprise, then, that ToTheArk becomes entwined with the central narrative as not only a commenter but as someone prompting the central characters. For a follower of the series, the interplay between the two sets of videos, and the resulting immersive engagement for those who sought to solve the puzzle, offers a clear demonstration of how new media structures present exciting narrative potential for filmmakers. However, this is but one of the ways in which *Marble Hornets* might be said to alter the dynamics of spectatorship.

Thomas Elsaesser and Malte Hagener contend that

> [d]igital cinema [. . .] lays out several paths into the future, where films will come in all lengths and genres, are shown on screens of all sizes, are available in all program formats and at a cost that is determined by the value we put on the occasion, not by the price of the product.[6]

Situated in the intersection between digital cinema aesthetics, new media and horror, *Marble Hornets* initiates provocative questions about the post-cinematic experience of spectatorship, particularly regarding the status and cinematic capacities of the 'third' and 'fourth' screens of media theory, the computer and the smartphone or tablet (positioned historically after the 'first' and 'second' screens of the cinema and television). In order to examine these questions most effectively, however, it is crucial to consider them through the frame of the horror genre's inextricable connection to the body of the viewer, as argued in the previous chapters.

The 'monster' of *Marble Hornets*, The Operator, is, like many found footage horror 'monsters', captured only in tantalising glimpses. It appears to have no ability to communicate, outside of the interference it causes to video and audio recordings, and its motivations are largely inscrutable. Its appearance and influence generate an unusual 'sickness', the symptoms of which include a hacking cough, recurrent bouts of amnesia, and an escalated level of aggression in those who are exposed to it, but it rarely acts directly against the protagonists. When it does appear, it is often out of focus, obscured behind visual layers, or at the edges of frame (Figure 7.3).

The Operator is, in a visual sense, largely indecipherable; as we are unable to ever clearly see The Operator, we are unable to understand its motives or its meaning. While this visual impenetrability does fit with Carroll's contention that horror often proceeds from our pursuit of the 'unknowable', it does not explain the deeply felt bodily intensity of experience in the moments that

Figure 7.3 The 'obscured' Operator of *Marble Hornets*.

border The Operator's appearance, and in response to the ToTheArk videos. This suggests that the horror of these short films resides not primarily in The Operator's presence, but in its combination with the digital aesthetic and the delivery modality of the computer screen or smartphone. This consideration actively questions a hierarchy of perception and cognition that places the semantic content of the image at its centre. Instead, it reframes horror as primarily a sensory-affective experience. It returns to the embodied manner in which we first experience the image as the driver of the viewer–image interface. It is not through an appraisal of the image's semantic content when viewing new media artefacts such as *Marble Hornets* and the post-cinematic horror short that affective responses emerge. It is through the process of how these works implicate the body of the spectator.

The Embodied Experience of New Media Artefacts

The implication of the body of the viewer is especially true of new media artefacts that are primarily experienced via smartphone, tablet or computer screens, which is how most consumers of *Marble Hornets* engage with the series. While each of these media generates its own relations of embodied experience, there are similarities between the three. Ingrid Richardson draws attention to how these screens produce distinct differences from traditional televisual and cinematic screens, in terms of 'proximity, orientation and mobility'.[7] She also contends that these screens draw us into the image, arguing that 'we are no longer "lean-back" spectators or observers but "lean-forward" users'.[8] Our interaction with the images on these screens involves physical engagement, whether it be through the tactile manipulation of the smartphone screen or the instrumental use of the mouse or keyboard of the computer. As such, it produces a unique type of engagement. That is not to say that an embodied experience of the cinematic image requires spectatorial movement, but that, in their requisite physical engagement, new media forms produce an altered body–tool relation which has effects on the corporeal schematic that usually dominates the experience of cinema.

Found footage horror, particularly those films viewed on the smartphone or computer screen, capitalises on and distorts this relationship through its presentation of horrific imagery on devices which we are familiar with as recording devices. While conventional films such as *[REC]* (2007) present a recording of an explicit confrontation with the monster as the site of their horrifying imagery, *Marble Hornets* depicts a rupture of the image itself, which potentially surpasses the power of the unambiguous presence of the monster as a semantic presence. *Marble Hornets* becomes the site of a liminal space for a spectator, in which our conceptions of cinematic reality and unreality are unmoored by the complex relations we have with screens and cameras.

The internet – particularly YouTube – is one of the most recent sites to be infiltrated by the spectral stain that arises in all new technologies. *Marble Hornets* capitalises on this in a manner that conventional cinematic found footage horror film cannot. It does so in three specific ways: by exploiting the particular kinaesthetic qualities that advances in digital camera technology allow; by manipulating the sound and image to increase its sensorial properties; and by employing the hypertextual, non-hierarchical nature of new media to alter the spectator's experience of duration and proximity.

The dynamics of the camera movement in projects like *Marble Hornets* have specific kinaesthetic qualities that are the result of advances in camera technology. *Marble Hornets*, like all found footage, exists only through the pervasive presence of cameras within the diegetic world. Excluding the ToTheArk video responses mentioned earlier, everything we see throughout the series is captured by a camera either carried or mounted on the body of one of the protagonists. One of the biggest innovations of digital cinema is the mobility and economy of camera size, and economy of camera price, that allows for greater access to recording devices for filmmakers and more dynamic uses of camera within the construction of the film. Horror is one genre where filmmakers actively experiment with this new flexibility in order to best intensify the spectatorial experience: we see this in films such as *Blair*

Witch (2016), a sequel to *The Blair Witch Project*, in which the protagonists take to wearing portable Bluetooth earpiece cameras. The protagonists in this film also utilise a drone camera to produce inventive cinematic images, such as that which shows the drone's ascent away from the group, revealing in a single unedited shot their complete isolation and the density of the woods surrounding them.

As paranoia grips the protagonists of *Marble Hornets*, they take to recording everything. While the use of the handheld camera is not particularly innovative in and of itself, having origins in the Direct Cinema movement of the late 1950s, the manner in which *Marble Hornets* engages with its particular rhythms and movement has different effects. As previously discussed, the genre of found footage has often played with loss of focus, incongruent framing and camera shake in an effort to conjure verisimilitude that evokes the documentary mode. *Marble Hornets* extends this technique: as the characters become compelled by an obsessive need to record, they begin wearing body-mounted cameras that are positioned at the sternum and record the world from a fish-eye perspective. The particular cadence of movement produced by the bodily attached camera in *Marble Hornets* has different effects, while promoting the same sense of realism. The qualities of its distorted, wide angle view on the world, and the way its passage through spaces is united with the rhythmic movement of the body of the protagonist, are different to the handheld camera: the image seems to more fully unite with the body of the protagonist, moving in conjunction not only with his passage through space, but with his breathing and the dynamics of his movement. For example, his body falling to the ground is not simply represented by the camera being dropped or hitting the ground, as it would in some found footage horror films – the image is presented from the point of view of the body, in all the specificities of its fall. This unity heightens the sensory engagement of the viewer – not just of vision, but of the kinaesthetic qualities that vision is associated with – to the point where the spectator's body and its position in the world feels disrupted. Powell contends that this increase in sensory participation arises from pre-cognitive affect in our mechanisms of perception, arguing that horror's 'undermining of normative perspective' intensifies participation at the sensory level.[9] The images provided by the body-mounted camera are not 'normative perspectives', and they too intensify sensory integration between viewer and image.

To clarify, this heightened sensory engagement produced by the body-mounted camera is not akin to a visual identification with the camera as identical to the spectator's eye, but instead the ability of the image to engage all the senses and stimulate our entire corporeal presence through the particularities of camera movement through environment. This would concur with

Michele Guerra's assertion that '"biological movement" – the camera being mounted on the operator's body' elicits a stronger motor resonance between the camera operator's body, the film's body and the viewer's body, a claim backed up by an experiment Guerra references which studied motor cortex activation in relation to camera movement.[10]

Body-mounted cameras may stymie the visual identification with the eye and instead produce an experience of camera movement that dramatically reconfigures the body–image relationship; in *Entry #83*, for example, the character Tim is racked with coughing fits that portend the presence of The Operator (Figure 7.4).[11] His inability to stand and his struggle to breathe are visually reproduced by the camera more fully synchronising with the body of the performer, a body that the viewer becomes implicated with as they kinaesthetically synchronise with the movement of the image.

In *The Address of the Eye*, Sobchack offers perhaps the most comprehensive theorisation for how this synchronisation occurs, positing a reciprocal relationship between the viewer body and a filmic 'body', through an analysis of philosopher Don Ihde's embodiment relations. Sobchack examines how the tools of cinema, camera and projector are intricately connected to the perception of filmmaker and spectator. Utilising the work of Merleau-Ponty, Ihde uses the term 'embodiment relations' to label the imbrication of tools into our corporeality, and the way in which the artefacts of the world become

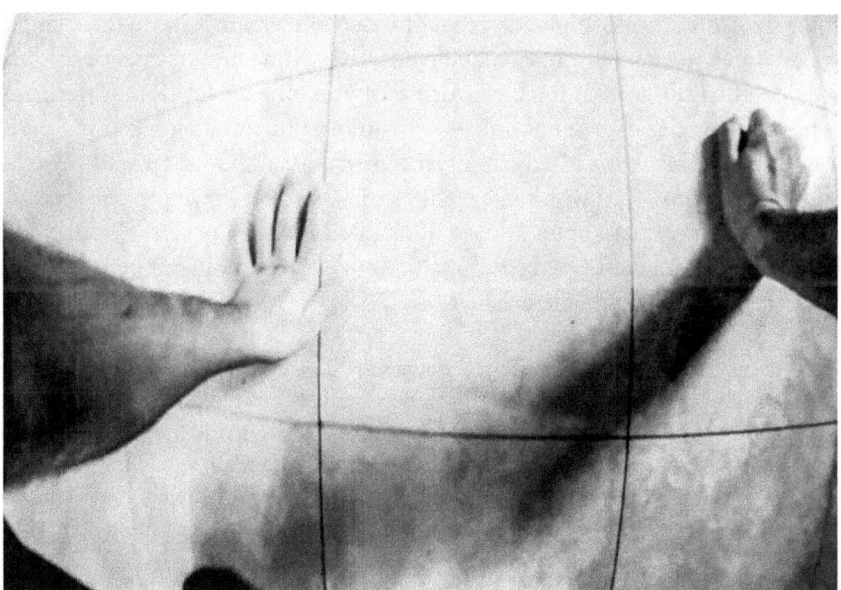

Figure 7.4 Camera attached to sternum in *Marble Hornets*.

part of our bodily experience. In an embodiment relation, Ihde argues, 'I take the technologies *into* my experiencing in a particular way by way of perceiving *through* such technologies and through the reflexive transformation of my perceptual and body sense.'[12] This leads to a symbiosis between user and artefact through action. The focus of Ihde's observations here is primarily the connection between perception and its object in the use of scientific instruments like the microscope or telescope. Sobchack, applying Ihde's philosophical investigation to cinema, notes a distinct conceptual difference when she writes:

> The single technological relations of individual embodied persons to instruments that Ihde describes are necessary but not sufficient to the film experience. They are imbricated in, but cannot, in themselves or in their sum, account for the *doubled* and *inclusive* machine-mediation of the film experience, an experience that results in the constitution of a *reversibly perceptive and expressive text* and in *intersubjective* communication.[13]

Sobchack further extrapolates the dynamics of relations between spectator–world–filmmaker as produced through the tools of camera and projector in a manner that exceeds the scope of this chapter. However, her investigation of embodiment relations in regards to cinema helps to rethink how our embodiment relations with smartphones or computers can contribute to a dynamic bodily synchronisation with the image, particularly when the series is viewed on a smartphone or computer screen. This occurs primarily due to the fact that many modern users of these technologies have a different experience of these devices than the conventional experience of watching a television or theatrical screen. These devices are not only viewing tools, but are often recording tools, and it is possible that a bleed-through occurs between the various existing relationships a person has with these technologies, and the viewing experience.

Sobchack touches upon how technologies of recording can reproduce the experience of an act of perception, although the 'technology' she refers to is camera and projector, when she writes:

> Insofar as it concerns the technology of the cinema, this embodiment relation between perceiver and machine genuinely extends the intentionality of both filmmaker and spectator into the respective worlds that provide each with objects of perception. It is this extension of the incarnate intentionality of the person that results in a sense of *realism* in the cinema. [. . .] What is experienced as the sense of realism *in* the phenomenon is genuinely lived *as* the experience of a real or existential act of perception.[14]

Sobchack goes on to refer to the camera's potential for 'amplification of perceptual experience', identifying the camera's potential to produce an experience of perception of the world that is 'unavailable to human vision', yet one that we still experience similarly to our direct lived-body engagement with phenomena.[15] *Marble Hornets* employs this amplification of perceptual experience through its body-mounted cameras: despite our relatively static position as viewers, there is a particular quality to the on-screen movement that transfers as a kinaesthetic sense. When this occurs, we move, fall, crouch, hide, run and struggle to breathe, all without ever leaving our seats. Sobchack refers to this as the spectator's body 'kinetically "listening" to the movement of another', 'another' here referring to the filmic body.[16]

Using 'gesture' as a term to codify expressive bodily movement that is directed towards the world, Barker argues that films also contain gestures in the form of cinematic devices or techniques.[17] Employing Stanley Kubrick's *The Shining* (1980) as an example, she argues that the 'repeated, slow moving surreptitious camera movement [. . .] demands a reply of some kind from the attentive spectator's body. It evokes a corresponding but not predetermined gesture from our bodies.'[18] In a similar manner, *Marble Hornets* has its own set of repeated gestures of camera movement: in the early episodes, the hand-held camera and its ability to zoom becomes like a searching eye, seeking clues or details in the image. In the latter episodes, the body-mounted camera and its particular rhythms becomes a particular type of passage through the world: apprehensive, paranoid, ever-vigilant.

It is not only the particular type of movement exemplified by the cameras of *Marble Hornets* that produces a specific bodily intensity for the viewer; it is also the qualities of the image itself. Digital cinema presents the horror genre with an extended playground of methods to heighten intensity, especially through digital manipulation of the image. *Marble Hornets* illustrates this in two ways: first, through the digital ruptures caused by the presence of The Operator; and second, through the form of the ToTheArk videos, which threaten the viewer through their destabilisation of sound and image.

Throughout the series, the majority of the videos recorded by Alex Kralie for his student project and, later, the videos of Jay and Tim's investigations, contain the trace of some form of digital decay, be it static, loss of tracking, desaturation or hyper-saturation of colour, loss of audio or distortion of audio, or digital bleed-through of the image. The cause of this, within the world of the story, is the presence of The Operator, whose manifestation appears to degrade or warp recordings. As a result, pivotal moments of narrative revelation are often lost or obscured by the degradation of the digital record. Capturing a clear image of The Operator on camera appears impossible, and direct confrontations between the characters and The Operator, such as in *Entry #43*, when Alex approaches it in the woods, are lost in a fog of image decay as the image polarises and fades away.[19]

Dialogue is also lost in a similar manner, drowned out by bursts of discordant noise or unexplainably muted. In *Entry #83* these tears in the image and audio become literal tears in space and time, as The Operator's presence appears to produce a temporal and spatial warp that envelops the fleeing Tim.[20]

The contention that certain filmic images destabilise or frustrate the conventional links that hold action and situation together is one that Deleuze first posited in *Cinema 2*. Deleuze contends that a rupture and imagistic shift arose, after World War II, in films such as those made by the Italian neorealist and French New Wave filmmakers. These films emerged as a counter-response to cinema's general movement towards the rigidity of cliché and repetition. Ronald Bogue identifies these clichés in the manner in which Hollywood created 'an integrated system of practices [. . .] that ensures a seamless and continuous presentation of action within a single time and space'.[21] He argues that a 'commonsense, rational sensori-motor schema informs the Hollywood system'.[22] *Marble Hornets*, as an outlier to the Hollywood system in its independent production and release, is more freely able to transgress the limits of this 'rational' system in favour of images and sounds that are counter to or excessive to a 'seamless' presentation. As such, it shares qualities with what Deleuze identifies as a mutation that occurred in neorealist cinema that challenges the chain of situations and actions that continually create the same types of images. Deleuze labels this mutation the 'time-image'. The cinema of the time-image, he argues, is more productive of 'opsigns' and 'sonsigns': pure optical and audio images that facilitate the potential collapse of the sensory-motor process, in that they interrupt the coherent flow from situation to action or action to situation.[23] As a post-cinematic artefact, *Marble Hornets* can also more fully experiment with the elements that Deleuze sees at the heart of the time-image: the dispersive situation, characterised by multiple characters and less defined narrative arcs; the voyage form, where the protagonist's journey is meandering, somewhat aimless; the production of any-spaces-whatever, which are locations that are not intimately tied to narrative or locations that are undefined; and the capacity for the action to be disengaged from the situation.[24]

While it would be incorrect to equate the post-cinematic horror of *Marble Hornets* with the time-image in any wholesale way, Deleuze's description of the new sensory-motor schema presented by the post-war art cinema can expand our understanding of how the somewhat indistinct approach to characterisation and narrative in the series has unique effects on the spectator. The characters of Deleuze's time-image cinema are, like those of *Marble Hornets*, often trapped in a disjointed or opaque world where their perceptions and actions are no longer in synchronisation. For Deleuze, it is 'the purely optical and sound situation which takes the place of the faltering sensory-motor situations' in this kind of cinema, a statement that could also apply to the irruption of the ToTheArk videos.[25]

In the cinema of the time-image, traditional notions of identification with a character can be inverted, so that the character themselves becomes a kind of viewer of the diegetic world they inhabit. Deleuze describes the situation of this character in this way:

> He shifts, runs and becomes animated in vain, the situation he is in outstrips his motor capacities on all sides, and makes him see and hear what is no longer subject to the rules of a response or an action. He records rather than reacts. He is prey to a vision, pursued by it or pursuing it, rather than engaged in action.[26]

This is an apposite description of the constantly recording protagonists of *Marble Hornets*, and provides another way to comprehend the extended duration of some of its images, and how this duration is all too often disturbed by dissonant sound and image. The genre of horror offers a natural state for these dissonant experiences of image and sound. For Powell, much of the affect of horror originates in the incongruous colours, distorted sounds and hallucinatory images of the genre.[27] Each of these contributes to an experience of spectatorship as a Deleuzian assemblage between viewer and text, an assemblage that is, in Deleuzian terms, molecular and corporeal. This allows for an experience that can transcend the normative, static structure of the 'molar plane' – the register of film that, in del Río's interpretation, is analogous to traditional narrative – as opposed to the 'molecular plane', which she argues is home to the affective-performative register of cinema.[28] This affective-performative register, for del Río, focuses on the way 'bodily forces or affects are thoroughly creative and performative in their ceaseless activity of drawing and redrawing connections with each other through a process of self-modification or becoming'.[29]

The molar plane of horror film corresponds to the reified structures of conventional narrative that promote a film's purpose as a logical progression of cause and effect leading to a satisfactory narrative conclusion. In brief sketch, the presence of the monster would destabilise the environment of the main characters, a disruption that would be stabilised by the struggle against and eventual destruction of the monster (however, often with the possibility of the monster's rebirth or resurrection). Each scene in this model performs a vital role in the narrative chain that leads to this conclusion. *Marble Hornets* subverts these conventions through its repeated presentation of actions and situations that frustrate the sensory-motor schema of conventional narrative in favour of the disjointed and uncoordinated (in)actions and situations of the time-image.

THE AESTHETICS OF DISTORTION: SYNAESTHETIC QUALITIES OF SOUND AND IMAGE

In 'Glitch Gothic', Marc Olivier contends that a 'glitch aesthetic' is common to found footage horror films and that 'visual glitches, or temporary disruptions to the flow of information such as unexpected pixilation [sic], chromatic shifts, and other error-based distortions, now constitute essential tropes in the language of cinematic ghost stories'.[30] He also poetically argues that '[t]he jarring spectacle of data ruins is becoming to the twenty-first century what the crumbling mansion was to gothic literature of the nineteenth century: the privileged space for confrontations with incompatible systems, nostalgic remnants, and restless revenants.'[31]

These digital ruptures are, however, more than just spectacle or the visual representation of the frustration of narrative progression or resolution: they also produce an intensification of our bodily engagement through synaesthetic means; synaesthesia being the 'neurological phenomenon that occurs when a stimulus in one sense modality immediately evokes a sensation in another sense modality'.[32] Applying this synaesthetic capacity to cinema, Marks claims that vision itself can be tactile, 'as though one were touching a film with one's eyes': she terms this process 'haptic visuality'.[33] Marks draws her theoretical frame from art historian Alois Riegl's interrogation of the hierarchy of perception.[34]

This notion of haptic visuality is central to the claim that images of this kind can exceed the boundaries of Heller-Nicholas's 'active horror fantasy', which includes a conscious or unconscious denial of the verisimilitude of the image. Vision, particularly in the horror film, can produce an immersion in the filmic space: its atmosphere, its spatial relations, and its texture. Rather than processing a film purely on the level of comprehension of narrative and character, haptic visuality involves a sensorial relationship that brings into play a synaesthetic exchange between light, colour, sound, mood and texture.

The defining feature of haptic imagery is its reciprocal nature: Marks refers to the 'erotic' quality of the 'intersubjective relationship' that occurs 'between beholder and image' when the viewer 'relinquishes her own sense of separateness from the image', producing an intimate meeting between viewer and work of art that questions any clear delineation between the two.[35] This hapticity is not solely a link between image and body, but also extends to a kind of inhabitation of filmic geography. Giuliana Bruno describes this intersubjective form of space as a 'geopsychic architexture'.[36]

Entry #40 of *Marble Hornets* serves as a cogent example of this creation of space through images that stimulate our sense of tactility, creating a 'geopsychic architexture' of location that is immersive and potent for the viewer.[37] The combination of Jay's movement through the environment, the aural landscape of the various surfaces underfoot, the hyper-saturated colour and, towards the end of the video, the textural contrast between the organic and the man-made, allows the viewer to inhabit this location in a sensory way. These images are clear examples of Marks's definition of haptic visuality, where a viewer's interest is not so much in the textual elements of the image but in the textural. As Marks says, '[h]aptic looking tends to move over the surface of its object rather than to plunge into illusionistic depth, not to distinguish form so much as to discern texture.'[38] She argues that these types of images draw on the viewer's resources of memory and imagination, two capacities that are especially powerful in the realm of horror.

Found footage horror films in particular use an aesthetic of distortion for thematic purposes, drawing on the way haptic imagery 'puts the object into question, calling on the viewer to engage in its imaginative construction'.[39] This is most evident in the ToTheArk videos, where the filmmakers have intentionally 'corrupted' the images to produce vividly textural and macabre imagery (Figure 7.5).

The sensory engagement heightened by the visual 'tears' in the image, the auditory 'tears' that accompany them, and the viewer's synaesthetic responses to the imagery draw them into a new kind of relationship where control over

Figure 7.5 Corrupted imagery in *File*.

their experience of the film through mastery of plot and narrative may be disrupted. By dislocating the image from its semantic role, the relationship between film and viewer is disrupted. As these videos reject the patterns of cause and effect motivated by narrative demands, they potentially heighten the viewer's entanglement, and thus arguably their tension and fear. This de-emphasis on the visual component of the videos is a movement away from ocularcentric logic, where an understanding of the image is designed to be clear and unambiguous, to a sensory logic, one that accentuates the other senses in order to generate fear. As a result of this move away from the viewer's central engagement with the series as one of comprehending the semantics of the image, the image no longer becomes simply an enigma, puzzle, or code that requires solving; the videos are instead 'opened up' and are able to generate an affective response regardless of the viewer's facility to decode them.

The auditory distortions mentioned above are not the only method *Marble Hornets* employs to capitalise on the audio-visual capacities of new media artefacts. A consideration of the interrelation of sound and image requires that we question any hierarchical arrangement between the two. When Chion contends that 'there is no soundtrack', he is arguing that a film's images cannot be studied independently of its sound, and vice versa.[40] Like the post-cinematic horror shorts discussed in the previous chapter, *Marble Hornets* engages sound as but one element of a heterogeneous ensemble. Returning to Chion's insistence that polyphony challenges the hierarchy of the visual, it can be argued that an audience's 'rendering' of the scene involves a complex intertwining of each of the senses in the articulation of both film's auditory *and* visual texture. Irrespective of their fidelity to a reproduction of the scene's reality, the sensations produced are congruent to the experience of viewing. The synaesthetic foundations of 'haptic visuality' can be expanded to explain how these auditory components intertwine with our other sensory responses. Chion proposes the term 'trans-sensory perceptions' for perceptions that 'belong to no one particular sense but that may travel via one sensory channel or another without their content or their effect being limited to this one sense'.[41] In this understanding, the aural dimensions of these videos are not only heard, but have the capacity to be translated into other sensory dimensions.

As the post-cinematic horror short demonstrates, it is not uncommon in new media for distorted sounds, particularly those that operate at either extreme of high or low frequencies, to work in combination with the image and activate a marked corporeal response. However, while the use of specific sounds or sound frequencies can produce the desired physiological response of shock, such as that of the 'sting' scare of conventional horror film, it cannot account for the nuanced multifaceted sensory response that the ToTheArk videos such as *Decay* produce: a low rumble underscores an undulating irruption of inorganic or mechanical noise that 'renders' sensations of materiality, heaviness and potential danger in its combination with the image.[42] Returning to Chion's 'trans-sensory perceptions', this may be due to what he terms the essential trans-sensory dimension: rhythm, within which he includes audio texture and grain.[43] Rhythm is the earliest sensory perception (Chion points to the rhythms experienced by the foetus in utero) and is perceived by each of the sensory channels.

This rhythmic quality is also evident when we look at the videos recorded by the protagonists. One example is *Entry #60*, where Jay investigates a tunnel under an original *Marble Hornets* filming location.[44] The claustrophobic crawl space is lit only in glimpses by passing torchlight, and the echo of Jay's breathing and the clatter of his passage constitute much of the sequence. This rhythmic combination is interrupted by *Marble Hornets*' version of the 'sting' scare: the audio-visual distortion that signals the arrival of The Operator. However, prior to The Operator's arrival, the soundscape of this sequence is a fitting example of the particular auditory rhythms that are unique to this form of found footage, where diegetic sound is the predominant auditory accompaniment to the image. This auditory texture would, in conventional cinema, most often be added to with either score or effects that would further paint in the soundscape. The unadorned verisimilitude of found footage, with its lack of score or sound effects, is more fully accepted by the viewer, given its fidelity to the large proportion of existing non-fictional streaming video content, and the viewer's familiarity with this, particularly when viewed on a computer or phone screen.

New Modalities, New Tensions

Any argument that advocates the equivalence of third and fourth screen media to cinema has in the past been met with resistance and conjecture by many critics. Raymond Bellour contends that 'neither television nor computers, not the Internet, mobile phones or a giant personal screen can take the place of cinema'.[45] Hanich argues that the theatrical experience is crucial, in that it 'dialogically intertwines' an individual's immersion with the collective experience, producing a pleasurable fear in the meeting point of individuality and collectivity.[46] It is important to acknowledge that these new experiences do not replace cinema, but instead utilise the respective technologies of the computer and the smartphone to create a unique experience of spectatorship that shares characteristics with traditional horror spectatorship, but has capacities the conventional theatrical experience cannot afford.

The form of the Internet video archive and its potential for user interaction is one capacity that has been skilfully utilised by the *Marble Hornets* creators. Smartphones and computers, while limited in terms of being experienced by a unified collective in a shared space, open up new methods of communal media experience through online social interactivity. The genetic elements of *Marble Hornets* were formed in the online community of the Something Awful website, and the interactivity and formation of community of that site carried over in the DNA of the initial *Marble Hornets* video posts, which led to the creation of new networks in order to speculate on both the meaning and the authenticity of the videos.

The videos themselves also promote greater individual immersion, through the spectator's control over duration, proximity and chronology. With its intentionally fractured chronology, *Marble Hornets* is an apposite example of this interactive potential for re-mix and the concomitant increase in spectatorial immersion. The *Marble Hornets* wiki promotes several playlists of the series, including 'release order', 'a tentative chronology' and 'suggested order' (which places the response videos in context). Each variation of the series not only produces new understandings of the narrative content, but in the dynamics of its grouping, a new affective resonance can form between the videos: for example, the infected imagery of a shadow passing a doorway in the entry *Admission* carries over into *Entry #23*, where every doorway in the dilapidated house seems to portend doom.

Duration and proximity are also altered through this modality. Sequences can be re-watched on loop, a compulsion that is inevitable when visual clues are hidden in the dense digital textures, and when the presence of The Operator threatens to infect every frame. The many online communities that were drawn into the mystery, much like the characters, encouraged avid viewers of the series to capture and parse still frames, searching for answers. Watching the videos on smartphone or computer screen offers the spectator the opportunity to literally 'lean in' to the image, a compulsion that arises for many viewers in the temporal elongation of scenes of dread (the flipside of this lean-in is the discomfort experienced by those for whom the palpability of dread is too extreme, which results in aversion). The prologue of this chapter is intended as a vivid example of how and why this compulsion to lean in is generated as much by the video's sensory aspects as by its narrative content: watching on my computer screen, I am not only figuratively drawn into the image but often find myself drawing closer in physical proximity, the intensified sound and image luring me in.

Each of these observations about *Marble Hornets*' distinctive properties draws attention to how, in relation to corporeal engagement, form is as crucial as content. Adrian Martin argues that the categorical distinction of representational and non-representational elements in film is false and misleading. He contends that our spectatorial engagement with 'colour, texture, movement, rhythm, melody [and] camera work' is as important as setting, story, dialogue and plot.[47] He writes:

> There is another register of feeling in our contact with the arts (and especially film). It is the moment when, in the imaginary experience of viewing, hearing and being absorbed in something that is unfolding, we pass out of ourselves, just a precious little bit for a precious little while. We become rivers, pylons, doors, tin cans. And we join, also, with the flux of the non-representational: the colours, shapes and edits, those gestures of the film itself as a living, breathing, pulsating organism.[48]

This 'living, breathing, pulsating organism' can sometimes be horrific. It can destabilise our comfortable distance from the image and bring us closer than we want to be. It can both fascinate and repel us, and it can affect us in viscerally intense ways: in our muscular response, our breathing, at the level of our skin. Heller-Nicholas argues that some of the power of *Marble Hornets* resides in its 'mistrust of language – paralysed by paranoia, its protagonists are notoriously incapable of discussing even with each other the terrifying supernatural forces that plague them'.[49] This recourse to something other than language to understand the events of the series is echoed in the experience of the spectator. With only vague and unsettling hints at the origins of The Operator and its true connection to the myriad occurrences of the series, the viewer processes the images of *Marble Hornets* in a different way: at the level of the body, and its powerful and unruly response to the sensory excess of the series and the immersive properties of the modality through which it is delivered. *Marble Hornets* demonstrates how the combination of digital cinema aesthetics and new media structures of content delivery can combine to accentuate the existing powers of the subgenre of found footage horror. As a series, it pushes back against the homogenising forces of Hollywood horror filmmaking and illustrates the potential of cinema narrative that is unshackled from conventional structure. The modalities of the third and fourth screens offer a fascinating potential for genre filmmakers who wish to challenge these existing paradigms.

'SCREENLIFE' HORROR AND *UNFRIENDED*

Post-cinematic horror films can arguably work more effectively on alternative screens, such as computer screens or television screens, than they do in the theatrical environment. In fact, 'Screenlife' films such as Levan Gabriadze's *Unfriended* (2014) are most effective when they share the same delivery modality as their diegetic source. 'Screenlife' is a term coined by creator Timur Bekmambetov to describe films such as *Unfriended*, *Searching* (2018) and *Unfriended: Dark Web* (2018), where the entire narrative takes place on a screen. In the case of *Unfriended*, the screen belongs to a teenage girl whose group chat with her friends is invaded by a supernatural force that appears to be able to infiltrate each of their electronic devices. Watching *Unfriended* on a computer screen heightens its effectiveness for a viewer, as the film soon convincingly replaces the screen of the viewer's real world with its diegetic version.

From its very first moments, *Unfriended* signals that it too is engaging with an aesthetics of distortion, in the corruption of the pre-credits Universal logo, a deformation that occurs on both a visual and an aural level. The familiar musical refrain first crackles, and then is further warped by what sounds like an otherworldly chorus of moaning voices, punctuated by a higher-pitched growl. On a visual level, the galactic background echoes fractal art, as the black space is riven with bleeding colours. It is an image that clearly echoes both the ToTheArk videos of *Marble Hornets* and the post-cinematic horror shorts previously discussed.

The screen fades to black and we are then immediately presented with the film's central visual conceit: that it takes place (almost entirely) on a computer screen. Unlike the premise of found footage, this is not a recording of a computer screen that is being later assembled by an unseen hand. Instead, it is offered as a presentation: the live actions of teenager Blaire's negotiations of the various computer screens that gradually come to be digitally haunted by the ghostly manifestation of her dead friend Laura Barns. We see Laura's death, by her own hand, in the very first scene of the movie, as a recording that was illicitly uploaded to video website Liveleak.

The haunting, like many supernatural cinematic narratives, is almost innocuous at its inception. It begins as a Facebook message from the deceased girl, leading Blaire to immediately suspect she is being pranked by one of her friends. The friends, who appear on screen in various configurations via a Skype conference call, are initially unaware of the incipient taunting by the dead girl, but they too are gradually made cognisant through the presence of an unknown entity in their conference call: an intruder using the Skype account of the deceased Laura Barns, and whose on-screen avatar is that of the blank icon. Almost playful in its initial manifestations, Laura's intrusion eventually spills outside of the confines of the screen, as the spirit enacts its vengeance one by one on Blaire and her friends for their role in the cyberbullying that led to Laura committing suicide.

The film's form exists on a spectrum between pleasurable and frustrating, most likely dependent on the viewer's exposure to the technologies it integrates into its narrative. As a regular user of Skype, chat messaging and social media, I was drawn into the film early, through the almost rhythmic quality to the way Blaire skips between windows and attempts to interrogate the puzzle of Laura's first cryptic message. The term 'Easter Eggs' has been coined to describe the way in which postmodern texts 'hide' visual clues or insider knowledge in the frame, and part of the appeal of *Unfriended* is also the manner in which the film encourages us to search the various foreground and background screen windows for further clues as to who or what is responsible for the messages. The film also preys in various ways upon our postmodern anxieties about technology being infiltrated or hacked by agents outside of our control: directly, in the appearance of on-screen advertisements that ask explicitly 'Who is following me? Find out now!' and indirectly, in the way in which Blaire's computer auto-fills text fields or answers a Skype conference call without her intervention (among many other examples).

'Dude, weird computer shit happens to me all the time,' Laura's friend Jess says later in the film, as the group of friends attempt to uncover the identity of the interloper on their group chat. On one level, *Unfriended* continues the interrogation of our unease and anxieties about technology's relentless progression and our inability to understand both its function and its dysfunction. In this understanding, technohorror works explicitly to exploit the omnipresent potential of the 'glitch', by presenting its origins as malevolent and supernatural: faced with an inability to understand the cause or to 'debug' it (as Ken tries to do with his software patch), the characters' attempts to escape it are also futile. Every malfunction of the computer is a metaphoric representation of the haunting.

However, like the aforementioned projects in this chapter, there is also a particular affective resonance in the corruption and distortion of the sound and image in *Unfriended* that furthers our imbrication with the work. This distortion manifests visually in the following ways: a ghostly static or 'haloing' effect that surrounds the characters; distortion and pixellation of the faces; and frozen frames (Figure 7.6). Aurally, it is present through a pervasive background hum that rises and falls, depending on the tension, and a static crackle that indicates the intensity of Laura's manifestation (echoing here The Operator's effects on the sound recording technology of *Marble Hornets*).

Returning to Denson's concept of post-cinematic horror and 'discorrelation', in his analysis of *Unfriended* he contends that the film's glitch events '[open] a gap between the experiential and the computational', confronting the viewer with the existence of a material and temporal difference.[50] For Denson, the shared screen of the material and diegetic world is revealed through the glitch to be a 'membrane between the discorrelated levels of the phenomenal/visual and the computational/avisual'.[51]

Figure 7.6 Facial distortion in *Unfriended*.

While *Unfriended* works effectively as a theatrical experience, and performed reasonably well at the box office, the full potential of its skilful manipulation and degradation of the sound and image becomes particularly evident when viewing *Unfriended* on a computer or laptop. Visually, the frame becomes filled with mini-frames, each with its own narrative visual content, a configuration that is more akin to our experience of the television or computer screen than cinema. The moving cursor becomes a narrator of sorts for the viewer, drawing their attention from frame to frame (although they often escape to its periphery) (Figure 7.7).

When these frames begin to become 'infected' with the haunting, and begin to display the visual traits described above, the viewer's response while watching on a computer is distinct from the theatrical experience. The 'infection' no longer works only as a metaphor, but now carries over to a specific contamination of *their* viewing device, the one resting on their laps or at the edge of their fingers.

Unfriended also employs a visual technique that uniquely capitalises on this specific type of engagement: the frozen frame. Unlike classical Hollywood film, where the frozen frame occurs for the totality of the image and denotes a pause in time, *Unfriended*'s frames-within-frames allows for one frame to be 'frozen' while the others continue to be animated by sound and movement. This frozen image again utilises our familiarity with 'frozen' computer windows but to macabre effect: while the viewer waits for the character within the frame to become reanimated, the eerie stillness draws them phenomenologically closer. Their intentionality likely becomes riveted to

Figure 7.7 *Unfriended*'s screens within screens.

the one still section of an otherwise still 'alive' scene. In a clever moment, *Unfriended* recognises this and builds on this tension: when the Skype call to Val becomes 'frozen' on her alarmed face, Jess attempts to call her to circumvent the supposedly broken connection – only to find that that, in the corner of the image, Val's ringing cellphone gradually buzzes into frame as it vibrates on the table. This disjunction, between movement and stasis within the one frame, is horrifying. Denson's key insight into these frozen moments is that they serve as 'micro-cliffhangers' that focus our attention on 'the material infrastructure of experience itself'.[52] He writes:

> And in this space of the screen, seemingly unitary but, as we have seen, doubled and in fact multiplied even further by the machinic and social networks in which it participates (both diegetically and materially), our vision is dispersed, divided. We are forced to scan the screen for relevant information; our gaze is not sutured, not directed, and to this extent we are hailed not as an integral subject, but as a bundle of affects engaged in a collective effort to perceive – an effort that is both enabled and hindered by the protocols and agencies of the media environment, out of which our subjectivities are wrought.[53]

Millennial media consumers live in a multi-window world. By expanding the frame to include not only the specific aesthetics of many post-cinematic horror works, but also their primary location (the computer screen) and its own multi-window properties, *Unfriended* has expanded its affective capacities. It has also created an opportunity, through its 'short-circuiting' of perception and temporal flow, to, as Denson says, 'make sense' of the discorrelation which underpins the difference between the experiential and computational.[54]

On the Threshold

In 'Sunset with Chainsaw', Evan Calder-Williams stakes out the political relevance of reading horror outside of an allegorical interpretation, arguing that such a reading forecloses 'more provocative possibilities of interpretation', particularly around those visual environments that are more 'aberrant'.[55] He argues for resisting the 'who-is-threatening-whom mode of reading', in favour of 'letting our eyes be drawn to background patterns and flows, to aberrations of form and intrusive details', as a means of considering the amorphous and unconstrained qualities of the economic and social order.[56]

'Aberrations of form' are at the heart of this chapter. By examining the experimentations with form that these new media horror works present, specifically the manner in which they seem to undermine the primacy of the image, both in its regular operation as part of the sensory-motor schema, and in its supposed hierarchical relationship to sound, we can better understand how their evolution has led to an intensified corporeal response in the viewer. Each of the works described in this chapter engages with form in a manner that deprioritises its visual content, emphasising an expanded sensory engagement that is less reliant on semantic decoding.

The renewed emphasis on expanded sensory engagement has been key to understanding how these works provoke such intense bodily reciprocity with sound and image. A new 'economy of the senses', as Shaviro describes it, comes to the fore in these works, producing an engagement with the work that surpasses the relative shortcomings of its horrific contents. The stress is on heightening the sensory aspects: as a result, the cross-modal synaesthetic qualities of experience are more vividly awakened, wherein a sound can transmute an image, rather than simply being an 'add-on'. Similarly, the aesthetics of distortion promote a heightening of the haptic dimensions of the sound and image. In horror, this suddenly alien sense of tactility, where we are unfamiliar with it, can be far more frightening than a well-composed 'bogeyman'.

In Chapter 6, I used the term 'liminal state' to describe a specific type of spectatorial engagement. Turning to the etymological root of liminal, we find the Latin turn *limen*, meaning threshold. The experience of the horror works discussed in this chapter also places us on a similar threshold – between that which we think does not threaten us and that which our body tells us otherwise.

Notes

1. To view, go to <bit.ly/mhconversion> (last accessed 9 September 2019).
2. The entire archive is available at <https://www.youtube.com/user/MarbleHornets> (last accessed 9 September 2019).
3. Knudsen, 'Victor Surge, Deviant Art'.
4. The Slender Man mythology was also central to the case of an attempted murder in Waukesha, Wisconsin in 2014, when, in an attempt to prove their worth as proxies to The Slender Man, two 12-year-old girls allegedly enticed a third 12-year-old girl to follow them into the woods and stabbed her multiple times.
5. To view the ToTheArk videos, go to <https://www.youtube.com/user/totheark> (last accessed 9 September 2019).
6. Elsaesser and Hagener, *Film Theory*, p. 176.
7. Richardson, 'Faces, Interfaces, Screens', p. 8.
8. Ibid. p. 3.
9. Powell, *Deleuze and Horror Film*, p. 5.
10. Guerra, 'Modes of Action at the Movies', p. 153.
11. To view, go to <bit.ly/Entry83> (last accessed 9 September 2019).
12. Ihde, *Technology and the Lifeworld*, p. 72; original emphasis.
13. Sobchack, *The Address of the Eye*, p. 191; original emphasis.
14. Ibid. p. 181; original emphasis.
15. Ibid. p. 183.
16. Ibid. p. 186.
17. Barker, *The Tactile Eye*, p. 78.
18. Ibid. p. 78.
19. To view, go to <bit.ly/Entry43> (last accessed 9 September 2019).
20. To view, go to <bit.ly/Entry83> (last accessed 9 September 2019).
21. Bogue, *Deleuze on Cinema*, p. 109.
22. Ibid. p. 109.
23. Ibid. p. 6.
24. Deleuze, *Cinema 2*, pp. 18–24.
25. Ibid. p. 3.
26. Ibid. p. 3.
27. Powell, *Deleuze and Horror Film*, p. 11.
28. Del Río, *Deleuze and the Cinemas of Performance*, p. 16.
29. Ibid. p. 3.
30. Olivier, 'Glitch Gothic', p. 253.
31. Ibid. p. 253.
32. Campen, *The Hidden Sense*, p. 1.
33. Marks, *The Skin of the Film*, p. xi.
34. Riegl, *Late Roman Art Industry*, p. 28, cited in Marks, *The Skin of the Film*, p. 161.
35. Marks, *The Skin of the Film*, pp. 182–3.
36. Bruno, *Atlas of Emotion*, pp. 9–10.
37. To view, go to <bit.ly/Entry40> (last accessed 9 September 2019).
38. Marks, *The Skin of the Film*, p. 162.

39. Marks, *Touch*, p. 16.
40. Chion, *Film, a Sound Art*, p. xi.
41. Ibid. p. 496.
42. To view, go to <bit.ly/mhdecay> (last accessed 9 September 2019).
43. Chion, *Film, a Sound Art*, p. 496.
44. To view, go to <bit.ly/Entry60> (last accessed 9 September 2019).
45. Bellour, 'The Cinema Spectator', p. 211.
46. Hanich, *Cinematic Emotion in Horror Films and Thrillers*, pp. 248–9.
47. Martin, 'Delirious Enchantment'.
48. Ibid.
49. Heller-Nicholas, 'Gothic Textures in Found Footage Horror Film'.
50. Denson, 'The Horror of Discorrelation'.
51. Ibid.
52. Ibid.
53. Ibid.
54. Ibid.
55. Calder-Williams, 'Sunset with Chainsaw', p. 28.
56. Ibid. p. 33.

CHAPTER EIGHT

The Embodied Player of Horror Video Games

A black computer screen. Before I see anything, I hear a sound that is familiar to those of a particular age: the nostalgic clunk of a VHS tape being loaded into a player, and the soft whirring of the machinery. A title page, bearing the hallmarks of a degraded VHS tape, reads: ANATOMY. At the base of the screen: 8_18_94. The screen freezes, accompanied by a high-pitched buzz.

I am suddenly transported to the foyer of a darkened house. Ahead is a murky hallway. To my left, a doorway; to my right, stairs leading to the second floor. My light source only stretches a few feet into the darkness. With trepidation, I begin to investigate the house.

As I explore, the static of scan lines intermittently rolls up the screen. It should signal to me that the experience is only a fiction, but somehow it adds to its authenticity: my exploration feels like it is simultaneously a recording of sorts.

Soon, I am prompted to make my way into the basement. I open the door and navigate down the stairwell, into an inky blackness broken only by the scan line distortion. It feels as though the edges of the computer screen are lost to me. There is only the basement now, and my anxious journey edging along the walls. I can't risk going to the centre of the room. The light does not reach back to the walls.

FEAR IN THE FIRST PERSON

For many who enjoy horror cinema, the lure of horror video gaming is strong. Gone is the frustration of watching protagonists make the wrong decision by fleeing upstairs from the knife-wielding maniac; instead, it is replaced by the more active identification of the player as participant in the diegetic world. Now it is *you* who will be forced to make the decision to traipse down into the murky basement.

In this chapter I examine the aesthetics of several exemplar works of horror video gaming that operate to produce a defined embodied experience, one that is altered from the dynamics of cinema spectatorship but one that can be explained by drawing from similar foundational approaches. The first two exemplar games surveyed are not traditional 'survival horror', and thus they provide an opportunity to extend the thesis of previous chapters and ask whether the 'monster' in these games, and its horrific affect, can emerge instead from the intensification of sound and image, as opposed to the representational presence of monsters. The second half of the chapter looks at a video game adaptation of the *Alien* franchise, *Alien: Isolation*, where the monster is well and truly present, and asks how the concept of 'cinematic dread' described in earlier chapters can be transposed to a gaming environment.

To begin, it is worthwhile to delineate the difference between 'survival horror' video games and other types of horror games. Bernard Perron, in his thorough and in-depth examination of horror gaming, makes a distinction between 'horror video games', 'survival horror games' and 'scary video games'.[1] While the first label covers all works associated with horror, the second refers to a particular idiomatic label that arose in the 1990s to describe third-person action-adventure games such as *Resident Evil* and *Silent Hill*, where old-fashioned adventure game puzzle solving was combined with action sequences wherein the player confronts the various in-game monsters. The third, Perron's nomenclature, refers to games that 'take fear explicitly and intentionally as an object'.[2] He chooses 'scary' over 'horror' to accentuate that the main design intention in these games is the elicitation of fear.[3]

The genre of horror, and particularly horror cinema, has long played a role in influencing video game design. Geoff King and Tanya Krzywinska, while examining the 'broad points of contact, and departure, between cinema and games at the aesthetic, formal or textual level', note that genre is 'an obvious point of contact', as many games occupy a 'territory familiar from the generic categories of cinema – and often [draw] on devices specific to these genres in the cinema'.[4] While this chapter will explore a variety of these devices, the first I will turn to is the similarity between found footage horror and the first-person perspective employed by many of these games, including my exemplars.

First-person perspective in games typically refers to the lack of an on-screen avatar. Kai Vogeley and Gereon Fink define it as the 'centeredness of one's own multimodal experiential space upon one's own body, thus operating in an egocentric reference frame'.[5] That is to say, because there is no on-screen character that is visible, the player frames their experience as a mental and corporeal integration with the unseen body. This differs from the third-person point of view, wherein the player is more likely to ascribe mental states to their avatar, and there is a disjunction in corporeal integration.[6] King and Krzywinska concur with this, arguing that first-person perspective produces 'the greatest sense of presence, or sensory immersion in the gamescape'.[7]

Importantly, first-person perspective in the video game assists in enabling what Timothy Crick labels 'a fluent engagement with the virtual world'.[8] Interrogating video games through a comparison to Sobchack's phenomenological approach to cinema, Crick contends that video games and cinema have similar spatio-temporal qualities, and share a phenomenology that is 'embodied, immersive, interpellative, visceral, [and] mobile'.[9] Acknowledging that video games cannot offer the same 'concreteness and inexhaustible detail of indexical cinematic images', Crick argues that they compensate through the manner in which the virtual world of the game 'can be roamed like the physical one and thus is experienced as an inter-enactment as well as an embodiment of vision'.[10] This is ostensibly connected to the notion of first-person perspective through the way the player in this mode of game rarely thinks about 'controlling' the avatar in a reflective or intellectual sense: as Crick contends, we think 'as the avatar, from the point of view of the avatar . . . The avatar's [. . .] movement is incorporated with my corporeal schema and, as such, becomes an extension of my bodily basis of consciousness.'[11] Here again we are dealing with an approach that acknowledges the indivisibility of the subject/object dichotomy, this time of player and video game.

Lo-fi, High Tension: *Marginalia* and *Anatomy*

While not widely known, Connor Sherlock and Cameron Kunzelman's *Marginalia* (originally released in 2014 and updated and re-released in 2017) and Kitty Horrorshow's *Anatomy* (2016) both offer ideal illustrations of how the horror video game can be affectively intense without the overt presence of a monster, and without an avatar body that is under threat.[12] There are various other similarities that bond these two games, but the primary one, following on from the various examples in previous chapters, is their shared experiential qualities: both games build a tension and dread that transcends their lo-fi design.

Marginalia, by independent game designer Sherlock and writer Kunzelman, is a walking simulator game that revels in its ominous mood and atmosphere. Walking simulators are a genre that has existed since the 1980s but has seen a boom in popularity in the last decade. These types of games typically lack puzzles or obstacles to experiencing the narrative (which is why they have been pejoratively dismissed by some as not meeting the criteria of a game), and do not allow the player to fail or die. These games often prioritise the storytelling aspects of the game, be it linear or interactive. Crucially, in walking simulators, there are no monsters or enemies to kill. Adam Charles Hart notes that this is a trend of recent years in relation to first-person horror video games, which have sought to distinguish themselves from first-person shooters by 'minimizing, obscuring, or simply doing away with the player's capacity for combat'.[13]

Presented as a first-person experience, *Marginalia*, according to its teaser blurb, 'transports you to Kestlebrook, a secluded valley where history becomes enmeshed with a strange present. Weeks ago Eric left. Days ago you got a letter telling you to come to him. Now you're here, but precisely where is here? And better yet, when?' We will see how, in analysing *Anatomy*, this destabilisation of the player's knowledge of the space and time of the story-world is a useful trope in generating suspense and unease. The plot of *Marginalia* is relayed through an intermittent voice-over narration that describes both some of the events that occurred before the game narrative began, and some that the player will experience as the game continues. A male narrator, unnamed, tells of how a friend (or perhaps, romantic partner, it is never made clear) named Eric left in the middle of the night. When the narrator receives a mysterious letter from Eric, he takes a train ride to the valley of Kestlebrook and, on the way, reads through Eric's journals, looking for answers. The unresolved revelations of those journals, and the player's experiences as they journey through the valley as this unnamed and unseen protagonist, are purposefully enigmatic and narratively opaque.

The game begins with the player arriving at a campground car park. An adjacent forest descends into a valley beside the car park. As the player proceeds down into the valley, they are inevitably drawn towards common repeated light sources: lamps that illuminate the rough trail. As they pass each lamp, a fragment of the narrative is revealed in on-screen text and through voice-over, metaphorically 'illuminating' a fragment of the narrative.

At the base of the valley there is another light source that invariably draws the player's attention, only it is far more ominous and mysterious than the lamps. In the far-off distance, jagged beams of purple light hover in the sky. As the player approaches, they find the lights floating above what appears to be a set of rune stones. Ineffable and oddly portentous, the beams are nonetheless compelling for a player to pass underneath and examine. While nothing momentous occurs in this singular moment, it is illustrative of one of the ways *Marginalia* is effective as a 'scary video game' (although it is arguable that the designers are not so much interested in eliciting fear so much as tension and unease). As the narrative unfolds, revealing Eric's research into the history of the valley, this sense of unease is intensified by the incongruous nature of further abstract visual elements. While the player feels compelled and drawn to further explore the virtual space of the game, the discoveries revealed in the journey offer few answers, and often more questions. In a second forest, after crossing the plain where the rune stones are located, the player locates another path and comes across a series of glowing red, flame-shaped objects bordering it. The glow of their distant presence draws the player on. These red objects will later become tendrils of glowing red light that lead the player, like a thread, through the woods on the other side of the valley, into a second, deeper valley. The narrator, while wondering if Kestlebrook is 'haunted', remarks instead that 'someone went there a long time ago and planted a seed. All seeds want to grow.' These tendrils of light may also remind a player of the roots of a plant, stretching out beyond its natural borders.

Sound in *Marginalia* plays a crucial role, and the soundtrack of the game contains an ominous synth drone that repeats, building tension. The drone later becomes an organ, and then builds into a cacophonous symphonic blast as the player makes their way into an enveloping red light, a space that confounds the player's sense of geography. It is only through experimental movement that the space reveals a doorway, and the player can conclude that it is a portal of sorts. This portal leads them to the final space of the game: a vast alien terrain, and a bridge that leads to a shadowy figure encased in purple light at the top of a temple-like structure. As the player journeys towards this temple (and perhaps towards Eric?), jagged shards of black invade the visual space of the game, simulating a breakdown of the screen. The visual content is restricted as the player approaches the figure, obstructing the player's full knowledge of what and where this alien space is, and who the figure in the distance might be. Finally, the last glimmer of vision is stymied, the screen becomes completely black, and the player is returned to the opening screen of the game. In these final moments, *Marginalia* utilises the 'delayed, blocked or partial vision' that Giles refers to as common to horror cinema to intensify the affect of the game's conclusion.[14]

The above description is an apt example of the connection between first-person horror games and found footage horror that Hart identifies: that they are both 'built around a camera that is constantly searching, and which is always inherently inadequate to that task'.[15]

Anatomy, by Kitty Horrorshow, shares many similarities with *Marginalia*. Horrorshow is, like Connor Sherlock, an independent game designer who primarily self-distributes her games. *Anatomy* is essentially also a walking simulator, although unlike *Marginalia* it does force the player to fail on several occasions (each 'failure' results in a new iteration of the game when reloaded).

Another distinction is found in how *Anatomy* heightens its affect through the way the story-world of the game is progressively corrupted. The game, as described in the chapter introduction, begins with a sound familiar to most children of the 1980s: the whirring of electronics of a VHS tape being loaded into a player. The image is immediately disrupted by rolling scanlines – the bars of static that would also be familiar to those who have ever watched a VHS. The integration of these distortions plays cleverly on the tropes of found footage, and helps unify the first-person perspective of the game with the affective properties of subjective perspective in films such as *The Blair Witch Project* and *V/H/S*.

Anatomy is a haunted house story. The player begins in a relatively featureless hallway of a darkened house. They soon determine their purpose is to find audio cassette tapes located in the various rooms. Each time the player finds a tape, they must take it to the tape player in the kitchen of the home. Each tape contains a section of a monologue, ruminating on the relationship between humans and their homes, specifically the shared similarity between the 'anatomy' of the two. As the game progresses into its various iterations through a forced 'reboot', the tone of the voice on the tapes shifts, and the messages become sinister and threatening.

Each time the player is forced to recover a new tape, and thus forced further into the depths of the house, the fear of what could be lurking unseen in the darkness escalates. The search for the cassettes forces the player into these spaces, making them an unwilling participant in the intensification of this disquiet. In the basement, as in several of the rooms, the centre of the room is so dark that nothing can be seen – it is only by moving to the walls at the edges of the room that you can determine where the room starts and ends.

The aforementioned scanlines, horizontal bars of static, intermittently roll up and down the screen, another level of obstruction beyond the darkness. The VHS introduction scene, however, does more than introduce the glitch aesthetic. While the game seems to end abruptly on first play after an exploration of the house, this is only a temporary ending, and each time you reload the game (until you reach the final level) the VHS tape which appears to be recording (or replaying?) your actions is further degraded.

Restarting the game forces the player to repeat scenes so that they have an eerie, uncanny sense of déjà vu. In the second and third iterations, the tapes begin to be filled with static, and the voice on them becomes warped. This warping is matched by the story, which begins to describe the house as both 'hungry' and 'awake'. The geography of the rooms also begins to break down, and they become filled with abstract, non-geometric shapes (like the lights of *Marginalia*, oddly sinister in their abstraction). This further destruction of the logic of the space leads to more grotesque appearances, like fleshy walls, doors and windows that blink in and out of existence, and furniture and objects that hang in the air (Figure 8.1). Despite all the warnings from the tapes, the player feels compelled to push on, even after hearing the implicit threat on the tapes that 'when a house is both hungry and awake, every room becomes a mouth'. Like *Marginalia*, the game ends with little narrative

Figure 8.1 A floating tape recorder in *Anatomy*.

resolution, instead leaving the player with the residual of a deepened feeling of unease and apprehension that is the mark of horror's affect.

Each of these games borrows elements from horror's techniques of affective intensification examined in previous chapters: the aesthetics of found footage, the destabilisation of the image through glitch and distortion, the tension of the out-of-frame and the heightened subjectivity of first-person perspective. As they do not fall under the rubric of survival horror, it is only apposite that they eschew what Perron refers to as the main event schema of single-player horror video games: 'the confrontation', where a gamer must 'face the monster' or 'avoid it by hiding and fleeing from threat'.[16] Instead, they build their affect not through confrontation, but through an experience of a gradual intensification of sound and image. Each game begins with an innocuous space that, through the player's journey, is progressively destabilised (through the breakdown of sound and image in *Anatomy*) or amplified (through the ruptures of colour and the augmentation of score in *Marginalia*). These acts of destabilisation or amplification fit with Krzywinska's assertion that horror games 'explore ways to play with, and against, game media's normative expectations of mastery and its concomitant representational, symbolic, and emotional contours'.[17] She further contends that this obstruction of mastery may also be bolstered by the way in which 'the most effective and affective Horror games [. . .] make a play through representation and performance to work against the usual Vitruvian coordinates of games (used to work with the types of affect associated with pleasure, agency and assuredness)'.[18]

Video games arguably extend cinema and the other new media forms examined in this book in relation to their application of the out-of-frame because, as Perron asserts, a gamer 'is not just a witness to the scene'.[19] Drawing on Pascal Bonitzer's work on the 'blind space', which is roughly equivalent to the out-of-frame as previously discussed, Perron contends that the video game screen is 'more centripetal than the movie screen', because it 'elicits fear based on gameplay by constantly showing a space that extends into a nightmarish universe into which gamers have to immerse themselves. As a result, the enemy is indeed virtually everywhere and the whole audio-visual field is dramatized.'[20] In this consideration, the only shelter from fear comes from the player refusing to play, as every moment traversing the game world brings about the possibility of an encounter with something from the 'blind space'; even in games like *Anatomy* and *Marginalia*, where the lack of an enemy becomes quickly evident, the fear endures.

DELEUZE AND THE VIDEO GAME

What was until recently a relatively underexplored area of scholarship, the relation between affect and video games, has in recent years seen fruitful explorations, among them Deleuzo-Guattarian approaches such as that advanced by Colin Cremin. Cremin contends that the video game aesthetic is 'affective' and that, as a medium in which action is integral, video game theory requires non-representational approaches.[21] The angle Cremin takes is a consideration of affect in a Deleuzian sense as 'a force rather than emotion, a force that varies in intensities as it combines with multiplicities of different objects and assemblages: exceeding a body defined by an identity society prescribes to it and endlessly produces the new'.[22] This concept of affect shares certain affinities with the approach I have used within this book, and provides us with a way of thinking through how the experiential dimension of games such as *Anatomy* and *Marginalia* transcends their representational content.

While Cremin's rhizomatic reading of video game 'play' might run contrary to a consideration of walking simulators as a fully-fledged 'game' (Cremin's description of the inhabitation of 'rhizome-play' could well apply to the way walking simulators to some degree force the player into 'arborescent tracings'), there is still value in assessing how the concept of assemblages may provide new ways of thinking through the gaming experience.[23] In Cremin's reading, video games are assemblages of 'forces, of affects and pre-personal becomings; they are multiplicities, not closed systems at all, rather open to infinite variation and invention'.[24] This occurs through the way in which the player becomes, in a sense, 'an artist in becoming', transforming the designer's intention through every choice that is made within the game.

The subjectivity that Cremin describes is not so much an inhabitation of the virtual world of the game, but an emancipation of the affects of the game. He writes: 'We do not put ourselves in [video game worlds] as such, we put ourselves in proximity with the affects that are stored in them by the developer and "liberated" in the event of play.'[25] This proximity is not an interaction, but an 'assemblage'; the implication of interaction is a dualism, as opposed to Cremin's concept of the video game plane as a place where 'forces are selected and bodies without organs composed; the motion of the hand that connects to the controller augments or decomposes by our actions and relations the possibilities for new becomings, new actions and multiplicities'.[26] Video games in this model are 'compositions' of creative forces.

With this understanding, we can open up a consideration of why games like *Anatomy* and *Marginalia* produce an affective intensity that belies the scarcity of horrific representational content. Horror in these games emerges from the multiplicities presented by the spatial and temporal freedom for the player, in combination with the amplification or distortion of the image and sound. While there are clear boundaries to the virtual world of the game, the player is at liberty to navigate it with relative spatial freedom, and with almost complete temporal freedom. What may materialise from this 'infinite variation and invention' is a type of transition between states which is difficult to codify into purely emotional terms.

SPATIAL AND TEMPORAL APERTURES IN *ALIEN: ISOLATION*

The spatial and temporal elasticity described above is also crucial to the operation of the horror game that does have an explicit monster, and in the remainder of this chapter I will examine the game experience of *Alien: Isolation* in consideration of this. Based on the *Alien* series of films, and released on Xbox, PlayStation and PC in 2014, *Alien: Isolation* is a first-person perspective game wherein the player's avatar is Amanda Ripley, daughter of Ellen Ripley from the films. The game begins when Amanda's search for her mother is interrupted by a rescue mission on a derelict space station. While the game operates through the logic of assigning various missions to the game world avatar, underneath this straightforward narrative is the portentous dread of a surprise confrontation with the titular alien. Any savvy, game-literate player would comprehend that an interaction with the alien is inevitable, yet each meeting is a jarring and fear-inducing experience in the way it is staged, and each meeting brings about a corporeal intensification.

Figure 8.2 *Alien: Isolation* motion sensor.

There are two elements of the game that contribute much to this intensified bodily experience. The first is the in-game use of a motion sensor device, which, when activated, appears in the player's view like a real-world handheld tool: the game designers cleverly shift the focal plane to the device each time it is used, which replicates the perceptual directedness we have with our real-world use of tools. The device tracks the movement of the alien and its proximity (Figure 8.2). The second element is the game's architectural design of interior space and how it is utilised in the narrative. For example, throughout the space station there are lockers, cupboards and storage spaces whose only purpose within the narrative is as a place of refuge, and, when employed as a hiding place, their claustrophobic sense of containment feels strikingly real.

Perron argues that the involvement of the gamer may be 'intensified by the deadly menace endangering a protagonist, especially since the latter is under their control'.[27] He also asserts that the 'optimal ludic experience' of horror video games occurs when 'a gamer's survival skills are dynamically balanced with the deadly threat they face'.[28] *Alien: Isolation* provides a compelling support for Perron's argument, especially in those moments when, while moving through the space station, the alien suddenly descends into the player's field of vision from the air vents above. In these moments the intensification of shock hijacks the body and prompts a flight response similar to that of real life.

In my first experience of this moment within the game, I fled towards the safety of a room I had recently departed, knowing a locker in the room offered some form of safety. Taking refuge inside it, I noticed my real-world breathlessness and racing heart, an experience that was to me more akin to the experience of shock while viewing a film than any previous gaming experience. As I waited inside the locker, my vision reduced to staring through the gaps of the locker's vents, there was a coalescence of dread. The thickening of time that Hanich proposes in his work on dread was, upon later reflection, evident, and although I could rationalise the fear of the computer-generated image as unnecessary, my bodily reaction denied any form of rationalisation. The previously mentioned motion sensor device, when activated, showed the movement of a green dot heading towards my location. In the specific sense of helplessness, there was also a passive voyeurism that echoed the best cinematic horror. Yet, despite this, it *was* coming for *me*.

For what felt like far longer than the objective ten or so seconds of the experience, the vision of my avatar remained glued to the entry to the room from inside the confinement of our hiding space. Suddenly, the door retracted, and the creature entered the room. It paced throughout the room, moving into the periphery of the sightlines afforded by the locker. Time continued to stretch – until a huge obsidian head appeared, directly in front of the locker, sniffing the vents. Here the game designers of *Alien: Isolation* create a fascinating requirement for the player: the game prompts them to hold their breath (through a controller action) and draw back against the rear wall of the locker.

Here I would like to briefly diverge from my description of the traditional game playing experience to discuss the phenomenological implications of playing *Alien: Isolation* in virtual reality. Although it was never officially released for virtual reality, modifications (or mods) were made available so that the game could be experienced in the Oculus Rift. The intensified bodily experience described above escalates dramatically in virtual reality. Although the game requires a controller to allow the players to traverse their environment, the headset allows a freedom of perceptual direction which is very much akin to cinematic virtual reality (which will be the focus of the next chapter).

In the virtual reality experience, the mobility of the player through the haptically charged environment facilitates a deeper form of connection to the space surrounding them: the game design brilliantly recreates textures like stagnant water, claustrophobic air vents, and the glass shield of a spacesuit facemask. While the player still has the given mission goals to achieve, the relative freedom with which they can move through the labyrinthine space station helps build the 'geopsychic architexture' that Bruno postulates, no doubt aided by the particularly haptic qualities of the animation.[29]

In the virtual reality version of the game, the experience of being trapped in the locker, and the recoil it demands, shifts; it becomes both a gaming process and a physical recoil. Playing the game in virtual reality, I could do nothing but shrink away from the rows and rows of serrated teeth that remained on the other side of the vents. The game sets up the premise that, if the player can withdraw to an acceptable degree, the alien will move on to investigate other rooms. Thankfully this is what the predator did, stalking back out into the corridor, unsatiated.

In both regular gaming and virtual reality, every moment after this first meeting becomes saturated with the anticipation that the alien is around the next corner, an effect that is sustained and complemented by the ambisonic sound design, which indicates the approaching footsteps of the returning predator, along with its passage through the space station's ventilation system. The entire territory of the space station becomes imbued with dread. Here we can return to Perron's acknowledgement of the 'centripetal' force of gaming's 'blind spaces'.

That spatial elasticity contributes to this dread is, of course, but one half of the equation – the second half is the temporal elasticity of the gaming environment. In *Alien: Isolation*, each confrontation with the xenomorph has an unbounded temporal frame: if retreat is successful, it may still involve minutes of being stalked by the alien. If unsuccessful, there may only be seconds before it strikes. When Hanich argues that we indulge in horror 'because it gives time temporarily back in our hands', he draws attention to the way horror in particular can make duration palpable.[30] This palpability counters what he labels the 'fragmentation of time experience' in modern life.[31] For Hanich, this time experience comes about in two forms, acceleration and deceleration, both of which *Alien: Isolation* puts to great use.

In conventional horror cinema, scenes of cinematic shock bring the present moment to the fore, while scenes of cinematic dread produce a density in duration, a stillness that extends enigmatically into a potential terrifying future moment. In the realm of gaming, both virtual reality and traditional, this concept of dread can evolve and transform to produce an exceptionally intense experience. The experience is heightened further by the extended duration of the gaming experience, wherein players can spend hours navigating the labyrinthine corridors, and the completely randomised potential for further confrontations with the alien. Each experience is unique, and uniquely embodied.

Attempts by the player to rationalise their fear, in that it is produced by a computer-generated image, are in part denied by the bodily intensification that occurs. This intensification is greater in virtual reality, which fuses the inevitable horrific outcome for both the avatar of Amanda Ripley and the player who shares a more embodied sense of her vision. But it is not only this shared vision which is key: it is also the combination of the fluid duration of the experience and the continuous spatial reconfiguration which comes with the expanded freedom of interaction and movement within the diegetic world. The combinatorial power of these elements allows for Hanich's cinematic dread to reach its apogee in the virtual reality environment.

The virtual reality experience of the game *Alien: Isolation* offers one such ideal example. The game convenes a player who becomes, to some degree, less a player than a spectator-interactor, although this notion of spectatorship is very different from conventional cinematic spectator. The game achieves this through the way it synthesises what could be considered a cinematic style of narrative with the greater temporal and spatial capacities of gaming: the viewer/gamer becomes a participant in an environment that changes moment to moment and makes active choices that alter the dimensions of their experience. In the following chapter we will investigate how cinematic virtual reality may employ similar dimensions of experience, and what cinema can offer back to this burgeoning technology.

Notes

1. Perron, *The World of Scary Video Games*, p. 4.
2. Ibid. p. 4.
3. Ibid. p. 4.
4. King and Krzywinska, *Screenplay*, p. 10.
5. Vogeley and Fink, 'Neural Correlates of the First-Person-Perspective', p. 38.
6. Lim and Reeves, 'Being in the Game', p. 353.
7. King and Krzywinska, *Tomb Raiders and Space Invaders*, p. 10.
8. Crick, 'The Game Body', p. 267.
9. Ibid. p. 261.
10. Ibid. p. 265.
11. Ibid. p. 267.
12. Both games are available via indie games online store itch.io.
13. Hart, 'The Searching Camera', p. 88.
14. Giles, 'Conditions of Pleasure in Horror Cinema', p. 39.
15. Hart, 'The Searching Camera', pp. 74–5.
16. Perron, *The World of Scary Video Games*, p. 110.
17. Krzywinska, 'Gaming Horror's Horror', p. 293.
18. Ibid. p. 297.
19. Perron, *The World of Scary Video Games*, p. 262.
20. Ibid. p. 263.
21. Cremin, *Exploring Videogames with Deleuze and Guattari*, p. 2.
22. Ibid. p. 2.
23. Ibid. p. 94.

24. Ibid. p. 16.
25. Ibid. p. 19.
26. Ibid. p. 20.
27. Perron, *The World of Scary Video Games*, p. 346.
28. Ibid. p. 106.
29. Bruno, *Atlas of Emotion*, pp. 9–10.
30. Hanich, *Cinematic Emotion in Horror Films and Thrillers*, p. 239.
31. Ibid. p. 239.

CHAPTER NINE

The Spectator-Interactor of Virtual Reality Horror

I pick up the black headset, attached to the computer by a knot of cables, and slide it over my eyes. Headphones cover my ears. Wearing both, I feel a little like I've slipped under the surface of some obsidian lake, into dark water. I press play.

The darkness dissipates, replaced by a gauze-like film covering the only light source. I hear distant footsteps, but also something much closer. It's approaching from in front. I hear its heavy breath and instinctively hold my breath . . . then the gauze is withdrawn, the blindfold removed. Immediately there is a sense of presence to this world: visually, aurally, bodily.

My first instinct is primal, to observe my surroundings for threat. Freed to look in any direction, I peek over both shoulders, up at the roof, down at the floor. I'm in a dark, catacomb-like chamber. Whoever removed my blindfold is now retreating away from me, a shadowy figure. He pauses in the entrance doorway, silhouetted by light, and then closes the door. The experience of these events is unlike watching them occur on a screen – instead, I am in this space, in a moment of encounter.

The sound of slow-running water suggests that perhaps I am underground. Suddenly, unintelligible whispers orbit me, voices without a source. I twist and turn, trying to pinpoint their origin. They fade away.

Time stretches as the water continues its gurgle. The stasis is broken by flashing fluorescents, illuminating the room in blasts of white. I can now see that I am in the centre of what appears to be a circular room, with four arched doorways leading to a larger surrounding chamber. My reconnaissance is interrupted by what the strobing light suddenly reveals – a woman, in the chamber with me, facing the wall.

As the light flickers and strobes, she disappears – and reappears fractions of a second later, closer now, facing me. Approaching, and then retreating. She lurches and trembles. The light continues to obfuscate her movements. The whispers return, ominous and threatening. The light goes out . . .

When it returns, they are screaming at me – not just one woman, but three, madly shrieking. And then, just as suddenly, they are gone again, obscured by darkness. In the eerie gloom another figure appears now, more nightmarish in its abstraction. It appears to be a child, with the head of a pig, holding a dead fox. He is looking directly at me. Again, darkness conceals his departure.

My angst and growing bodily discomfort are prolonged by seconds of darkness and then, slowly, the light in the surrounding alcoves returns. More footsteps. Accompanied by a pulsing score, a man in a dark suit enters the room. The most disturbing thing is his movement: languorous and somehow dreamlike. I can see that he is shadowed by another version of himself, his movements echoed by this ghostly halo. He too is able to instantaneously shift his position in the room. He dances, dances, and then reaches out towards me, hands reaching for my eyes.

Another cut to black. When the strobe-like lighting returns, both the man and the woman are sitting beside me: the man to my left, the woman to my right, each staring at me with blank indifference. There is a slightly maniacal chuckle, and then a child's voice says: 'She's coming.' The others remain mute. The light continues to strobe, as I relentlessly scan for the promised arrival.

A screeching metallic door directs my attention to the end of the room. From the silhouette, I can determine it is someone wearing a dress. She enters the room, letting the door thud closed behind her (Figure 9.1). *The presence of the visitor has also captured the attention of the others. In glimpses it appears to me to be a little girl, but then, fractions of a second later, a woman. The sporadic illumination refuses any attempts to resolutely classify her. She begins to walk slowly towards me.*

Accompanied by a shrill scream, she abruptly rushes forward, and now finally I can see her features, although I wish I couldn't – pallid face, white hair, black cavities for eyes, a gaping black mouth, and a blood-spattered white gown. She strikes and I tip over, falling horizontally to the ground. It's an eerie sensation, a

Figure 9.1 The woman in *11:57*.

type of kinaesthetic reaction where my real-world senses are incongruent with my visual processes and my appraisal of danger. Still sitting in my chair in the real world, I feel, just for a moment, like I have fallen, and my body tenses for the expected impact with the floor.

Now lying on my side in the virtual world, I can still tilt my head, and out of the corner of my eye I can see the woman slink away into the darkened alcoves surrounding this chamber. A strobe light continues to flash. The pulsing score returns, as the end credits appear before me. Yet even with the intrusion of non-diegetic credits, the music cues me to continue looking, to continue to be on guard.

Rightfully so – if I hadn't continued scanning the room, I wouldn't have seen her return, moments later, from behind. The white-faced woman approaches, crouches down, and stretches her pale fingers towards my face . . .

THE MEETING PLACE OF VIRTUAL REALITY AND HORROR CINEMA

The sequence described above is an experience of the short film *11:57*, a pioneering cinematic virtual reality horror project from the Sid Lee Collective. Although only four and a half minutes in length, it demonstrates some of the embryonic strengths and the possible pitfalls of the synthesis of cinema and virtual reality. The previous chapters have focused on how the reduced presence of on-screen bodies in certain horror texts does not necessarily negate the generation of affect, and can in turn lead to the employment of textual strategies that amplify the affective possibilities of the genre. Virtual reality cinema works somewhat differently to these texts: by its general visual negation of the actual spectatorial body, which is instead replaced with a virtual bodily presence that is also experienced in an intensified manner.

Horror as a genre is the prevailing location of much of the contemporary experimentation in merging cinematic storytelling with this new technology, perhaps due to how its explicit sensory engagement and immediately immersive quality allow a circumvention of the conventional hierarchical importance of narrative. In many of these short projects, the filmmakers forgo narrative depth in favour of intensity of immersion and affect. However, this approach may be problematic for the long-term future of virtual reality cinema, as will be discussed. This chapter will also focus on the following questions: what are the potential ramifications to the experience of horror spectatorship in the burgeoning world of VR filmmaking? Does VR as an environment open up new capacities for cinematic storytelling? If so, how do these new capacities alter our understandings of our embodied relationship to sound and image? And what are the implications of the new cinematic space constructed in VR for cinematic experience, both positive and negative? These questions will be examined through an analysis of the short 360-degree video VR films *11:57*, *The Black Mass Experience*, *Catatonic* and *Escape the Living Dead*. It should also be acknowledged that the technologies discussed in this chapter are in flux, with rapid developments occurring across a variety of related fields, including haptics, volumetric photogrammetry, artificial intelligence and hyper-narratives. This chapter is in some ways a speculative consideration of where the art form may go, as well as an analysis of how early virtual reality filmmakers are attempting to formulate a new cinematic grammar.

The integration of virtual reality and cinema has been the elusive dream for cinephiles and technophiles since the first wave of virtual reality in the early 1990s. It is, however, only recently that the technology for both production and reception of virtual reality has developed to the point where this integration has been achieved, and many independent content developers have begun to experiment specifically with virtual reality filmmaking. On a larger scale, while they have yet to produce significant content, companies such as Disney and filmmakers such as Steven Spielberg are already staking bold financial investments in the continued development of these tools for filmmakers. As early as 2002, Jeffrey Shaw argued that 'the hegemony of Hollywood's movie-making modalities is increasingly being challenged by the radical new potentialities of the digital media technologies'.[1] He then located these challenges in video games, location-based entertainment, and contemporary new media art.[2] These challenges have now evolved into the fuller explorations into virtual reality filmmaking that several large Hollywood studios are currently undertaking. Experimentation in the field continues at a rapid pace, with Disney and Lucasfilm currently developing multiple virtual reality projects set in the *Star Wars* universe.

The technological advances that have hastened this development are intimately tied to enhancements in the quality of the verisimilitude in the VR experience. They include an improved graphics frame rate, increased capacity for body tracking, reduction in movement latency, accommodation of sensory modalities such as touch (haptics integrated into gloves and controllers, for example), improvement in the quality of the images (in terms of brightness, colour, contrast and resolution), enlarged field of view and visual fidelity of the rendered scene.[3]

The immersive properties of the current wave of virtual reality technology are second to none. High-end headsets such as the Oculus Rift and HTC VIVE allow for what is known as 6DoF – six degrees of freedom of movement in a three-dimensional space (although even the limited properties of a viewer such as the Google Cardboard, which utilises a mobile phone as a VR screen, and works only in three degrees of freedom of movement, can have dramatic effects for a first-time viewer of virtual reality).

In 2002, Sabine Himmelsbach wrote: '[v]irtual reality seeks to create a synthesis of observer and computer-generated visual environment, converting data into sense experience. The distance between visual space and observer is abolished. The latter is now literally in the picture.'[4] This observation still holds true for virtual reality cinema. There are, however, two distinct types of experience within this domain, which are predominantly separated by the degree of movement offered. The first is generally labelled 360-degree video. This is video filmed by a 360-degree camera with 'ambisonic' sound recording (a technique that uses a spherical microphone to capture the same range of sound), where the viewer is placed in the position of this camera in the environment it has recorded. In this configuration, there is no facility for 6DoF.

The second type of production is what is commonly known as 'room-scale' design, which is a paradigm for VR which allows the users to freely move through a limited space, with their real-life motion reflected in the VR environment. Although the term refers to 'room-scale', these spaces vary in dimension. Cinema in this environment requires direct integration with game engines, which facilitate the 6DoF movement within the filmic world. These projects often integrate 360-degree video with other cinematic elements, such as computer-generated imagery (CGI), and often involve interactive elements. An apt example here is *VR Noir*, a VR project produced by the Australian Film Television and Radio School in 2016. It features acting sequences that were shot on a stereoscopic camera rig (to create the illusion of depth) that have been integrated into a six-dimensional CGI environment (Figure 9.2). The focus of the first part of this chapter is primarily 360-degree

Figure 9.2 *VR Noir.*

video; however, the chapter will explore how room-scale productions address some of the limitations of the 360-degree video, particularly in relation to horror projects.

One common aspect within the limited albeit varied field of 360-degree VR films currently available, even in those that poorly utilise the mode, is the remarkable potential presented by a somewhat 'frameless' experience of a filmic world, and the enhanced corporeality this experience brings to the fore. 'Frameless' here refers to the perceptual freedom given to the virtual reality spectator: in the diegetic world of virtual reality, the spectator is free to direct their own attention at any time to any point in the entire range of vision. For the genre of horror, this freedom has tremendous significance, as it intensifies the push–pull imperative of the desire to look versus the trepidation about doing so, discussed earlier in this book. To recapitulate, in conventional horror cinema the composition of the frame is a delimiting device, used to elicit our attention to both what is shown and what threatens to be shown. Through the judicious manipulation of on-screen and off-screen content, filmmakers can create and amplify various forms of cinematic fear. Virtual reality, on the other hand, induces a mode of image perception that is essentially a brain–body simulation of the perceptual choices of the viewer: the vision supplied to us through the binocularity of the headset mimics the manner in which perception works in the world outside of VR. For a filmmaker, this produces a filmic world that is, in essence, 'frameless': now that the viewer can look anywhere when confronted with a horrifying situation, the question becomes: *where do they look?* Not surprisingly, this newfound freedom can conflict with the requirements of a rigidly constructed narrative, which is dependent on directing the spectator's attention. Therefore, it requires VR filmmakers to rethink one dominant paradigm of constructing the cinematic image: harnessing spectatorial gaze.

Instead of the process of manipulating the spectator's attention to certain aspects of the frame, or the imposed dialectics of the linking of images via the process of montage, virtual reality activates our bodies as spectators in a new and revolutionary way, due to the unique interface of our bodies with this type of digital image. As much as it shares the ethic of astonishment with Tom Gunning's 'cinema of attractions', VR transforms this astonishment into a recalibration of our bodily experience as viewers.[5] This bodily experience is radically different to conventional cinema, in that it foregrounds our bodily presence and impels us to 'interact' with the image, through bodily movement. Miriam Ross contends that virtual reality's distinct ability to separate the viewer from the outside world also 'establishes the potential for synesthetic interactions to take place with greater proximity and in a more enveloping manner', and makes valuable observations about the specific factors that can affect this synaesthetic transference, such as the emphasis on a 'tactile sensorium', the 'doubled embodiment' that may occur in the presence of a visual avatar, and the interplay between live action and digitally created visual fields.[6]

The genre of horror is a fertile field for the study of this recalibration, because, as established throughout this book, horror film's various affects are catalysed in the fluid, dynamic relationship between our bodies, the image and our viewing environment. This interchange is prompted not only in the reception of a cinematic story, but in how cinema, in the words of Rutherford, mobilises 'the corporeality, the embodied responsiveness of the spectator'.[7] Examining the viewer's skin in a metaphoric sense, Rutherford delineates the boundary between spectator and image as akin to a 'permeable membrane'.[8] Virtual reality accentuates the permeability of this membrane, eliciting a heightened form of embodied experience. Jessica Brillhart, Google's chief virtual reality filmmaker, cites Dziga Vertov's 1929 description of the cinema's 'fresh perception' of the world: 'I'm an eye. A mechanical eye. I, the machine, show you a world the way only I can see it. I free myself for today and forever from human immobility.'[9] Brillhart takes issue with Vertov's assertion of disembodiment resulting from a melding of viewer and camera. In her speculative article on the future of VR, she states that 'VR isn't a disembodied medium at all. It's quite the opposite, because its whole end-goal is embodiment.'[10] Brillhart links this to how VR emphasises the intersubjectivity of the viewer's *experience* of the VR world, as opposed to the reception of a pre-established narrative. In Brillhart's opinion, VR filmmakers should be less interested in compelling the viewer to follow a sequential and linear narrative and more interested in creating cinematic moments that can be more freely inhabited by the viewer.

As this book contends, horror in conventional cinema also intensifies these bodily dimensions of spectatorship, albeit in a different way. Hanich proposes that the bodily response is foregrounded in horror in order to counter the 'disembodiment and acceleration' that modernity has wrought. For Hanich, the pursuit of a 'deep' experience, of both time and of our lived body in time and space, can be effectively met by the manner in which horror film generates a specific phenomenological spatiality and temporality of the lived body.[11] This is also evident in the experience of cinematic virtual reality horror.

Hanich's work on the paradoxical pleasure of horror and its ability to alter our experience of space and time, discussed in Chapter 3, presents a theoretical frame to examine how both horror cinema and virtual reality may best integrate their respective technologies. According to Hanich's paradigm, the intensification of bodily experience is intimately connected with the way horror film reconfigures our conventional everyday experience of time and space to one that expands or contracts these respective elements.

Virtual Reality and Presence

The articulation of a unique spatiality and temporality of the lived body is evident in the experience of virtual reality horror. The emphasis on corporeal interaction within the technology places the embodied viewer as the locus of the experience, open to a wide array of sensory influences. These sensory influences can be visual (what the spectator sees), aural (what is heard), haptic (sense of touch, temperature or pressure), proprioceptive (to do with the body's configuration in space) or vestibular (orientation, balance and movement). That these influences produce a corporeal response, despite their virtuality, is due to the body and brain's partial inability to distinguish many of these sensory engagements from their real-world counterparts.[12] While the body of the VR participant is rarely reproduced as a visual avatar within VR cinema, the indissoluble connection between movement and perception elicits both a conscious and unconscious awareness of the viewer's bodily presence within the virtual space. Even in the absence of a virtual body within the virtual environment, there is a bodily sense of 'being in' the virtual environment, rather than where the participant's body is actually located. Theorists use the term 'presence' to describe this sense of being there.[13]

Mel Slater offers one conceptual account for how this occurs, in his examination of this foundational presence. While Slater draws attention to how 'sensorimotor contingencies that approximate those of physical reality can give rise to the illusion that you are located inside the rendered virtual environment', he distinguishes presence, the 'qualia of having a sensation of being in a real place', into two distinct concepts: place illusion and plausibility illusion.[14]

This conception separates 'the strong illusion of being in a place in spite of the sure knowledge that you are not there' (place illusion) from 'the illusion that what is apparently happening is really happening' (plausibility illusion).[15] This spectrum of illusion contributes to the sense of immersion. For Slater, 'the body is a focal point where [place illusion] and [plausibility illusion] are fused'.[16] However, for Slater, the fullest extent of this fusion requires synchrony between a virtual body and the real-world body: that a visual avatar in the virtual environment can fully replicate the body of the actual participant.[17]

Kent Bye builds on Slater's concepts with his 'elemental theory of presence'.[18] Bye offers four types of presence that contribute to plausibility (and thus immersion): active presence, which is the creation of immersion through the use of handheld tools or devices in the VR experience; emotional presence, which occurs through the evocation of an emotional response; social presence, which is the active engagement with others in the VR space; and embodied presence, which is, for Bye, an acknowledgement of the existence of the real body within the VR space. Bye argues that by reducing one or more of these presences, the others are amplified, and that because 360-degree video reduces active and embodied presence, it strengthens the emotional and social presences.[19]

Both Slater's and Bye's concepts presented above are somewhat reliant on intensified embodiment as a result of a visual correspondence between a virtual body and the real body: that the body presented in the virtual environment matches the body outside of it. However, this understanding does not correlate with my experience of cinematic virtual reality; regardless of the presence of a virtual avatar, my bodily response is intensely attuned to the virtual environment of these cinematic experiences. The general 'presence' of the experience is sufficiently strong despite the lack of a virtual bodily avatar. While the presences that Bye argues for do have effects in intensifying immersion, to predicate the intensity of embodied presence on the presence of the body of a virtual avatar seems to echo the earlier understandings of cinematic affect that focus on the bodily presence of the protagonist, such as those presented by Reyes.

A deeper consideration of the experience of virtual reality cinema and its specific production of affect yields understandings that develop the broader arc of this book: that spectatorship occurs at the nexus of body, thought and image. Virtual reality cinema highlights the limitations in placing an emphasis on narrative progression as the primary driver for our interface with the image. The limitations of narrative in these projects, due to the exigencies of their production and the constraints of their short durations, reveal that it is not so much control of spectatorial attention that allows for virtual reality cinema's transformative dimension: it is its corporeal-affective dimensions. In its dépaysement of perception, cinematic virtual reality paradoxically implicates the body of the spectator more fully than previous imaging technologies.[20] It affectively charges the (unseen) body. This is not to say that conventional cinema does not carry its own affective charge, but what is vitally different is that VR cannot use the same techniques of narrative or identification to forge affective bonds with the viewer in the way Plantinga presents, which raises questions regarding how necessary these are to the production of affect. In the place of these techniques of narrative and identification, VR cinema instead seems to revel in the bodily surplus that emerges from this nexus of body, thought and image.

The horror short films of early cinematic virtual reality are a particularly productive site for the examination of this process, because they highlight the narrative limitations of the mode. Like many of the texts examined in the previous chapters, these virtual reality horror films also place great emphasis on what is *not seen*, on the *potential* for the monster to appear. They also heighten the non-visual sensory qualities of the experience to produce the kind of intensified interaction between spectatorial body and image argued for in previous chapters. This concept would seem to run counter to the ocularcentric nature of a head-mounted display that replicates vision, with its implication that the spectatorial body is somehow excluded or forgotten when we take away the actual presence of the body that occurs in real-world visual perception. However, it is precisely this disjunction which highlights virtual reality's action on the body. Far from media becoming simply 'eye-wash', as posthumanist theorists such as Friedrich Kittler suggest, all of the senses in virtual reality are activated in concert, bringing the spectatorial body to the fore.[21]

Analysing various works of virtual reality horror cinema allows us to further unpack the fallacy that vision is virtual reality's primary sensory mode. This move continues to develop an understanding of why it is it not so much that which is seen (the ghoulish woman of *11:57*, for example), but the viewer's entire embodied experience of the image that carries its power.

Virtual Reality and Cinema: Strange Bedfellows?

If cinema is said to have a spectrum that ranges from Lumière's first celluloid images to the optical–digital hybrid of the contemporary Hollywood high concept film (such as Ang Lee's *Billy Lynn's Long Half-Time Walk*) to the completely digital worlds of modern animation or animation/live action hybrids (such as Robert Zemeckis's *The Polar Express*), then it is arguable that cinematic virtual reality is a new divergent branch that, while not necessarily part of this continued evolution, perhaps harks back to the early magnetism of the turn of the century novelty that Tom Gunning terms 'the cinema of attractions'.[22] Traced to the period between 1895 and 1904, this cinema capitalised on what Gunning calls 'an aesthetic of astonishment': its ethic was direct and exhibitionist, the pleasure it produced for audiences often deriving from 'the energy released by the play between the shock caused by (an) illusion of danger and delight in its pure illusion'.[23] Gunning argues that, while they were not aware of how the illusions of cinema were created, the audiences of this period were more sophisticated than some conventional claims, and took great pleasure in both the illusion itself and the knowledge that it was manufactured. Virtual reality also seems drawn to this combination of illusory danger and delight, with many early projects centred around simulations of situations or experiences that are unattainable to most: for example, climbing Mount Everest, flying in a wingsuit, or rock climbing in Yellowstone National Park.[24]

The early iteration of cinema that Gunning details was far less subject to the demands of narrative that would later hold sway over the medium, much like the simulations described above and the more narratively complex horror shorts discussed in this chapter. Gunning draws a comparison between early cinema and trompe l'oeil, the art technique of 'aesthetic illusion': for many of its exemplars the raison d'être of trompe l'oeil was the simple capacity to confound or amaze, using optical tricks that exceeded reason.[25] Martin Battersby argues that one of the aims of trompe l'oeil is the emergence of 'a feeling of disgust in the mind of the beholder', arising from 'a conflict of messages' about the realism of the image.[26] The initial cinematic virtual reality horror shorts, such as *11:57*, appear to be driven by a very similar imperative, as they wrestle with how to best utilise the medium: the pursuit of plausibility, as Slater labels it. Many of these early films appear to be focused primarily on the verisimilitude of the virtual world, where the principal engagement is crafted around making the virtual world as real as possible, with the implicit understanding that if the situation is horrific enough, its production of 'place illusion' will be spectacle enough to thrill the spectator.

Bruce Isaacs argues that the move towards new variations of spectacle are pivotal to cinema's future relevance, stating that,

> [i]f cinema is to maintain its life for the foreseeable future, if it is to invigorate an image of the world growing ever distant from the celluloid century of the medium, the image must continue to manifest as astonishment, as novelty object.[27]

The meeting point of cinema and virtual reality is one such instance of a 'novelty object', one that may perhaps develop into an art form of its own. But is the spectacle of this new form sufficient to sustain it beyond the foreseeable future? Does cinematic virtual reality require something more in order for it to flourish as an art form?

Although published more than fifty years before the emergence of VR, Walter Benjamin's 'The Work of Art in the Age of Mechanical Reproduction' offers insight into the capacities of virtual reality as an art form, particularly when framed by the understanding of Mark B. N. Hansen, who argues that the 'aura' that Benjamin attributed to a singular, unique piece of art now 'belongs indelibly to [the] singular actualization of data in embodied experience'.[28] For Hansen, an auratic presence emerges from how the body acts as sole creator and 'en-framer' of the image, and it is this process itself that validates the aesthetic value of art forms like virtual reality.[29] Hansen's position supports the argument that the intersection of cinema and virtual reality requires that we consider each medium not as a fundamentally different form that requires interweaving, but as a unique and particularly potent form of its own that activates a singular embodied event each time it is experienced.

The two distinct components of the term 'cinematic virtual reality', cinema and virtual reality, have been synthesised by these early projects in a variety of ways. Given the ongoing process of experimentation in the field, it is unclear exactly which elements of the 'cinematic' will be appropriated and which will be left behind, although there are some early indications. Examining the sparse but fascinating world of the early virtual reality filmmakers who are pioneering this new form offers some tentative answers to this question. To begin with, the majority of 360-degree video projects are relatively simple at the level of narrative. They are primarily constituted as a record of an environment or consecutive environments in 360 degrees, in which the spectator as percipient takes the place of the camera. The camera, when moving, is often diegetically motivated (for example, in *Escape the Living Dead*, the camera/protagonist is fleeing a zombie invasion on the back of a moving utility). The spectator is generally expected to remain seated or standing in a relatively static position, although they can turn their head to look in any direction. Predominantly, the spectator is addressed as though they were a participant in the diegetic world. These current films also have a limited duration (generally five to fifteen minutes), although there are some projects currently in production that are experimenting with longer durations, including those that are feature length.

11:57 is an apposite example of the restricted mobility brought about by the technical limitations of some of the early 'live action' 360-degree video projects, as it places the viewer immobilised in a chair in the centre of the experiential world. This is primarily due to the fact that the camera is static, recording from a single locked position in a 360-degree radius. While experiencing *11:57*, viewers are afforded the capacity to look away from where the action takes place, although auditory cues continually position the various interlopers and their actions to within a roughly 130-degree arc from centre facing forward. The spectator is addressed by the diegetic characters as though they were a participant in the diegetic world: the man and woman sitting beside the spectator look at her when they speak, as do the various silent interlopers who enter the room.

Figure 9.3 *Catatonic VR.*

Catatonic, another short VR 360-degree video, also works to this template, placing the shackled spectator in a wheelchair as they are taken through a sinister psychiatric ward (Figure 9.3). The narrative is comparatively simple: the spectator is taunted by the ghoulish residents and the clearly insane doctor-in-charge, and then is killed by a medication overdose delivered by the doctor. In *Catatonic*, the viewer is free to examine the rooms they pass through, but has no control over their passage through the hospital or its duration. What makes *Catatonic* relatively unique, however, is its use of jump-cut editing within its various scenes; breaking with the convention that the spectator's experience is of a unified and coherent segment of time, *Catatonic* splices together disparate moments in the same location to unnerve the viewer and engage the startle effect of cinematic shock.

Escape the Living Dead follows many of the same formal rules as the works described above: in the beginning of this film, the spectator is situated on the back of a moving utility that is driving away from a horde of suburban zombies. Again the spectator is free to look in any direction, but the position they view this scene from is locked to a singular location on the back of the truck; nevertheless, the movement of the truck through the scene turns this static position into a mobile passage through the VR environment. The narrative is more complex, as the story sees the spectator's filmic avatar bitten by a zombie, at which point the scene changes and the viewer becomes a roaming member of the zombie horde. As with the other exemplars above, the diegetic characters address the spectator as though they were a participant in the world of the film (even when they become a zombie). The major formal exception to the other two projects in *Escape the Living Dead* is that it offers a 'god's eye' view of the climactic scene: an explosion that is detonated to wipe out the zombie horde of which the viewer is now a member.

This brief cataloguing of common elements allows us to see that the filmic grammar of these 360-degree videos is, at the moment, rather elementary. Outside of the genre of horror, certain documentary VR filmmakers working in 360-degree video have pushed back at these formal choices, by employing many varied scenes and locations, transitions, unmotivated movement through the scene (such as drone footage) and a choice to not directly address the spectator, but these elements are exceptions and not the rule.[30]

Filmmakers working with 'room-scale' or interactive productions also appear less beholden to these formal choices. A problematic common choice in the formal aspects of these videos is an implied equivalence between the VR spectator and the camera in the diegetic world. In making this choice, these films are constrained to narratives where the viewer is forced to be a participant, but one who is largely passive, apart from the capacity to choose where to look. This creative choice has been challenged in 360-degree video projects, such as Jaunt's *The Game*, where a woman's abduction and subsequent captivity by sinister forces is shown from a variety of objective camera positions; no effort is made to construct a connection between the camera and a subjective position in the diegetic world. However, the issue with the way *The Game* utilises this technique is that the camera placement appears to be simply replicating how this short film would be filmed conventionally, and there is little benefit to the capacity for 360-degree vision.

Another key common factor is that the examples above are still, like much of conventional cinema, materially shot and created in the lens-based real world. This is another vital element to consider in terms of virtual reality's position in the spectrum that is cinema. Rodowick offers a deliberate and thoughtful examination of the dynamic relation between digital images and the history of film forms, in which he argues that 'periods of intense technological change' allow us to ask the touchstone question of film studies, that raised specifically in the title of André Bazin's seminal work: '"What is Cinema?"'[31] While Bazin answered this question by focusing on film's ability to capture the materiality of objects in duration, to 'embalm time', Rodowick instead interrogates the expanded capabilities of the digital image, and asserts that 'an idea of cinema persists or subsists within the new media, rather than the latter supplanting the former as is typically the case in a phase of technological transition'.[32] It is evident that this idea of cinema manifests in virtual reality's adoption of some of the principal cultural and aesthetic models for engaging the vision and imagination of viewers: for example, basic narrative components, such as character psychology and narrative causality, temporal linearity and realism. All of these elements, while taking place in the open realm of the virtual world, work in a similar way to how they work in conventional cinema, as devices designed to corral a viewer's attention.

Lev Manovich goes beyond Rodowick, positing that cinema's cultural resonance is vital to how new media artefacts are shaped and delivered. He argues:

> A hundred years after cinema's birth, cinematic ways of seeing the world, of structuring time, of narrating a story, of linking one experience to the next, have become the basic means by which computer users access and interact with all cultural data. In this respect, the computer fulfils the promise of cinema as a visual Esperanto.[33]

However, some theorists challenge this insistence on the primacy of the cinematic paradigm in new media: amongst them is Mark B. N. Hansen, who sees this instantiation of cinema as the dominant aesthetic medium (or, at least, cinematic conventions as the dominant principles) as over-determining and limiting. He takes issue with the supposed consensus of cinematic immobility as a default condition, arguing that new media instead have the capacity to 'explode the frame' that delimits our mobility through their engagement with the motile body.[34] Hansen is writing here of new media installations that are designed for the dynamic movement of spectators; however, his point is equally relevant to virtual reality. He aptly summarises why virtual reality cinema offers us a chance to rethink the construction of a cinema experience that is reliant on binding the viewer's gaze, when he writes of the possibilities of new media and the digital image that

> digital data is in the most literal sense polymorphous: lacking any inherent form or en-framing, it can be materialized in an almost limitless array of framings; yet so long as it is tied to the image-frame of the cinema, this will remain an entirely untapped potential.[35]

This transcendence of the frame is one of the most exciting possibilities of cinema's interface with virtual reality. It creates a clear and demanding challenge to the dominant existing paradigms of cinematic praxis within the VR environment. It is also one of the most evident challenges for the early designers of cinematic virtual reality, as they try to synthesise over a hundred years of cinematic codes and conventions with the capacities of this new regime. It is vital that, to develop the potential Hansen identifies, any synthesis of traditional cinema and virtual reality require that filmmakers consider expanded narratives or modes that incorporate the fuller dimensions of time and space that VR cinema accentuates. This can, in part, be achieved through utilising three specific capacities available to virtual reality: the melding of spectator and interactor, the rejection of the frame, and the embrace of virtual reality's more radical capacities.

The Melding of Spectator and Interactor

The first wave of virtual reality horror films, although primitive in some aspects, clearly demonstrates for the spectator an ongoing evolution of a new form. The genre of horror appears to be a natural home for this experimentation. This emerges from the genre's capacity to accentuate the respective strengths of both cinema and VR: VR heightens the immersive properties of horror cinema, while the codes and conventions of horror film establish a generic playground for VR. Filmmaker Scott Stewart, speaking at Tribeca Film Festival 2016, concurs:

> The horror genre has always been on the frontlines of formal and stylistic innovation. With movies like *The Blair Witch Project* and *Paranormal Activity*, and even earlier back with *Halloween* and *Friday the 13th*, filmmakers had lower budgets and therefore had to rely on filmmaking techniques to engage an audience; they didn't do it with movie stars, pyrotechnics, and big special effects. Every generation has a movie like those, that has a huge impact on the language of not just horror but also other genres of entertainment. For this generation, that's *Paranormal Activity* and its 'found-footage' POV technique. VR feels like a natural extension or continuation of those kinds of first-person narrative techniques, the whole found-footage style of horror filmmaking. Found-footage has a first-person, you-are-the-camera-operator quality, so it's an easy leap from there to 360° VR.[36]

However, it is also evident that the spectatorial experience of virtual reality diverges sharply from that of mainstream cinema, which in turn raises questions about the limitations of conventional narrative-driven cinema in this mode. The leap Stewart speaks of becomes a hurdle when virtual reality cinema pushes up against the limitations of the spectator being forced to inhabit the position of the camera as a participant or spectator in the diegetic world. How can cinematic virtual reality overcome the limitations that emerge from this forced alignment between camera, viewer and diegetic participant? To answer this question, it is necessary to examine the unique temporal and spatial aspects of the expanded modes of virtual reality cinema outside of

360-degree video, such as those offered by 'room-scale' production, to determine if they offer other alternatives.

This concept can be productively investigated by considering the movement Stewart refers to above, from conventional horror film to found footage, to cinematic virtual reality, using the content of *11:57* as an exemplar. For example, one could envision *11:57* presented as an orthodox cinematic short film, composed of multiple shots and sequences to direct audience attention and to execute more effectively the imperatives of narrative and integration of the spectator as witness to the diegetic world (but crucially, not a participant). This could be done using the time-honoured conventions of montage: the situation of the hypothetical protagonist and her environment would be established through continuity editing, and the (admittedly limited) narrative would be executed through the logic of cause and effect. As a primitive example, the film could begin with a close up on the bound arms of the protagonist, a mid-shot of her struggling in her chair, a close up of her eyes brimming with panic, and a wide shot revealing the room in which she is held captive. Each of these is a conventional trope in horror that heightens engagement for the spectator through the construction of a narrative. The flickering of the lights and impending darkness could herald the threateningly close presence of the monster. However, if the conclusion of *11:57* was transposed to a conventional work, it would be inherently disappointing for an audience; it would seem thin, clichéd, unsatisfying.

Alternatively, the same material could be presented as a 'found footage scenario'; for example, the protagonist could be wearing glasses that have a built-in camera (a narrative device used in the short film *Amateur Night*, featured in the 2012 horror anthology *V/H/S*). Essentially, in this example, the images that are presented would be from the point of view of our protagonist – the viewer's experience as a spectator would be intended to mirror the perceptions of the main character. In this style, the filmmaker can capitalise on a somewhat subjective mode, which in turn can implicate the spectator, as discussed in Chapter 4. Yet, in this mode, engagement with the film comes about through the filmmaker's choices of how the character chooses to view or record the world: the filmmaker crafts the elements that the spectator will be shown and what will not be shown to construct the image in a manner that will contribute to a limited identification with the character and best facilitate the progression of narrative.[37]

Virtual reality, by contrast, offers both immersion and potential interactivity. As established, the spectator in this realm is free to direct their own attention to any point in the virtual space of the experience. In *11:57*, for example, viewers are given the capacity to look away from where the action takes place, although auditory cues continually position the various interlopers and their actions to within a roughly 130-degree arc from centre facing forward, motivating curiosity and attention. The other people in the diegetic world guide the viewer's attention with their focused gaze on the room's entrance.

The short VR horror film *The Black Mass Experience* handles things in a different way. Using the multi-dimensional ambisonic sound design, it draws the viewer away from the central position, with sounds originating at the periphery of their vision. It also uses the movements of various diegetic characters to guide the viewer's perceptual choices: when a character runs by, the viewer's natural curiosity will often prompt them to follow that character's passage. It is less restrictive in terms of motivating the viewer's gaze, but when it does stage moments, the action tends to take place within an invisible proscenium.

Where *The Black Mass Experience* and *11:57* both fail to capitalise on the capacities of VR is in their attempts to manipulate the viewer by replicating the framing of conventional filmmaking, or by using visual or auditory cues to attempt to shift the viewer's gaze to what the filmmaker hopes they will attend to. This has a two-fold problem: first, if the viewer somehow misses these cues, the experience becomes partial and incomplete, losing the power of its affect; and second, once the viewer has learned where to direct their attention, the experience becomes largely the same as each previous iteration. The possibility of cinematic dread, while present in the first experience, evaporates to a large degree on repeated viewings. This is the crux of the second major problem: by creating a linear time frame with a strictly delineated beginning and end point, 360-degree video VR filmmakers are failing to exploit the full dimensions of VR's revolutionary possibilities of time and space. Although they fill their filmic world with horror imagery for the viewer to be confronted with, the temporal and spatial economy of the films halts their capacity to produce deeper intensity and immersion. Traditional 360-degree video neglects the opportunities available to turn a spectator into a spectator-interactor.

Alternative modes of VR, such as 'room-scale' projects or those that are designed to encourage more complex interactivity, demonstrate how VR can take advantage of its more expansive spatial and temporal dimensions.[38] VR horror cinema can operate differently to the horror cinema examples discussed earlier in this book, in the ways it manipulates what Hanich states are two vital principles of conventional cinematic storytelling: 'maximum visibility and temporal economy'.[39] Hanich argues that the construction of cinematic dread necessitates working against these imperatives. Chapters 2 and 3 examined how found footage utilises its form to revel in the constriction of spatial information and delay of outcome, and how, in spite of this lack, it produces an intensity and increased proximity to the world of the image for the viewer. While its temporal economy is quite similar to this, VR horror cinema, by contrast, does not constrict spatial information – in fact, it does the opposite, opening up the potential for threat to the expanses of wherever the viewer chooses to look. In 360-degree video, however, once the viewer has determined the spatial coordinates and duration of the experience, the intensity of the experience is dramatically reduced.

11:57 and *The Black Mass Experience*, while effective on some levels, do not fully capitalise on the ability for VR to produce the most potent form of cinematic dread. Their temporal and spatial economy restricts the achievement of the kind of immersion Hanich argues for. A spatial and temporal elasticity, like that described in the previous chapter in *Alien: Isolation*, could, on the contrary, more fully exploit the full temporal and spatial aspects of the VR realm. This spatial and temporal elasticity is not equivalent to interactivity in the simple terms of allowing a spectator the choice to guide the narrative through various 'forking paths', or the utilisation of peripherals such as haptic controllers or 'wands' that integrate the movement of the viewer into the virtual environment. It is instead the creation of a space and duration that can be inhabited by a spectator who is also an interactor.

In order to integrate these elements with cinematic VR, filmmakers would require elaborate database logistics: the diegetic world would no longer be limited to a single duration, and the spectator's viewing point would no longer be limited to a static position but would have to account for alternative spatial locations and alternative temporal frames. Whether or not this integration could occur and allow the space to remain 'cinematic', in the Bazinian sense, is a complex question. Certainly, the technological advances that are required to perform the above have largely been achieved if provided with the required computational processing power to stitch the elements together. This process of building a three-dimensional environment that can be inhabited, or objects within that environment, is called volumetric photogrammetry and has seen dramatic advances in the last several years. Volumetric displays form a visual representation of an object in three dimensions. In virtual reality, volumetric photogrammetry can allow for three-dimensional objects and actors to be integrated into room-scale productions, so that the viewer's perception of the object or actor changes, based on their movement through the space. This is a further step towards overcoming the 'plausibility illusion' Slater refers to; however, it does present its own challenges. Performances recorded through volumetric photogrammetry, for example, can easily be a paradoxical presence, for even though the presence of the actor is more realistic in terms of its dimensionality in space, it has no dynamic qualities in terms of its interaction with the viewer; the volumetric capture is a fixed recording and cannot respond to or interact with the viewer in its current form.

Brillhart argues that the rapid development of artificial intelligence is integral to the future of virtual reality narratives, particularly to the possibility of dynamic interaction with volumetrics.[40] However, even without these technological advances, Brillhart contends that at its foundations virtual reality needs to operate differently to conventional cinema in terms of its storytelling principles. She writes that

> storytelling generally involves someone – the teller – filtering an experience and then trying to communicate that experience to someone else. That transfer will then evoke a translation in the mind of the person receiving the message. Most mediums do this. This is, for filmmaking, Vertov's camera – the disembodied mechanical eye. To show you the world the way he sees the world. To deliver the world to you anew [. . .] What I have to be as a VR creator is a story enabler, not the story dictator. Allow stories to unfold in a space. Start to rely more on feeling and atmosphere than on conventional narrative. Let it be a bit more like music. Like architecture. Like dance.[41]

A consideration of these principles further develops the critique of the 360-degree video VR horror works analysed above. There is in these projects an unnecessary emphasis placed on 'story dictating', as opposed to allowing the viewer to inhabit the space and time of these works in a way that adds experiential depth to the encounter. It is only through a concerted 'rejection' of the predetermined frame that 'story dictating' may be transformed into 'story enabling'.

THE RADICAL POTENTIAL OF VIRTUAL REALITY

The recognition of VR's capacities, and its potential for the creation of new experiences of the body, has radical implications outside of the genre of horror. Artist Diana Gromala eloquently argues for what she sees as the virtues of virtual reality. She challenges claims of post-human transcendence or disembodiment, when she writes:

> Recent media frenzies about virtual reality portray these technologies as promising a brave new world [. . .] What if, instead, we explore this notion turned in on itself—our travels not to an abstract virtual 'outer' space, but to the inner reaches of our body?[42]

Interactive media systems like VR can bring about an evolution by presenting new perceptual experiences, new temporal flows and new sensory syntheses. Hansen argues that they achieve this by

> catalysing those bodily 'senses' – proprioception, interoception, affectivity – that allow us to orient ourselves in the absence of fixed points or external orienting schema, or in other words, through the internal, intensive space of our affective bodies [. . .] That is to say, by placing us into 'direct coupling' with information, this technical extension not only dissolves the mediating (framing) function of the image, but it renders perception itself secondary in relation to the primary affective experience of self-enjoyment.[43]

This speaks potently to the immersive capacities that virtual reality may offer to cinema more widely, and horror specifically. While virtual reality is often presented as a type of *optical* illusion, there is always an awareness in the spectator that what they are experiencing is an illusion. However, Hansen's expanded mode of virtual reality, where our perception may potentially be undifferentiated from illusion, given the bodily self-affection is at the root of our perception, raises the question of the limits of this awareness. This could have resonant consequences for horror's affective power in this mode. The cognitive distancing which challenges the authenticity of the monster may be insufficient to overcome the intensity of this type of horror: which is to say, in this type of horror we are not perceiving an image of the 'monster', we are literally experiencing the monster's presence. The implication of this is that spectators are less likely to subject themselves to this experience, given that it no longer has the voyeuristic distanciation of watching on a screen.

There are even more controversial implications to experiments with this form. For instance, virtual reality introduces the potential for contradictory visual-sensory-motor solicitations, where our embodied habits are pitted against a virtual world that does not necessarily correspond to reality. What happens when the physical laws of normal perception, or normal geometric space, are broken or defied in horrific ways? What if the 'monster' is no longer derived from the tropes of horror narrative, but instead in the monstrous disruptions to the body–brain connection that brings about the image? Each of these questions has yet to be explored by VR filmmakers, but the creative capacities of cinematic virtual reality allow for them to be raised. These types of experience could hold the same thrill that attracts horror aficionados to the more emotionally and sensory-heightened aspects of the genre in cinema.

One could argue that the vicarious identification in conventional horror would be irrelevant to this type of experimental virtual reality cinema, in that the spectator no longer requires a proxy to draw them in to the story-world of the film; as we have seen, in virtual reality, the viewer may be a participant and not a witness. A further way of developing this concept is to look at how the horror experience of virtual reality could capitalise on this inability for a viewer to demarcate themselves from the image. Experimenting with manipulating the image to respond to our heart rate or brain-waves, as some new media art installations have already done, could further tighten this inextricable bond between viewer and image.[44] This reconfiguration of the stable, logically ordered world of sensation would certainly seem to tap into the Lovecraftian definition of horror as creating an

> atmosphere of breathlessness and unexplainable dread of outer, unknown forces [. . .] of that most terrible conception of the human brain – a malign and particular suspension or defeat of those fixed laws of Nature which are our only safeguard against the assaults of chaos and the demons of unplumbed space.[45]

Experimenting with these capacities would appear to shift emphasis even further away from cinema's existing techniques of spectatorial integration, via narrative and identification with character. There are larger ethical issues raised by these possibilities, that, while important, are outside of the scope of this chapter, the focus of which is on the aesthetic potential and problems of the early experiments in the art form; however, there is productive space to further examine the ethical boundaries of the form, particularly in relation to horror.

One path in continuing this process of examining the problematic aspects of the current works is to assess the contention that spectatorial identification is less relevant to virtual reality cinema than conventional cinema. The alternative conception, which contends that spectatorial identification is no less relevant, may be evidenced in the way that there is arguably something missing in the current wave of VR horror films: the production of empathic engagement.

What Cinema Can Return to VR

While it is certainly true that many of the existing cinematic virtual reality projects address the viewer as a diegetic participant and not a witness, there is an element to the cinematic experience that is lost under this configuration, and it is one that is particularly important to horror film. Christian Metz contends that much of cinematic pleasure is derived from the distance between the spectator and the image. This distance is defined in two senses: first, the physical distance from the events on the screen, and second, the temporal distance, in that the events occurred at an earlier point in time. This double distancing, for Metz, produces pleasure, in that the viewer has complete mastery over the image and does not fear any form of reprisal.[46]

This vicarious pleasure in being an observer at a distance is rarely offered in contemporary virtual reality cinema projects, perhaps because many of the filmmakers are mistaking perspectival situatedness for empathic engagement: empathic engagement may require more than just an acknowledgement that the viewer is a participant in the diegetic world. For theorist Pia Tikka, positing VR technology as a machine that is especially productive of empathy requires that we consider its perceptual equivalence and immersive capacities as dependent on 'experiencing embodiment as emotional situatedness, and not about the perfect image projection'.[47] She elaborates that, 'if the context of the perceived world – interpersonal relationships, causal events, nature's forces, or facial movements – is meaningful, it will enable immersion'.[48] This redefines immersion from the theoretical interpretation put forward by Hansen, and reminds us that, for spectators, it is these contextual elements that deepen an emotional engagement. The affective properties of the face, the interpersonal relationships amongst diegetic characters, even the cause and effect structure of narrative, all enrich the cinematic world; cinematic virtual reality projects that neglect to consider these elements will be the poorer for it. For while many VR cinema shorts are affectively rich in the embodiment they produce, they often neglect elements like the ones listed above, that conventional cinema has refined in order to produce emotional engagement.

Another issue to consider is the potential reduction of the cinematic to the largely subjective response of a viewer as 'locus of experience', which has ramifications for cinema's social and cultural significance. Isaacs, for instance, argues that 'cinema cannot merely be about personal, individual experience', questioning the loss of cinema's cultural and social significance if experienced in isolation.[49] Isaacs is arguing for the image as a shared 'pathway', and making a link between how the images of the world are rendered in the image of cinema and how, through cinema's position as a popular and pervasive art form, these images become 'cultural and aesthetic object(s) of enormous significance'.[50] If the experience of virtual reality is largely unique, in the sense that each iteration is dependent on the smallest fractional movement of the spectator's body or vision, does this freedom unmoor cinematic virtual reality from its ability to become a shared 'cultural and aesthetic object'?

Films seemingly provide a static and repeatable artefact which reflects a culture and which a culture can reflect on, whereas virtual reality may only reach its full potential through its creation of unique and responsive 'events' where the viewer is co-creator. This has particular relevance to horror as a cinematic genre, which, as Hanich astutely points out, is often embraced as a shared theatrical experience due to the 'emphatic feeling of belongingness' that is brought about by what he labels a 'collectivity'.[51]

One way in which virtual reality cinema may address this is through its potential to uniquely energise and engage each viewer in a shared *experience*; in other words, how the bodily experience of spectators may become synchronous through their shared presence within the virtual world. *Life of Us*, which premiered at Sundance Film Festival 2017, is an animated VR project that allows four participants to experience it concurrently; although primitive in how it executes this concept, it demonstrates the potential of this new mode.[52] The aspirational notion of how cinematic virtual reality may embrace these possibilities would perhaps see it fulfil the mythic potential of cinema to instantiate new perceptual and psychological experiences.

The Future of Cinematic VR

Cinematic virtual reality, while only in its infancy, requires far more creative experimentation if it is to integrate cinema with the strengths of its particular form.[53] While this form will no doubt evolve with the expansive current and future development of content, it must also be noted that the technology is constantly evolving. Existing research argues persuasively that the more 'invisible' the interface with the body, the greater its affective capabilities.[54] While the binocular vision provided by headsets like the Oculus Rift may surpass traditional modes of cinematic perception, it still requires the wearing of a headset, one that is currently tethered to a computer (in the case of high-end virtual reality experiences). It also still needs further development in its optical resolution, range of optical periphery, and potential integration with other sensory stimuli. In addition, there is much work remaining for both filmmakers and developers to deepen their understanding of the physiological limitations and advantages of virtual reality; while the makers of the various headsets have amassed a large repository of information on the neurological and physiological responses to virtual reality, there is still only a small number of projects that have begun to comprehensively experiment with the wider range of aesthetic techniques discussed in this chapter, such as volumetric integration, hyper-narrative and expanded forms of interactivity. It is vital for filmmakers to consider the manner in which the bodily experience of virtual reality requires that they rethink some aspects of cinema's formal conventions.

Peter Weibel offers a potential riposte to the charge that virtual reality may contribute to the loss of cinema as cultural object. He sees virtual reality as expanding and revolutionising the existing cinematographic code, and points to the experimental placement of multiple simultaneous participants in new media installations, and in video games, as the future direction: this is the creation of virtual spaces, like *Life of Us*, that can be inhabited by more than one person at a time. The evolution of this, he sees, is an image technology shaped by 'massive parallel virtual worlds' (also known as multi-user virtual environments, or MUVEs) which are tele-correlated or 'entangled'.[55] This would facilitate a shared virtual reality experience between participants, reinstating its social and cultural significance. As mentioned previously, this 'entanglement' is only currently hindered by technical limitations and Weibel's hypothetical mode is no doubt on the horizon. What is up for debate is how much these virtual environments would draw from established cinematic paradigms, such as linear narrative progression or the use of diegetic characters to promote emotional engagement.

Another vital question raised by the emergence of this new form is the lack of political or ethical engagement with virtual reality as a technology. Erkki Huhtamo labels the field as dominated by a 'demo-aesthetic', wherein most projects 'have concentrated on exploring the expressive potential of the medium, instead of using it for ideologically charged critical purposes'.[56] For three-dimensional image-making to progress, technologically and culturally, Huhtamo requires that it become 'integral, constructive, and "deep"'.[57] Certainly, this is a valid criticism for much of the early cinematic virtual reality, and given the radical potential spelled out by Hansen, there is much room for development and expansion of the political and ethical capabilities of this new mode.

Ross Gibson sheds an idealistic light on his hopes for the transformative potential of virtual reality, and sees the cinematic in this new art form, in that cinema already segments and attenuates time, and that 'the art of time' will be vital to the development of these new experiences.[58] He posits this art as a 'phenomenological routine [that] will offer each participant a compelling, fully conscious experience of perceptive intensification followed by alteration'.[59] The alteration he refers to is that of the participant's understanding of experiential time.

Each of these futurists addresses the preliminary aspects of the cinematic virtual reality form, and how it demands evolution in various ways in order to reach maturity. To these various philosophical approaches, this chapter suggests the addition of key obstacles that need to be addressed by creatives: the melding of spectator and interactor, the 'rejection' of the frame, and the embrace of virtual reality's more radical capacities.

The production of a spectator-interactor balances the existing immersive elements of cinema spectatorship with the facility for the spectator to engage with the space in a manner that fully utilises virtual reality's unique spatial and temporal capacities. While this requires the integration of database logic and a reconsideration of linear narrative, two changes that may be outside the scope of what we currently consider 'cinema', introducing these elements would only strengthen what is cinematic about the experience: the further heightening of a synthesised bodily and emotional engagement.

A nascent understanding of virtual reality would suggest the 'rejection' of the frame as a necessity, given the perceptual freedom afforded to the spectator. However, it is evident, based on the current crop of cinematic virtual reality horror films, that the convention of 'framing' content in order to direct spectatorial engagement is a technique that filmmakers find hard to let go. It is also evident that those projects that do engage with the principle of allowing the viewer to inhabit an experience and 'direct' their own engagement are those that are the most stimulating and enjoyable, because they do not draw attention to the artifice of the form and instead capitulate to a sense of the naturalistic real world process of being-in-an-environment. This involves, in part, a surrender to virtual reality's fundamental differences to cinema, and perhaps an acquiescence to what Massumi presents as the defining asset of interactive media, when he writes that its strength is

> to take the situation as its 'object'. Not a function, not a use, not a need, not a behavior, exploratory or otherwise, not an action-reaction. But a situation, with its own little ocean of complexity. It can take a situation and 'open' the interactions it affords. The question for interactive art is, [h]ow do you cleave an interaction asunder? Setting up an interaction is easy. We have any number of templates for that. But how do you set it up so you sunder it, dynamically smudge it, so that the relation potential it tends-toward appears? So that the situation's objectivity creatively self-abstracts, making a self-tending life-movement, a life-subject and not just a setup. How, in short, do you make a semblance of a situation? [. . .] [W]here you are polling styles of being and becoming, not just eliciting behaviors.[60]

This creation of 'semblance' is the employment of interaction away from its instrumental function. For Massumi, the move towards 'relation' instead of 'interactivity' allows the semblance to express the dynamic qualitative differences of lived reality. He sees the emerging lived relation to an artwork as capable of producing an awareness of how 'every moment is intensely suffused with virtuality'.[61] To further articulate the differences, Massumi argues that '[w]hen what is concentrated on are instrumentalized action-reaction circuits, what gets foregrounded is the element of nextness in the flow of action. The voluminousness of the experience, its all-aroundedness [. . .] shrinks from feeling.'[62] Thus, cinematic virtual reality that allows for the emergence of these 'situations', as opposed to the attempted creation of environment-action/spectator-reaction, may utilise its interactive potential to the fullest.

Finally, it is perhaps in the more radical capacities of virtual reality that cinematic virtual reality, and horror in particular, will find the defining aspects of its new form. Virtual reality could examine that which terrifies us from a totally new perspective, where we are no longer tethered to allegorical monsters, but instead are subject to the possibilities for the brain–body image to itself become monstrous in the destabilisation of our everyday sensory-motor linkages. Each of these aspects requires further experimentation, but each also holds great significance for the advancement of virtual reality cinema, as not merely a hybrid combination of the two forms, but an art form in its own right.

Notes

1. Shaw and Weibel, *Future Cinema*, p. 19.
2. Ibid. p. 19.
3. Slater, 'Place Illusion and Plausibility', p. 2.
4. Himmelsbach, 'The Interactive Potential of Distributed Networks', p. 531.
5. Gunning, 'An Aesthetic of Astonishment'.
6. Ross, 'Virtual Reality's New Synesthetic Possibilities', pp. 4–6.
7. Rutherford, 'Cinema and Embodied Affect'.
8. Rutherford, 'Precarious Boundaries', pp. 63–84.
9. Vertov, *Kino-Eye*, cited in Brillhart, 'These Uncomfortably Exciting Times'.
10. Brillhart, 'These Uncomfortably Exciting Times'.
11. Hanich, *Cinematic Emotion in Horror Films and Thrillers*, pp. 222–3.
12. Slater and Wilbur, 'A Framework for Immersive Virtual Environments'.
13. Sanchez-Vives and Slater, 'From Presence to Consciousness through Virtual Reality', p. 333.
14. Slater, 'Place Illusion and Plausibility', p. 1.
15. Ibid. pp. 5–9.
16. Ibid. p. 10.
17. Ibid. p. 10.
18. Bye, 'An Elemental Theory of Presence + The Future of AI & Interactive Storytelling'.
19. Ibid.
20. Dépaysement is a French term to describe 'the feeling that comes from not being in one's home country', used here to refer to a form of disorientation.
21. Kittler, *Gramophone, Film, Typewriter*, pp. 1–2.
22. Gunning, 'An Aesthetic of Astonishment', p. 121.
23. Ibid. p. 129.
24. In the VR experiences *Everest VR*, *The Drop* and *Yellowstone VR*.
25. Gunning, 'An Aesthetic of Astonishment', p. 117.
26. Battersby, *Trompe l'Oeil*, p. 19, cited in Gunning, 'An Aesthetic of Astonishment', p. 117.
27. Isaacs, *The Orientation of Future Cinema*, p. 5.

28. Hansen, *New Philosophy for New Media*, p. 3.
29. Ibid. p. 3.
30. For example, the work of VR filmmaker Chris Milk. Milk uses sequences in which no one addresses the presence of the spectator, includes conventional transitions such as fade-outs, and works with a moving camera that is not diegetically motivated (see *Clouds Over Sidra, Evolution of Verse* and *Walking New York*).
31. Rodowick, *The Virtual Life of Film*, p. 9.
32. Bazin, *What Is Cinema?*, p. 14; Rodowick, *The Virtual Life of Film*, p. viii.
33. Manovich, *The Language of New Media*, pp. 78–9.
34. Hansen, *New Philosophy for New Media*, p. 35.
35. Ibid. p. 35.
36. Barrone, 'Virtual Reality's Horror Potential Is So Great That It's Scary – Pun Intended'.
37. For example, we do not immediately see the outcome of the monster's attack at the conclusion of *Amateur Night*; we are shown it through Clint's eventual surreptitious peeking around the corner of the bed he is hiding behind, and then only in glimpses.
38. *VR Noir*, for example, contains a sequence where the spectator needs to actively search for the target of the investigation by scanning various apartment windows.
39. Hanich, *Cinematic Emotion in Horror Films and Thrillers*, p. 163.
40. Brillhart, 'These Uncomfortably Exciting Times'.
41. Ibid.
42. Gromala, 'Dancing with the Virtual Dervish', p. 281.
43. Hansen, *New Philosophy for New Media*, p. 205.
44. Pavel Smetana's *Rooms of Desire* (1996) and Alan Dunning and Paul Woodrow's *Einstein's Brain* (2006), for example, both utilise bio-feedback in the production of the image.
45. Lovecraft, *Supernatural Horror in Literature*, p. 15.
46. Metz, *The Imaginary Signifier*, pp. 42–66.
47. Tikka, 'Cinema as Externalization of Consciousness', p. 151.
48. Ibid. p. 151.
49. Isaacs, *The Orientation of Future Cinema*, p. 11. This point has a heritage that traces back to Walter Benjamin's film theory, and has been examined in detail in Miriam Hansen's work on Benjamin.
50. Ibid. pp. 9–11.
51. Hanich, *Cinematic Emotion in Horror Films and Thrillers*, p. 249.
52. For a video demonstration of the kind of shared world experience created, go to <bit.ly/lifeofus> (last accessed 9 September 2019).
53. Ross asks if a formal system akin to the Classical Hollywood Cinema will emerge for cinematic virtual reality, or if it will simply contain 'a more multifarious combination of media styles and innovation', like those seen in contemporary video games; see Ross, 'Virtual Reality's New Synesthetic Possibilities', p. 14.
54. Hansen, *New Philosophy for New Media*, p. 200.
55. Weibel, 'The Intelligent Image', p. 601.

56. Huhtamo, 'Media Art in the Third Dimension', pp. 471–2.
57. Ibid. p. 473.
58. Gibson provocatively also proposes: 'Artists won't be fabricating objects so much as *experiences* – they will offer us intensely "moving" immersion in (or perhaps *beyond*) the objective world. The immersion will be so *moving* that the "objective world" will cease to be sensible in the ways we thought normal. Which means we will develop new options for agency or subjectivity in a world no longer composed of stable settings and props, a world no longer sensibly "objective"' (Gibson, 'The Time Will Come When . . .', p. 570; original emphasis).
59. Ibid. p. 570.
60. Massumi, *Semblance and Event*, p. 52.
61. Ibid. p. 46.
62. Ibid. p. 46.

Conclusion

Tonight, I'm watching a film on my computer screen. It's a found footage horror film with a great concept: the film is presented as a faux-documentary about the attempt to discover the identity of the mysterious creators of a sinister batch of viral non-fiction horror videos, similar to those examined in Chapter 6.

A man on my computer screen sits in front of a computer, his colleague standing behind him. 'Go ahead, press play,' the colleague says.

A title card appears on my screen, exactly as it does on the screen inside the film. It tells me: This is a snuff video. You actually see this girl commit suicide on camera. It is one of the most gruesome acts of violence ever captured on video.

On screen, the film cuts to a graveyard in the daytime. Blue-tinged and wintry. The camera pans across the headstones, coming to rest on a young woman off in the distance. The camera reframes, then zooms in as she walks towards the camera, oblivious to the fact she is being filmed. She wears what looks like a wedding dress and appears forlorn and distressed. She stops suddenly, clutching her wrists (Figure 10.1).

Another title card appears: You can see her veins ripped out of her wrists.

The title card fades away. The shot returns to the graveyard, and the woman.

Sitting at my computer, I realise I am mirroring the man in the narrative: we are both watching this video simultaneously. Although I can no longer see him, I am an echo of him. There is something potent in this interplay. We both know nothing about this woman. We know nothing of this cemetery. We know nothing of why she may be committing suicide, if that is even what she is doing. We know *nothing, and yet . . .*

My body is like a twisted rope, ever tightening. I feel as though I am being inexorably drawn into the image. The woman on screen continues to clutch her hands together, and lowers her head. The moment swells, distends, as I wait for what comes next.

This description of personal experience, like each of those presented in the preceding chapters, provides a first-hand account of one of the ways in which the modern experience of watching cinema has evolved and transformed. Whereas the traditional theatrical experience still has great value, advances in technology, and mutations in how horror stories are told cinematically, have

Conclusion 201

Figure 10.1 The woman in the graveyard in *#Screamers*.

led to reconfigurations of the viewer's bodily experience. Each of these new forms facilitates its own juncture with the spectatorial body. Importantly, in spite of claims from some cultural critics that increasing technological development devalues the body, these cinematic experiences revalorise this integration between spectator and film at a corporeal level. They defy any disembodying tendencies, in the way they produce an experience that many horror viewers seek from the genre – a proximity to the image that goes beyond our engagement with its narrative.

Through an analysis of the evolving forms of horror media presented in each chapter, this book has asked how cinema's affective capacities are transformed by these modifications in form. The answers are distinct to the modality examined; however, what each has in common is an intensification of bodily presence. Found footage heightens the viewer's engagement, not through richly drawn narrative or compelling characterisation, but by its distinct application of capacities of the out-of-frame, and its expanded temporal economy. Because found footage consciously experiments with subjective perspectives, it opens up a space for a consideration of flux in the distinction between subjective and objective images, such as that proposed by the perception-image. That these images are indistinct in perspective produces a complex interaction between viewer and film, and accentuates a 'being-with' the image, in a Deleuzian sense. These films also may markedly replicate the instinctual human drives of foraging, investigation, curiosity and expectancy of the SEEKING system that Panksepp proposes, in the way that their diegetic cameras often scan or search their environment.

The post-cinematic videos examined in Chapters 6 and 7 accentuate their synaesthetic and haptic qualities through the employment of an 'aesthetics of distortion', both visually and aurally. These aberrations of form heighten the sensory aspects of the sound and image, promoting the potential for cross-modal sensory experience. As with the lo-fi video games examined in Chapter 8, a concerted amplification of the non-representational content emerges often as a creative response to limitations in the practicalities of their production, be those limitations budgetary, or technical, or simply relating to the scope of the project. Like found footage horror cinema, these games and videos build on the inherent myth-building compulsion of some viewers, where they often make an imaginative leap from incredulity to ambiguity. This myth-building is insufficient, however, to fully explain how a viewer interfaces with this media; there has to be something more than just the viewer's imagination breathing life into a previously inert object. This 'something more' is at the heart of this book. It is the affective charge that image and sound can carry, in excess of the representational content, that allows these new media texts to become, in the words of Martin, 'living, breathing, pulsating organism[s]'.[1]

Importantly, the interface between the film as an 'organism' and the human body is just as dynamic as our interaction with any other organism; both are best thought of as Deleuze does:

> a body is not defined by either simple materiality, by its occupying space ('extension'), or by organic structure. It is defined by the relations of its parts (relations of relative motion and rest, speed and slowness), and by its actions and reactions with respect both to its environment or milieu and to its internal milieu.[2]

The meeting point of virtual reality and horror cinema has tremendous implications for how we consider the body of the spectator. Virtual reality promotes an embodied response in its construction of presence. Importantly, it highlights the fallacy of visual engagement as the primary sensory interface in the human interaction with media. Although a nascent art form, virtual reality demands that filmmakers consider an embodied response at the foundations of their interface with this 'frameless' media. In some vital sense the body is now the frame in virtual reality.

While psychoanalytic, representational and hermeneutic models are important to an analysis of how horror works, they often place the spectatorial body as second to cognitive response, contending that our physiological response emerges from our appraisal of the sound and image. By focusing on how the body is the primary interface between viewer and image, and by demonstrating how the somatic response to horror arises from horror's recurrent destabilisation of the image's semantic content, this book has shown the value of approaches to horror scholarship that reframe these questions through the presence of an embodied spectator. So too has it demonstrated some of the limitations of representational and hermeneutic models. By drawing on the work of theorists of embodied spectatorship and, more broadly, theorists of embodied cognition, I highlight how inseparable cognitive appraisal is from corporeal response, and offer a counter to a hierarchical approach that places cognition over corporeality.

The perpetually changing forms of horror examined, and the technological modalities through which they are delivered, alter the dynamics of spectatorship and, in doing so, often intensify embodied experience. On the level of the various senses, these new forms create new relations of sensory response, highlighting the cross-modal potential of cinema more broadly. The viewer does not simply watch or listen to these films, but as Ndalianis writes, they feel their 'sensorial enactments' across their entire bodies.[3] This is a consideration of horror cinema as a point of contact, but one that does not necessarily require the presence of on-screen bodies in order to generate this affective exchange.

A common factor of the works examined in this book is the reduced presence of on-screen bodies. Found footage, through the exigencies of its generic boundaries, commonly does not use the on-screen body in the same way that horror films outside of the subgenre do, as a location for implied threat or, in some cases, actual mutilation or torture. While these applications of the on-screen body in horror do intensify the affective response of the viewer, they are not the only way to consider horror's affect. Extending the consideration of horror's affect to the way the non-representational aspects of the image work, and how affect does not, in Massumi's terms, correspond to the semantic content, allows us a way to think through the intensities generated by forms that place less importance on elements such as narrative and spectatorial identification (for example, the YouTube videos discussed in Chapter 6). By employing Massumi's concept of affect, as the 'passing of a threshold, seen from the point of view of [the body's] change in capacity', we can also see how horror media often tries to direct this change in capacity, to either enhance it or diminish it.[4] The conclusions of this book do not establish a concrete articulation of what cinematic affect is; they are instead a thinking through of horror media's affective possibilities from the understanding of affect that Massumi advances. It may, in fact, be easier to articulate what affect is not, in the scope of this book: affect is not coterminous with emotion; it does not only emerge from the non-representational aspects, although they do have the possibility of amplifying it; similarly, it is not pure sensation, although the intensification of cinema's sensory aspects plays a major role in the generation of affect; crucially, its emergence does not require the presence of on-screen bodies. It may be beyond the scope of this book to fully codify cinematic affect, given that the way that we truly *understand* it is in the experience of viewing itself.

This understanding has obvious resonances with the conception of affect proposed through Deleuze's movement-image, where affection resides in-between perception and action. For Deleuze, affect emerges from the change or alteration that occurs when 'bodies' come into contact with each other. Powell establishes the value of Deleuzian concepts in understanding a genre that so often works to complicate its semantic content. Her application of Deleuze gives us ways of understanding how horror films employ the material force of their images, their shades of colour, intensities of light and timbres of sound, to affectively imbricate the viewer. I have attempted to expand these understandings outside of her work on conventional horror cinema, into these new modalities.

This book is intended as an amalgamation and synthesis of existing scholarship. It pays tribute to Deleuze's concept of 'machinic assemblage', by taking heterogeneous fields of thought and placing them into interaction and imbrication with one another, without reducing one domain of thought to another. This is why it links Deleuzian thought with reconceptions of the perception-image, with neuroscientific concepts such as Embodied Simulation Theory and Panksepp's SEEKING system, with existing theories of embodied spectatorship and phenomenological approaches to understanding the film–viewer dynamic. My approach is made with a consideration of the 'lived body' as the grounds of experience: in order to understand the world (and cinema), the body must be conceived not as a 'screen' between us and the world, but as that which forms our way of 'being-in-the-world'. The embodied self is the ground of perception.

I have synthesised these various fields of existing scholarship with an aim to understand horror cinema through the type of experience it produces for a viewer. This analysis shifts the emphasis from horror's representational content to how the affective properties of horror media can exceed the symbolic powers of language or the image. In the field of horror scholarship, this is crucial, as the more common approach to these texts is to either unpack their representational aspects, or to employ psychoanalytic theory to decode their production and reception. While both of these methods are effective in part, the approach proposed by this book expands our understanding of how horror works. It provides a framework which could be applied to further evolutions in the form, be they technological or generic; it demonstrates how, in order to productively analyse these future developments, cinematic artefacts should be examined for their modifications to the viewer's phenomenological experience of the image.

This book has several limitations. It has not focused on the political implications of the understandings it presents, although it does have potential value as a method of further extending Deleuze's critique of representational thinking, and in the ways it has considered the mutability of cinematic subjectivity. It has also largely bypassed the ethical quandaries raised by this bodily intensification, particularly in relation to developing technologies such as virtual reality, where the 'reality' of the horror has the potential to be misappropriated, or employed without the full understanding of it consequences.[5] There is value to further scholarship in the emerging field of cinematic virtual reality, particularly in relation to these ethical questions. There is also significant value in the further study of the development of a new cinematic grammar in this incipient mode. It would be productive to experiment further with the concept of 'story-enabling' in virtual reality cinema in a diverse set of genres, to establish whether the domain of horror can perhaps more fully integrate these qualities.

At the heart of this project has been an investigation of what horror cinema is capable of as it moves beyond the theatrical screen. Moments of viewing like the one described in the opening of this Conclusion will always hold appeal for the horror cinephile, in the intensification of experience they generate, in the way they promote entwinement with that which is often at the borders of our understanding. This book has been written for those who share this compulsion to 'go ahead, press play' and wait, on the edge of this border, for the image to grasp us, startle us, unnerve us.

Notes

1. Martin, 'Delirious Enchantment'.
2. Baugh, 'Body', p. 35.
3. Ndalianis, *The Horror Sensorium*, p. 3.
4. Massumi, *Politics of Affect*, pp. 3–4.
5. *Playtest*, an episode of the TV series *Black Mirror*, narratively wrestles with some of these implications in a profound and compelling way.

Bibliography

BOOKS, ARTICLES AND WEBSITES

Anderson, Joseph D. *The Reality of Illusion: An Ecological Approach to Cognitive Film Theory*. Carbondale: Southern Illinois University Press, 1998.

Badt, Karin Luisa. 'A Dialogue with Neuroscientist Jaak Panksepp on the SEEKING System: Breaking the Divide between Emotion and Cognition in Film Studies'. *Projections* 9, no. 1 (2015): 66–79.

Barker, Jennifer M. *The Tactile Eye: Touch and the Cinematic Experience*. Berkeley: University of California Press, 2009.

Barrone, Matt. 'Virtual Reality's Horror Potential Is So Great That It's Scary – Pun Intended'. *TribecaFilm*, 1 March 2016. <https://tribecafilm.com/stories/horror-virtual-reality-holidays-christmas-scott-stewart-killer-deal-anthony-c-ferrante> (last accessed 9 September 2019).

Battersby, Martin. *Trompe l'Oeil*. New York: St. Martin's Press, 1974.

Baugh, Bruce. 'Body'. In *The Deleuze Dictionary*, edited by Adrian Parr. Edinburgh: Edinburgh University Press, 2005.

Bazin, André. *What Is Cinema?: Volume 1*. Berkeley: University of California Press, 2005.

Bellour, Raymond. 'The Cinema Spectator: A Special Memory'. In *Audiences: Defining and Researching Screen Entertainment Reception*, edited by Ian Christie. Amsterdam: Amsterdam University Press, 2012.

Benson-Allott, Caetlin. *Killer Tapes and Shattered Screens: Video Spectatorship from VHS to File Sharing*. Berkeley: University of California Press, 2013.

Bergson, Henri. *Matter and Memory*. London: George Allen, 1912.

Bergson, Henri. *Time and Free Will: An Essay on the Immediate Data of Consciousness*. London: George Allen and Unwin, 1910.

Berliner, Todd. 'Hollywood Storytelling and Aesthetic Pleasure'. In *Psychocinematics: Exploring Cognition at the Movies*, edited by Arthur P. Shimamura. Oxford: Oxford University Press, 2014.

Black, Joel. *The Reality Effect: Film Culture and the Graphic Imperative*. New York: Routledge, 2002.

Blake, Linnie, and Xavier Aldana Reyes, eds. *Digital Horror: Haunted Technologies, Network Panic and the Found Footage Phenomenon*. London: I. B. Tauris, 2016.

Blumstein, Daniel T., Richard Davitian and Peter D. Kaye. 'Do Film Soundtracks Contain Nonlinear Analogues to Influence Emotion?' *Biology Letters* 6, no. 6 (2010): 751–4.

Bogue, Ronald. *Deleuze on Cinema*. New York: Taylor & Francis, 2003.

Bordwell, David. 'Convention, Construction, and Cinematic Vision'. In *Post-Theory: Reconstructing Film Studies*, edited by David Bordwell and Noël Carroll. Madison: University of Wisconsin Press, 1996.

Bordwell, David. *Narration in the Fiction Film*. New York: Taylor & Francis, 2013.
Bordwell, David, and Noël Carroll, eds. *Post-Theory: Reconstructing Film Studies*. Madison: University of Wisconsin Press, 1996.
Bordwell, David, and Kristin Thompson. *Film Art: An Introduction*. New York: McGraw Hill, 2008.
Bordwell, David, and Kristin Thompson. *Minding Movies: Observations on the Art, Craft, and Business of Filmmaking*. Chicago: University of Chicago Press, 2011.
Branigan, Edward. *Narrative Comprehension and Film*. New York: Taylor & Francis, 1992.
Branigan, Edward. *Point of View in the Cinema: A Theory of Narration and Subjectivity in Classical Film*. New York: Mouton, 1984.
Briefel, Aviva, and Sam J. Miller, eds. *Horror after 9/11: World of Fear, Cinema of Terror*. Austin: University of Texas Press, 2012.
Brillhart, Jessica. 'These Uncomfortably Exciting Times'. *Filmmaker Magazine*, 18 January 2017. <http://filmmakermagazine.com/101220-these-uncomfortably-exciting-times/> (last accessed 9 September 2019).
Brinkema, Eugenie. *The Forms of the Affects*. Durham, NC: Duke University Press, 2014.
Brown, William. *Supercinema: Film-Philosophy for the Digital Age*. New York: Berghahn Books, 2013.
Bruno, Giuliana. *Atlas of Emotion: Journeys in Art, Architecture, and Film*. New York: Verso, 2002.
Bye, Kent. 'An Elemental Theory of Presence + The Future of AI & Interactive Storytelling'. *Voices of VR*, 8 February 2017. <http://voicesofvr.com/502-an-elemental-theory-of-presence-future-of-ai-interactive-storytelling/> (last accessed 9 September 2019).
Calder-Williams, Evan. 'Sunset with Chainsaw'. *Film Quarterly* 64, no. 4 (2011): 28–33.
Campen, Crétien van. *The Hidden Sense: Synesthesia in Art and Science*. Cambridge, MA: MIT Press, 2008.
Carroll, Noël. *Engaging the Moving Image*. New Haven, CT: Yale University Press, 2008.
Carroll, Noël. *The Philosophy of Horror, or, Paradoxes of the Heart*. New York: Routledge, 1990.
Carroll, Noël. 'The Power of Movies'. *Daedalus* 114, no. 4 (1985): 79–103.
Carroll, Noël. *Theorizing the Moving Image*. Cambridge: Cambridge University Press, 1996.
Carroll, Noël, and William P. Seeley. 'Cognitivism, Psychology, and Neuroscience: Movies as Attentional Engines'. In *Psychocinematics: Exploring Cognition at the Movies*, edited by Alfred P. Shimamura. Oxford: Oxford University Press, 2013.
Chamarette, Jenny. *Phenomenology and the Future of Film: Rethinking Subjectivity beyond French Cinema*. London: Palgrave Macmillan, 2012.
Chion, Michel. *Audio-Vision: Sound on Screen*. New York: Columbia University Press, 1994.
Chion, Michel. *Film, a Sound Art*. New York: Columbia University Press, 2009.
Clark, Andy. *Being There: Putting Brain, Body, and World Together Again*. Cambridge, MA: MIT Press, 1998.
Clover, Carol J. *Men, Women, and Chain Saws: Gender in the Modern Horror Film*. Princeton: Princeton University Press, 1993.
Coëgnarts, Maarten, and Peter Kravanja, eds. *Embodied Cognition and Cinema*. Leuven: Leuven University Press, 2015.
Coëgnarts, Maarten, and Peter Kravanja. 'Film as an Exemplar of Bodily Meaning-Making'. In *Embodied Cognition and Cinema*, edited by Maarten Coëgnarts and Peter Kravanja. Leuven: Leuven University Press, 2015.
Colebrook, Claire. 'Disjunctive Synthesis'. In *The Deleuze Dictionary*, edited by Adrian Parr. Edinburgh: Edinburgh University Press, 2005.

Colman, Felicity. *Deleuze and Cinema: The Film Concepts*. Oxford: Berg, 2011.
Crary, Jonathan. *Techniques of the Observer: On Vision and Modernity in the Nineteenth Century*. Cambridge, MA: MIT Press, 1992.
Creed, Barbara. *The Monstrous-Feminine: Film, Feminism, Psychoanalysis*. New York: Taylor & Francis, 2012.
Cremin, Colin. *Exploring Videogames with Deleuze and Guattari: Towards an Affective Theory of Form*. New York: Routledge, 2015.
Crick, Timothy. 'The Game Body: Toward a Phenomenology of Contemporary Video Gaming'. *Games and Culture* 6, no. 3 (2011): 259–69.
Currie, Gregory. *Image and Mind: Film, Philosophy and Cognitive Science*. Cambridge: Cambridge University Press, 1995.
Curtis, Robin. '*Einfühlung* and Abstraction in the Moving Image: Historical and Contemporary Reflections'. *Science in Context* 25, no. 3 (2012): 425–46.
del Río, Elena. 'The Body as Foundation of the Screen: Allegories of Technology in Atom Egoyan's *Speaking Parts*'. *Camera Obscura* 38 (1996): 92–115.
del Río, Elena. 'Cinema's Exhaustion and the Vitality of Affect'. *In Media Res*, 29 August 2011. <http://mediacommons.org/imr/2011/08/19/cinemas-exhaustion-and-vitality-affect> (last accessed 9 September 2019).
del Río, Elena. *Deleuze and the Cinemas of Performance: Powers of Affection*. Edinburgh: Edinburgh University Press, 2008.
Deleuze, Gilles. *Cinema 1: The Movement Image*. Minneapolis: University of Minnesota Press. 2013.
Deleuze, Gilles. *Cinema 2: The Time Image*. Minneapolis: University of Minnesota Press. 2013.
Deleuze, Gilles. *Difference and Repetition*. New York: Columbia University Press, 1994.
Deleuze, Gilles, and Félix Guattari. *A Thousand Plateaus: Capitalism and Schizophrenia*. Minneapolis: University of Minnesota Press, 1987.
Denson, Shane. 'Crazy Cameras, Discorrelated Images, and the Post-Perceptual Mediation of Post-Cinematic Affect'. In *Post-Cinema: Theorizing 21st-Century Film*, edited by Shane Denson and Julia Leyda. Falmer: REFRAME Books, 2016.
Denson, Shane. 'The Horror of Discorrelation: Mediating Unease in Post-Cinematic Screens and Networks'. *Journal of Cinema and Media Studies* 59, no. 4 (Summer 2020, forthcoming).
Denson, Shane, and Julia Leyda. 'Perspectives on Post-Cinema: An Introduction'. In *Post-Cinema: Theorizing 21st-Century Film*, edited by Shane Denson and Julia Leyda. Falmer: REFRAME Books, 2016.
Denson, Shane, and Julia Leyda, eds. *Post-Cinema: Theorizing 21st-Century Film*. Falmer: REFRAME Books, 2016.
Dowd, A. A. 'Bobcat Goldthwait's *Willow Creek* Is Basically *The Blair Bigfoot Project*'. *A/V Club*, 5 June 2014. <http://www.avclub.com/review/bobcat-goldthwaits-willow-creek-basically-blair-bi-205236> (last accessed 9 September 2019).
Duchaney, Brian N. *The Spark of Fear: Technology, Society and the Horror Film*. Jefferson: McFarland, 2015.
Ebisch, Sjoerd, Mauro Perrucci, Antonio Ferretti, Cosimo Gratta, Gian Romani and Vittorio Gallese. 'The Sense of Touch: Embodied Simulation in a Visuotactile Mirroring Mechanism for Observed Animate or Inanimate Touch'. *Journal of Cognitive Neuroscience* 20, no. 9 (2008): 1611–23.
Egginton, William. 'Reality Is Bleeding: A Brief History of Film from the Sixteenth Century'. *Configurations* 9, no. 2 (2001): 207–29.
Egoyan, Atom. 'Surface Tension'. In *Speaking Parts*. Toronto: Coach House Press, 1993.

Elsaesser, Thomas, and Malte Hagener. *Film Theory: An Introduction Through the Senses*. New York: Taylor & Francis, 2009.

Flaxman, Gregory, ed. *The Brain Is the Screen: Deleuze and the Philosophy of Cinema*. Minneapolis: University of Minnesota Press, 2000.

Gallagher, Shaun. *How the Body Shapes the Mind*. Oxford: Clarendon Press, 2006.

Gallagher, Shaun, and Dan Zahavi. *The Phenomenological Mind*. New York: Routledge, 2013.

Gallese, Vittorio. 'Embodied Simulation Theory: Imagination and Narrative'. *Neuropsychoanalysis* 13, no. 2 (2011): 196–200.

Gallese, Vittorio. 'Mirror Neurons, Embodied Simulation, and the Neural Basis of Social Identification'. *Psychoanalytic Dialogues* 19, no. 5 (2009): 519–36.

Gallese, Vittorio, and Michele Guerra. 'Embodying Movies: Embodied Simulation and Film Studies'. *Cinema* 3 (2012): 183–210.

Gallese, Vittorio, and Michele Guerra. 'The Feeling of Motion: Camera Movements and Motor Cognition'. *Cinema & Cie* 14, no. 22–3 (2014): 103–12.

Gallese, Vittorio, and Hannah Wojciehowski. 'How Stories Make Us Feel: Toward an Embodied Narratology'. *California Italian Studies* 2, no. 1 (2011).

Gibson, Ross. 'The Time Will Come When . . .'. In *Future Cinema*, edited by *Jeffrey Shaw* and Peter Weibel. Cambridge, MA: MIT Press, 2003.

Giles, Dennis. 'Conditions of Pleasure in Horror Cinema'. In *Planks of Reason: Essays on the Horror Film*, edited by Barry Keith Grant and Christopher Sharrett. Oxford: Scarecrow Press, 2004.

Glendinning, Simon. *In the Name of Phenomenology*. New York: Routledge, 2007.

Grant, Barry Keith. 'Digital Anxiety and the New Verité Horror and SF Film'. *Science Fiction Film and Television* 6, no. 2 (2013): 153–75.

Gregg, Melissa, and Gregory J. Seigworth, eds. *The Affect Theory Reader*. Durham, NC: Duke University Press, 2007.

Grierson, John, and Forsyth Hardy. *Grierson on Documentary*. Berkeley: University of California Press, 1966.

Grisham, Therese, Julia Leyda, Nicholas Rombes and Steven Shaviro. 'The Post-Cinematic in *Paranormal Activity* and *Paranormal Activity 2*'. In *Post-Cinema: Theorizing 21st-Century Film*, edited by Shane Denson and Julia Leyda. Falmer: REFRAME Books, 2016.

Grodal, Torben. *Embodied Visions: Evolution, Emotion, Culture, and Film*. Oxford: Oxford University Press, 2009.

Grodal, Torben. *Moving Pictures: A New Theory of Film Genres, Feelings, and Cognition*. Oxford: Clarendon Press, 1999.

Gromala, Diane. 'Dancing with the Virtual Dervish: Virtual Bodies'. In *Immersed in Technology*, edited by Mary Anne Moser and Douglas MacLeod. Cambridge, MA: MIT Press, 1996.

Grosz, Elizabeth. 'A Thousand Tiny Sexes: Feminism and Rhizomatics'. *Topoi* 12, no. 2 (1993): 167–79.

Grusin, Richard. 'DVD, Video Games and the Cinema of Interactions'. In *Post-Cinema: Theorizing 21st-Century Film*, edited by Shane Denson and Julia Leyda. Falmer: REFRAME Books, 2016.

Guerra, Michele. 'Modes of Action at the Movies, or Re-thinking Film Style from the Embodied Perspective'. In *Embodied Cognition and Cinema*, edited by Maarten Coëgnarts and Peter Kravanja. Leuven: Leuven University Press, 2015.

Gunning, Tom. 'An Aesthetic of Astonishment: Early Film and the (In)Credulous Spectator'. *Art and Text* 34 (1989): 31–45.

Gunning, Tom. *D. W. Griffith and the Origins of American Narrative Film: The Early Years at Biograph*. Urbana: University of Illinois Press, 1994.

Hahner, Leslie A., Scott J. Varda and Nathan A. Wilson. '*Paranormal Activity* and the Horror of Abject Consumption'. *Critical Studies in Media Communication* 30, no. 5 (2013): 362–76.

Hallam, Julia, and Margaret Marshment. *Realism and Popular Cinema*. Manchester: Manchester University Press, 2000.

Hanich, Julian. *Cinematic Emotion in Horror Films and Thrillers: The Aesthetic Paradox of Pleasurable Fear*. New York: Routledge, 2011.

Hansen, Mark B. N. *New Philosophy for New Media*. Cambridge, MA: MIT Press, 2004.

Hansen, Miriam Bratu. 'Benjamin and Cinema: Not a One-Way Street'. *Critical Inquiry* 25, no. 2 (1999): 306–43.

Hantke, Steffen. 'Network Anxiety: Prefiguring Digital Anxieties in the American Horror Film'. In *Digital Horror: Haunted Technologies, Network Panic and the Found Footage Phenomenon*, edited by Linnie Blake and Xavier Aldana Reyes. London: I. B. Tauris, 2016.

Hart, Adam Charles. 'Killer POV: First-Person Camera and Sympathetic Identification in Modern Horror'. *Imaginations* 9, no. 1 (2018): 69–86.

Hart, Adam Charles. 'The Searching Camera: First-Person Shooters, Found-Footage Horror, and the Documentary Tradition'. *The Journal of Cinema and Media Studies* 58, no. 4 (Summer 2019): 73–91.

Heller-Nicholas, Alexandra. *Found Footage Horror Films: Fear and the Appearance of Reality*. Jefferson: McFarland, 2014.

Heller-Nicholas, Alexandra. 'Gothic Textures in Found Footage Horror Film'. University of Stirling. <http://www.gothic.stir.ac.uk/guestblog/gothic-textures-in-found-footage-horror-film/> (last accessed 9 September 2019).

Higley, Sarah Lynn, and Jeffrey Andrew Weinstock, eds. *Nothing That Is: Millennial Cinema and the* Blair Witch *Controversies*. Detroit: Wayne State University Press, 2004.

Hills, Matthew. *The Pleasures of Horror*. London: Bloomsbury Academic, 2005.

Himmelsbach, Sabine. 'The Interactive Potential of Distributed Networks'. In *Future Cinema: The Cinematic Imaginary after Film*, edited by *Jeffrey Shaw* and Peter Weibel. Cambridge, MA: MIT Press, 2003.

Huhtamo, Erkki. 'Media Art in the Third Dimension'. In *Future Cinema*, edited by Jeffrey Shaw and Peter Weibel. Cambridge, MA: MIT Press, 2003.

Husserl, Edmund. *Zur Phänomenologie der Intersubjektivität II*. New York: Springer, 1973.

Ihde, Don. *Bodies in Technology*. Minneapolis: University of Minnesota Press, 2002.

Ihde, Don. *Technology and the Lifeworld: From Garden to Earth*. Bloomington: Indiana University Press, 1990.

Isaacs, Bruce. *The Orientation of Future Cinema: Technology, Aesthetics, Spectacle*. London: Bloomsbury Publishing, 2013.

Jackson, Kimberly. *Technology, Monstrosity, and Reproduction in Twenty-First Century Horror*. Basingstoke: Palgrave Macmillan, 2013.

Jancovich, Mark. *Rational Fears: American Horror in the 1950s*. Manchester: Manchester University Press, 1996.

Joy, Stuart. 'The Patriarchal Construction of Hysteria: Examining the Possessed Woman in the *Paranormal Activity* Franchise'. *Monsters and the Monstrous* 3, no. 1 (2013): 1–18.

Keller, James. '"Nothing That Is Not There, and the Nothing That Is": Language and the Blair Witch Phenomenon'. *Studies in Popular Culture* 22, no. 3 (2000): 69–81.

Kinder, Marsha. 'Narrative Equivocations between Movies and Games'. In *The New Media Book*, edited by Dan Harries. London: BFI Publishing, 2002.

King, Geoff, and Tanya Krzywinska, eds. *Screenplay: Cinema/Videogames/Interfaces*. New York: Wallflower Press, 2002.

King, Geoff, and Tanya Krzywinska. *Tomb Raiders and Space Invaders: Video Games in the 21st Century*. London: I. B. Tauris, 2006.

Kittler, Friedrich. *Gramophone, Film, Typewriter*. Stanford: Stanford University Press, 1999.

Knudsen, Eric. 'Victor Surge, Deviant Art'. *Deviant Art*. <http://victor-surge.deviantart.com/> (last accessed 9 September 2019).

Kristeva, Julia. *Powers of Horror: An Essay on Abjection*. Edited by Leon S. Roudiez. New York: Columbia University Press, 1982.

Krumins, Aaron. 'Haptic Bodysuits and the Strange New Landscape of Immersive VR'. *ExtremeTech*, 4 January 2017. <https://www.extremetech.com/extreme/241917-haptic-bodysuits-strange-new-landscape-immersive-virtual-reality> (last accessed 9 September 2019).

Krzywinska, Tanya. 'Gaming Horror's Horror: Representation, Regulation, and Affect in Survival Horror Videogames'. *Journal of Visual Culture* 14, no. 3 (2015): 293–7.

Leyda, Julia. 'Demon Debt: PARANORMAL ACTIVITY as Recessionary Post-Cinematic Allegory'. In *Post-Cinema: Theorizing 21st-Century Film*, edited by Shane Denson and Julia Leyda. Falmer: REFRAME Books, 2016.

Lim, Sohye, and Byron Reeves. 'Being in the Game: Effects of Avatar Choice and Point of View on Psychophysiological Responses during Play'. *Media Psychology* 12, no. 4 (2009): 348–70.

Livesey, Graham. 'Assemblage'. In *The Deleuze Dictionary*, edited by Adrian Parr. Edinburgh: Edinburgh University Press, 2005.

Lovecraft, H. P. *Supernatural Horror in Literature*. New York: Dover, 1973.

Lowenstein, Adam. 'Living Dead: Fearful Attractions of Film'. *Representations* 110, no. 1 (2010): 105–28.

McDowell, Scott Dixon, and Daniel Myrick. 'Method Filmmaking: An Interview with Daniel Myrick, Co-Director of *The Blair Witch Project*'. *Journal of Film and Video* 53, no. 2/3 (2001): 140–7.

McLuhan, Marshall. *Understanding Media: The Extensions of Man*. Berkeley: Gingko Press, 2013.

McRoy, Jay. *Nightmare Japan: Contemporary Japanese Horror Cinema*. Amsterdam, Rodopi, 2008.

Manovich, Lev. *The Language of New Media*. Cambridge, MA: MIT Press, 2001.

Marks, Laura U. *The Skin of the Film: Intercultural Cinema, Embodiment, and the Senses*. Durham, NC: Duke University Press, 2000.

Marks, Laura U. *Touch: Sensuous Theory and Multisensory Media*. Minneapolis: University of Minnesota Press, 2002.

Martin, Adrian. 'Delirious Enchantment'. In *Mysteries of Cinema: Reflections on Film Theory, History and Culture 1982–2016*. Amsterdam: Amsterdam University Press, 2018.

Massumi, Brian. *Parables for the Virtual: Movement, Affect, Sensation*. Durham, NC: Duke University Press, 2002.

Massumi, Brian. *Politics of Affect*. Cambridge: Polity Press, 2015.

Massumi, Brian. *Semblance and Event: Activist Philosophy and the Occurrent Arts*. Cambridge, MA: MIT Press, 2011.

Merleau-Ponty, Maurice. *Phenomenology of Perception*. New York: Routledge, 2002 (original publication 1962).

Meslow, Scott. '12 Years after "Blair Witch," When Will the Found Footage Horror Fad End?' *The Atlantic*, 6 January 2012. <https://www.theatlantic.com/entertainment/archive/2012/01/12-years-after-blair-witch-when-will-the-found-footage-horror-fad-end/250950/> (last accessed 9 September 2019).

Metz, Christian. *The Imaginary Signifier: Psychoanalysis and the Cinema*. Bloomington: Indiana University Press, 1982.
Mitry, Jean. *Esthétique et Psychologie du Cinéma*. Paris: Cerf, 2001.
Moretti, Franco. *Signs Taken for Wonders: On the Sociology of Literary Forms*. New York: Verso, 2005.
Moure, José. 'The Cinema as Art of the Mind: Hugo Münsterberg, First Theorist of Subjectivity in Film'. In *Subjectivity: Filmic Representation and the Spectator's Experience*, edited by Dominique Chateau. Amsterdam: Amsterdam University Press, 2011.
Mulvey, Laura. 'Visual Pleasure and Narrative Cinema'. In *Film Theory and Criticism: Introductory Readings*, edited by Leo Braudy and Marshall Cohen. New York: Oxford University Press, 1999.
Münsterberg, Hugo. *The Photoplay: A Psychological Study*. New York: D. Appleton, 1916.
Nagib, Lúcia, and Cecilia Mello. *Realism and Audiovisual Media*. New York: Palgrave Macmillan, 2009.
Nannicelli, Ted, and Paul Taberham. *Cognitive Media Theory*. New York: Routledge, 2014.
Ndalianis, Angela. *The Horror Sensorium: Media and the Senses*. Jefferson: McFarland, 2012.
Neill, Alex. 'Empathy and (Film) Fiction'. In *Philosophy of Film and Motion Pictures: An Anthology*, edited by Noël Carroll and Jinhee Choi. Malden: Basil Blackwell, 2006.
Nichols, Bill. *Introduction to Documentary*. Bloomington, Indiana University Press, 2010.
Noë, Alva. *Action in Perception*. Cambridge, MA: MIT Press, 2004.
Olivier, Marc. 'Glitch Gothic'. In *Cinematic Ghosts: Haunting and Spectrality from Silent Cinema to the Digital Era*, edited by Murray Leeder. New York: Bloomsbury, 2015.
Panksepp, Jaak. 'Affective Consciousness: Core Emotional Feelings in Animals and Humans'. *Consciousness and Cognition* 14, no. 1 (2005): 30–80.
Panksepp, Jaak. *Affective Neuroscience: The Foundations of Human and Animal Emotions*. Oxford: Oxford University Press, 2004.
Panksepp, Jaak. 'Cross-Species Affective Neuroscience Decoding of the Primal Affective Experiences of Humans and Related Animals'. *PLOS ONE* 6, no. 9 (2011): 1–15.
Panksepp, Jaak. 'Damasio's Error? Review Article: "Looking for Spinoza: Joy, Sorrow, and the Feeling Brain" by A. Damasio'. *Consciousness 38* 4, no. 1 (2003): 111–34.
Panksepp, Jaak, and Douglas Watt. 'What Is Basic about Basic Emotions? Lasting Lessons from Affective Neuroscience'. *Emotion Review* 3, no. 4 (2011): 387–96.
Pasolini, Pier Paolo. *L'Expérience Hérétique: Langue et Cinéma*. Paris: Payot, 1976.
Pepperell, Robert. 'Where's the Screen? The Paradoxical Relationship between Mind and World'. In *Screen Consciousness: Cinema, Mind and World*, edited by Robert Pepperell and Michael Punt. Amsterdam: Rodopi, 2006.
Perron, Bernard. *The World of Scary Video Games (Approaches to Digital Game Studies)*. New York: Bloomsbury Publishing, 2018.
Pinedo, Isabel. *Recreational Terror: Women and the Pleasures of Horror Film Viewing*. New York: State University of New York Press, 1997.
Pinker, Steven. *The Blank Slate*. New York: Viking, 2002.
Pisters, Patricia. '*Dexter's Plastic Brain*: Mentalizing and Mirroring in Cinematic Empathy'. *Cinéma & Cie* 14, 22/23 (2014): 53–63.
Pisters, Patricia. *The Matrix of Visual Culture: Working with Deleuze in Film Theory*. Stanford: Stanford University Press, 2003.
Pisters, Patricia. *The Neuro-Image: A Deleuzian Film-Philosophy of Digital Screen Culture*. Stanford: Stanford University Press, 2012.
Plantinga, Carl. 'The Affective Power of Movies'. In *Psychocinematics: Exploring Cognition at the Movies*, edited by Arthur P. Shimamura. Oxford: Oxford University Press, 2014.

Plantinga, Carl. *Moving Viewers: American Film and the Spectator's Experience*. Berkeley: University of California Press, 2009.
Powell, Anna. *Deleuze, Altered States and Film*. Edinburgh: Edinburgh University Press, 2007.
Powell, Anna. *Deleuze and Horror Film*. Edinburgh: Edinburgh University Press, 2006.
Powell, Anna. 'Kicking the Map Away: *The Blair Witch Project*, Deleuze and the Aesthetics of Horror'. *Spectator* 22, no. 2 (2002): 56–68.
Prince, Stephen. 'True Lies: Perceptual Realism, Digital Images, and Film Theory'. *Film Quarterly* 49, no. 3 (1996): 27–37.
Protevi, John. *Life, War, Earth: Deleuze and the Sciences*. Minneapolis: University of Minnesota Press, 2013.
Radford, Colin, and Michael Weston. 'How Can We Be Moved by the Fate of Anna Karenina?' *Proceedings of the Aristotelian Society, Supplementary Volumes* 49 (1975): 67–93.
Raz, Gal, Yael Jacob, Tal Gonen, Yonatan Winetraub, Tamar Flash, Eyal Soreq and Talma Hendler. 'Cry for Her or Cry with Her: Context-Dependent Dissociation of Two Modes of Cinematic Empathy Reflected in Network Cohesion Dynamics'. *Social Cognitive and Affective Neuroscience* 9, no. 1 (2014): 30–8.
Reyes, Xavier Aldana. *Horror Film and Affect: Towards a Corporeal Model of Viewership*. New York: Routledge, 2016.
Richardson, Ingrid. 'Faces, Interfaces, Screens: Relational Ontologies of Framing, Attention and Distraction'. *Transformations* 18 (2010): 1–15.
Riegl, Alois. *Late Roman Art Industry*. Rome: Giorgio Bretschneider Editore, 1985 (original publication 1927).
Rizzo, Teresa. *Deleuze and Film: A Feminist Introduction*. London: Bloomsbury Publishing, 2012.
Rizzolatti, Giacomo, and Corrado Sinigaglia. *Mirrors in the Brain: How Our Minds Share Actions and Emotions*. Oxford: Oxford University Press, 2008.
Rødje, Kjetil. 'Intra-Diegetic Cameras as Cinematic Actor Assemblages in Found Footage Horror Cinema'. *Film-Philosophy* 21, no. 2 (2017): 206–22.
Rodowick, David N. *The Virtual Life of Film*. Cambridge, MA: Harvard University Press, 2009.
Roscoe, Jane, and Craig Hight. *Faking It: Mock-Documentary and the Subversion of Factuality*. Manchester: Manchester University Press, 2001.
Ross, Miriam. 'Virtual Reality's New Synesthetic Possibilities'. *Television & New Media* (2018): 1–18.
Rushton, Richard. 'Passions and Actions: Deleuze's Cinematographic Cogito'. *Deleuze Studies* 2, no. 2 (2008): 121–39.
Rutherford, Anne. 'Cinema and Embodied Affect'. *Senses of Cinema*, March 2003. <http://sensesofcinema.com/2003/feature-articles/embodied_affect/> (last accessed 9 September 2019).
Rutherford, Anne. 'The Poetics of a Potato: Documentary that Gets Under the Skin'. *Metro Magazine: Media & Education Magazine* 137 (2003): 126–31.
Rutherford, Anne. 'Precarious Boundaries: Affect, Mise en scène and the Senses in Angelopolous' Balkans Epic'. In *Art and the Performance of Memory: Sounds and Gestures of Recollection*, edited by Richard Candida Smith. New York: Routledge, 2002.
Rutherford, Anne. *What Makes a Film Tick?: Cinematic Affect, Materiality and Mimetic Innervation*. Bern: Peter Lang, 2011.
Sanchez-Vives, Maria V., and Mel Slater. 'From Presence to Consciousness through Virtual Reality'. *Nature Reviews Neuroscience* 6, no. 4 (2005): 332–9.
Sayad, Cecilia. 'Found-Footage Horror and the Frame's Undoing'. *Cinema Journal* 55, no. 2 (2016): 43–66.

Schmitz, Hermann. *Der Gefühlsraum*. Bonn: Bouvier, 1969.
Schwartz, Louis-Georges. 'Typewriter: Free Indirect Discourse in Deleuze's Cinema'. *SubStance* 34, no. 3 (2005): 107–35.
Sconce, Jeffrey. *Haunted Media: Electronic Presence from Telegraphy to Television*. Durham, NC: Duke University Press, 2000.
Shaviro, Steven. *The Cinematic Body*. Minneapolis: University of Minnesota Press, 1994.
Shaviro, Steven. *Post Cinematic Affect*. London: John Hunt Publishing, 2010.
Shaviro, Steven. 'Post-Cinematic Affect: On Grace Jones, *Boarding Gate* and *Southland Tales*'. *Film-Philosophy* 14 (2010): 1–102.
Shaviro, Steven. 'Post-Continuity'. In *Post-Cinema: Theorizing 21st-Century Film*, edited by Shane Denson and Julia Leyda. Falmer: REFRAME Books, 2016.
Shaviro, Steven. 'Splitting the Atom'. In *Post-Cinema: Theorizing 21st-Century Film*, edited by Shane Denson and Julia Leyda. Falmer: REFRAME Books, 2016.
Shaw, Jeffrey, and Peter Weibel, eds. *Future Cinema*. Cambridge, MA: MIT Press, 2003.
Shaw, Spencer. *Film Consciousness: From Phenomenology to Deleuze*. London: McFarland, 2008.
Shimamura, Alfred P., ed. *Psychocinematics: Exploring Cognition at the Movies*. Oxford: Oxford University Press, 2013.
Sinnerbrink, Robert. *Cinematic Ethics: Exploring Ethical Experience through Film*. New York: Routledge, 2015.
Sinnerbrink, Robert. *New Philosophies of Film: Thinking Images*. London: Continuum, 2011.
Sinnerbrink, Robert. 'Questioning Style'. In *The Language and Style of Film Criticism*, edited by Andrew Klevan and Alex Clayton. New York: Routledge, 2011.
Skal, David J. *The Monster Show: A Cultural History of Horror*. New York: Farrar, Straus and Giroux, 2001.
Slater, Mel. 'Place Illusion and Plausibility Can Lead to Realistic Behaviour in Immersive Virtual Environments'. *Philosophical Transactions of the Royal Society B: Biological Sciences* 364, no. 1535 (2009): 3549–57.
Slater, Mel, and Sylvia Wilbur. 'A Framework for Immersive Virtual Environments (FIVE): Speculations on the Role of Presence in Virtual Environments'. *Presence-Teleoperators and Virtual Environments* 6 (1997): 603–16.
Smith, Murray. 'Empathy, Expansionism, and the Extended Mind'. In *Empathy: Philosophical and Psychological Perspectives*, edited by Amy Coplan and Peter Goldie. Oxford: Oxford University Press, 2011.
Smith, Murray. *Engaging Characters: Fiction, Emotion, and the Cinema*. Oxford: Clarendon Press, 1995.
Smith, Murray. 'On the Twofoldedness of Character'. *New Literary History* 42 (2011): 277–94.
Sobchack, Vivian. *The Address of the Eye: A Phenomenology of Film Experience*. Princeton: Princeton University Press, 1992.
Sobchack, Vivian. *Carnal Thoughts: Embodiment and Moving Image Culture*. Berkeley: University of California Press, 2004.
Stam, Robert. *Film Theory: An Introduction*. Hoboken: Wiley, 2000.
Storr, Anthony. *Music and the Mind*. New York: Ballantine, 1992.
Subramanian, Janani. 'Candid Cameras: Transmedia Haunting and the Paranormal Activity Franchise'. *Refractory Journal*, 22 June 2014. <http://refractory.unimelb.edu.au/2014/06/22/paranormalacitivity-subramanian/> (last accessed 9 September 2019).
Taussig, Michael. *Mimesis and Alterity: A Particular History of the Senses*. New York: Routledge, 1993.

Telotte, J. P. 'Faith and Idolatry in the Horror Film'. In *Planks of Reason: Essays on the Horror Film*, edited by Barry Keith Grant and Christopher Sharrett. Oxford: Scarecrow Press, 2004.

Thompson, Kristin. 'Categorical Coherence: A Closer Look at Character Subjectivity'. *Observations on Film Art*, 24 October 2008. <http://www.davidbordwell.net/blog/2008/10/24/categorical-coherence-a-closer-look-at-character-subjectivity/> (last accessed 9 September 2019).

Tikka, Pia. 'Cinema as Externalization of Consciousness'. In *Screen Consciousness: Cinema, Mind and World*, edited by Robert Pepperell and Michael Punt. Amsterdam: Rodopi, 2006.

Tirrell, Jeremy. 'Bleeding through, or We Are Living in a Digital World and I Am an Analog Girl'. In *The Scary Screen: Media Anxiety in the Ring*, edited by Kristen Lacefield. Burlington: Ashgate, 2010.

Tudor, Andrew. 'Why Horror? The Peculiar Pleasures of a Popular Genre'. *Cultural Studies* 11, no. 3 (1997): 443–63.

Turner, Peter. *Found Footage Horror Films: A Cognitive Approach*. New York: Routledge, 2019.

Urbano, Cosimo. '"What's the Matter with Melanie?": Reflections on the Merits of Psychoanalytic Approaches to Modern Horror Cinema'. In *Horror Film and Psychoanalysis: Freud's Worst Nightmares*, edited by Steven Jay Schneider. Cambridge: Cambridge University Press, 2004.

Varela, Francisco J., Eleanor Rosch and Evan Thompson. *The Embodied Mind: Cognitive Science and Human Experience*. Cambridge, MA: MIT Press, 1992.

Vertov, Dziga. *Kino-Eye: The Writings of Dziga Vertov*. Berkeley: University of California Press, 1984.

Vogeley, Kai, and Gereon R. Fink. 'Neural Correlates of the First-Person-Perspective'. *Trends in Cognitive Sciences* 7, no. 1 (2003): 38–42.

Wehner, Mike. 'The Most Disturbing Viral Video Now Has a Sequel, and We Spoke to the Creator'. *The Daily Dot*, 19 January 2016. <https://www.dailydot.com/debug/11b-x-1371-11b-3-1369-parker-wright/> (last accessed 9 September 2019).

Weibel, Peter. 'The Intelligent Image'. In *Future Cinema*, edited by *Jeffrey Shaw* and Peter Weibel. Cambridge, MA: MIT Press, 2003.

Wetmore, Kevin J. *Post-9/11 Horror in American Cinema*. New York: Bloomsbury Publishing, 2012.

Williams, Linda. 'Corporealized Observers: Visual Pornographies and the "Carnal Density of Vision"'. In *Fugitive Images: From Photography to Video*, edited by Patrice Petro. Bloomington: Indiana University Press, 1995.

Williams, Linda. 'Film Bodies: Genre, Gender and Excess'. *Film Quarterly* 44, no. 4 (1991): 2–13.

Wilson, Margaret. 'Six Views of Embodied Cognition'. *Psychonomic Bulletin & Review* 9 (2002): 625–36.

Wood, Andrea, and Brandy Schillace, eds. *Unnatural Reproductions and Monstrosity: The Birth of the Monster in Literature, Film, and Media*. Amherst: Cambria Press, 2014.

Wood, Robin. 'The American Nightmare: Horror in the 70s'. In *Hollywood from Vietnam to Reagan, and Beyond*, edited by Robin Wood. New York: Columbia University Press, 2003.

Yacavone, Daniel. 'Film and the Phenomenology of Art: Reappraising Merleau-Ponty on Cinema as Form, Medium, and Expression'. *New Literary History* 47, no. 1 (2016): 159–85.

Zacks, Jeffrey M. *Flicker: Your Brain on Movies*. Oxford: Oxford University Press, 2014.

Zimmer, Catherine. *Surveillance Cinema*. New York: New York University Press, 2015.

Videos

11:57. VR Short Film. Sid Lee Collective. <http://1157.pm/> (last accessed 9 September 2019).

11bx1371. Online Video. Parker Wright. <http://bit.ly/11bx1371> (last accessed 9 September 2019).

Admission. Online Video. ToTheArk. Joseph DeLage and Troy Wagner. <https://www.youtube.com/watch?v=rIe-a6-TNHI> (last accessed 9 September 2019).

The Black Mass Experience. VR Short Film. Jaunt and New Deal Studios. <https://www.jauntvr.com/title/NewDealStudios-BlackMassExperienceTrailer.2014-10-30_titles> (last accessed 9 September 2019).

Catatonic VR. VR Short Film. Guy Shelmerdine. <http://www.catatonic.co/> (last accessed 9 September 2019).

Clouds Over Sidra. VR Short Film. Chris Milk and Gabo Arora. Within. <https://with.in/watch/clouds-over-sidra/> (last accessed 9 September 2019).

Conversion. Online Video. ToTheArk. Joseph DeLage and Troy Wagner. <https://www.youtube.com/watch?v=-xX7-eFWmy8> (last accessed 9 September 2019).

Cursed Kleenex Commercial Changing at Midnight. Online Video. Shrouded Hand. <https://www.youtube.com/watch?v=9GIraEWMVHk> (last accessed 9 September 2019).

Decay. Online Video. ToTheArk. Joseph DeLage and Troy Wagner. <https://www.youtube.com/watch?v=XhwO6wm76-U> (last accessed 9 September 2019).

The Drop VR. VR Short Film. Inside360. <https://www.youtube.com/watch?v=SPmPU09GtHA> (last accessed 9 September 2019).

Entry #23. Online Video. Marble Hornets. Joseph DeLage and Troy Wagner. <https://www.youtube.com/watch?v=SzdZyZgCY58> (last accessed 9 September 2019).

Entry #40. Online Video. Marble Hornets. Joseph DeLage and Troy Wagner. <https://www.youtube.com/watch?v=p2Jo6yrUVwM> (last accessed 9 September 2019).

Entry #43. Online Video. Marble Hornets. Joseph DeLage and Troy Wagner. <https://www.youtube.com/watch?v=zqQIVmauiXI> (last accessed 9 September 2019).

Entry #60. Online Video. Marble Hornets. Joseph DeLage and Troy Wagner. <https://www.youtube.com/watch?v=6a-pO2Pm37A> (last accessed 9 September 2019).

Entry #83. Online Video. Marble Hornets. Joseph DeLage and Troy Wagner. <https://www.youtube.com/watch?v=Tb33j_DWu8Y&t=1s> (last accessed 9 September 2019).

Escape the Living Dead. VR Short Film. Jaunt. <https://www.jauntvr.com/title/0ed2a6b244> (last accessed 9 September 2019).

Everest VR. VR Short Film. Sólfar. <http://www.solfar.com/everest-vr/> (last accessed 9 September 2019).

Evolution of Verse. VR Short Film. Chris Milk. <https://with.in/watch/evolution-of-verse/> (last accessed 9 September 2019).

File. Online Video. Marble Hornets. Joseph DeLage and Troy Wagner. <https://www.youtube.com/watch?v=TNUweuEnBI0> (last accessed 9 September 2019).

The Game. VR Short Film. Jaunt. <https://www.jauntvr.com/title/e6a64293ee> (last accessed 9 September 2019).

Life of Us. VR Short Film. Chris Milk and Aaron Koblin. <http://www.zacharyrichter.com/life-of-us/> (last accessed 9 September 2019).

Spectrogram '11B X 1371'. Online video. Marasus 1922. <https://www.youtube.com/watch?v=cSPjWtAjlfM> (last accessed 9 September 2019).

Suicidemouse. Online Video. Nec1. <https://www.youtube.com/watch?v=C_h1dY66Rm4&> (last accessed 9 September 2019).

Unfavourable Semicircle. Online Video Channel. Unfavourable semicircle. <https://www.youtube.com/channel/UCA2j2wFhXsQej79c9V4v_Lg> (last accessed 9 September 2019).
Username: 666. Online Video. nana825763. <http://bit.ly/666vid> (last accessed 9 September 2019).
VR Noir. VR Short Film. AFTRS, FSM and StartVR. <https://startvr.co/project/vr-noir/> (last accessed 9 September 2019).
Walking New York. VR Short Film. Chris Milk. Within. <https://with.in/watch/nyt-mag-vr-walking-new-york/> (last accessed 9 September 2019).
Webdriver Torso. Online Video Channel. Webdriver Torso. <https://www.youtube.com/channel/UCsLiV4WJfkTEHH0b9PmRklw> (last accessed 9 September 2019).
Yellowstone VR. VR Short Film. Jaunt and Flex. <https://www.jauntvr.com/title/bbbb711213> (last accessed 9 September 2019).

FILMS

#Screamers. 2016. Directed by Dean Matthew Ronalds. Trick Candle Productions.
The American Nightmare. 2000. Directed by Adam Simon. Minerva Pictures.
The Amityville Horror. 1979. Directed by Stuart Rosenberg. American International Pictures, Cinema 77 and Professional Films.
Bird Box. 2018. Directed by Susanne Bier. Bluegrass Films, Chris Morgan Productions and Universal Pictures.
Blair Witch. 2016. Directed by Adam Wingard. Lionsgate, Room 101, Snoot Entertainment and Vertigo Entertainment.
The Blair Witch Project. 1999. Directed by Daniel Myrick and Eduardo Sánchez. Haxan Films.
The Cabinet of Dr Caligari. 1920. Directed by Robert Wiene. Decla-Bioscop AG.
Cannibal Holocaust. 1980. Directed by Ruggero Deodato. FD Cinematografica.
Chronicle. 2012. Directed by Josh Trank. Twentieth Century Fox Film Corporation, Davis Entertainment and Dune Entertainment.
Cloverfield. 2008. Directed by Matt Reeves. Paramount Pictures and Bad Robot.
The Conjuring. 2013. Directed by James Wan. New Line Cinema, Safran Company and The Evergreen Media Group.
Creep. 2014. Directed by Patrick Brice. Blumhouse Productions and Duplass Brothers Productions.
End of Watch. 2012. Directed by David Ayer. Exclusive Media Group, EFO Films and Hedge Fund Film Partners.
Eraserhead. 1977. Directed by David Lynch. American Film Institute and Libra Films.
The Exorcist. 1973. Directed by William Friedkin. Warner Brothers and Hoya Productions.
The Fly. 1986. Directed by David Cronenberg. SLM Production Group and Brooksfilms.
Forgotten Silver. 1995. Directed by Costa Botes and Peter Jackson. New Zealand Film Commission, New Zealand On Air and Wingnut Films.
Friday the 13th. 1980. Directed by Sean S. Cunningham. Paramount Pictures, Warner Brothers and Georgetown Productions.
Get Out. 2017. Directed by Jordan Peele. Universal Pictures and Blumhouse/QC Entertainment.
Hereditary. 2018. Directed by Ari Aster. PalmStar Media.
It Follows. 2014. Directed by David Robert Mitchell. Northern Lights Films, Animal Kingdom and Two Flints.
Lady in the Lake. 1947. Directed by Robert Montgomery. Metro-Goldwyn-Mayer.
The Last Broadcast. 1998. Directed by Stefan Avalos and Lance Weiler. FFM Productions.

The Last Exorcism. 2010. Directed by Daniel Stamm. Strike Entertainment, StudioCanal and Arcade Pictures.
The Lawnmower Man. 1992. Directed by Brett Leonard. Allied Visions, Fuji Eight Company and Lake Pringle Productions.
Le Manoir du Diable. 1896. Directed by Georges Méliès. Georges Méliès.
Le Squelette Joyeux. 1898. Directed by Louis Lumière. Lumière.
Man Bites Dog. 1992. Directed by Rémy Belvaux, André Bonzel and Benoît Poelvoorde. Les Artistes Anonymes.
Medium Cool. 1969. Directed by Haskell Wexler. H & J.
Mulholland Drive. 2001. Directed by David Lynch. Les Films Alain Sarde, Asymmetrical Productions, Babbo Inc. and Canal+.
Night of the Living Dead. 1968. Directed by George Romero. Image Ten, Laurel Group and Market Square Productions.
No Country for Old Men. 2007. Directed by Joel and Ethan Coen. Paramount Vantage, Miramax and Scott Rudin Productions.
Pandora's Box. 1929. Directed by G. W. Pabst. Nero-Film AG.
Paranormal Activity. 2007. Directed by Oren Peli. Solana Films and Blumhouse Productions.
Paranormal Activity 2. 2010. Directed by Tod Williams. Paramount Pictures, Solana Films and Blumhouse Productions.
Paranormal Activity 3. 2011. Directed by Henry Joost and Ariel Schulman. Paramount Pictures, Solana Films and Blumhouse Productions.
Paranormal Activity 4. 2012. Directed by Henry Joost and Ariel Schulman. Paramount Pictures, Solana Films and Blumhouse Productions.
Paranormal Activity: The Marked Ones. 2014. Directed by Christopher Landon. Paramount Pictures, Solana Films and Blumhouse Productions.
Paranormal Activity: The Ghost Dimension. 2015. Directed by Gregory Plotkin. Paramount Pictures, Solana Films and Blumhouse Productions.
Poltergeist. 1982. Directed by Tobe Hooper. Metro-Goldwyn-Mayer, Amblin Entertainment and SLM Production.
Project X. 2012. Directed by Nima Nourizadeh. Green Hat Films and Silver Pictures.
[REC]. 2007. Directed by Jaume Balagueró. Castelao Producciones, Filmax and Instituto de la Cinematografía y de las Artes Audiovisuales (ICAA).
[REC 2]. 2009. Directed by Jaume Balagueró and Paco Plaza. Filmax, Televisión Española (TVE), Canal+ España.
[REC 3]. 2012. Directed by Paco Plaza. Filmax.
[REC 4]: Apocalypse. 2014. Directed by Jaume Balagueró. Filmax.
Repulsion. 1965. Directed by Roman Polanski. Compton Films and Tekli British Productions.
The Ring. 2002. Directed by Gore Verbinski. DreamWorks, Parkes+MacDonald Image Nation and BenderSpink.
Ringu. 1998. Directed by Hideo Nakata. Basara Pictures, Imagica and Asmik Ace Entertainment.
The Shining. 1980. Directed by Stanley Kubrick. Warner Brothers, Hawk Films and Peregrine.
Sinister. 2012. Directed by Scott Derrickson. Alliance Films, IM Global and Blumhouse Productions.
Slither. 2006. Directed by James Gunn. Gold Circle Films, Strike Entertainment, Brightlight Pictures.
Strange Days. 1995. Directed by Kathryn Bigelow. Lightstorm Entertainment.
The Texas Chainsaw Massacre. 1974. Directed by Tobe Hooper. Bryanstown Pictures.
Them! 1954. Directed by Gordon Douglas. Warner Brothers.

Unfriended. 2014. Directed by Levan Gabriadze. Bazelevs Productions and Blumhouse Productions.
The Usual Suspects. 1995. Directed by Bryan Singer. PolyGram Filmed Entertainment, Spelling Films International, Blue Parrot, Bad Had Harry Productions and Rosco Film GmbH.
V/H/S. 2012. Directed by Matt Bettinelli-Olpin, David Bruckner, Tyler Gillett, Justin Martinez, Glenn McQuaid, Radio Silence, Joe Swanberg, Chad Villella, Ti West and Adam Wingard. 8383 Productions, Bloody Disgusting and Collective Studios.
V/H/S 2. 2013. Directed by Simon Barrett, Jason Eisner, Gareth Evans, Gregg Hale, Eduardo Sánchez, Timo Tjahjanto and Adam Wingard. 8383 Productions, Bloody Disgusting, and Collective Studios.
Videodrome. 1983. Directed by David Cronenberg. Filmplan International, Guardian Trust Company and Canadian Film Development Company.
The Visit. 2015. Directed by M. Night Shyamalan. Blinding House Pictures and Blumhouse Productions.
Willow Creek. 2013. Directed by Bobcat Goldthwaite. Jerkschool Productions.
Wolf Creek. 2005. Directed by Greg McLean. Australian Film Finance Corporation, South Australian Film Corporation and The 403 Productions.

TELEVISION

Black Mirror. 2011–Present. Created by Charlie Brooker. Zeppotron, Channel Four and Gran Babieka.
Most Haunted. 2002–Present. Antix Productions and Hanrahan Media.
The Twilight Zone. 1959–64. Created by Rod Serling. Cayuga Productions and CBS.
The X-Files. 1993–2018. Created by Chris Carter. Ten Thirteen Productions and Twentieth Century Fox.

GAMES

Sega. *Alien: Isolation*. 2014. Xbox One and Oculus Rift (via mod).
Kitty Horrorshow. *Anatomy*. 2016. PC.
Connor Sherlock and Cameron Kunzelman. *Marginalia*. 2017. PC.

Index

#Screamers, 200–1
11:57, 171–3, 180–2, 187–9
11bx1371, 117, 119–22, 126
4Chan, 117–18

aberration, 154, 202
acousmatic, 56, 126
acousmêtre, 56, 59, 61, 70–1, 126
affect, 31–2, 37, 51, 60–4, 109–12, 117,
    125, 129, 143, 163, 173, 179, 193
  affective intensities, 80
  affective neuroscience, 109
  affective surplus, 44–5, 47–8, 54
  and cognition, 16–20, 26, 50
  and the on-screen body, 5, 50
  studies of, 3–8
  see also Deleuze, Gilles; Massumi, Brian
Alien: Isolation, 11, 158, 161, 165–9, 189
alignment
  with character, 48, 99–100, 104
  and modes of looking, 32
  between viewer, camera and diegetic
    participant, 186
  between viewer and on-screen body,
    5–6
allegiance, 17, 58, 65, 99
The Amityville Horror, 41
Anatomy, 11, 157, 159–65
assemblage, 4, 7–8, 61, 79–80, 143,
    164–5, 204

Badt, Louisa, 110–11
Bardem, Javier, 85
Barker, Jennifer, 29, 107, 141

Battersby, Martin, 181
Baudry, Jean-Louis, 34, 83
Bazin, André, 42, 55, 184, 189
Bekmambetov, Timur, 150
Bellour, Raymond, 147
Benjamin, Walter, 61, 107, 181
Bergson, Henri, 18, 21–2, 28,
    80
Bigelow, Kathryn, 93
Bigfoot, 56–7, 59, 122, 124
Birdman, 116, 119–20, 126
Blair Witch, 137–8
The Blair Witch Project, 9, 39–41, 47–8,
    50, 55–6, 62–4, 77, 121, 138,
    162, 186
Bogue, Ronald, 81, 142
Bonitzer, Pascal, 164
Bordwell, David, 14–16, 26, 78, 93,
    104, 124
Branigan, Edward, 78, 85–6
Brentano, Franz, 28
Brice, Patrick, 75–6
Brillhart, Jessica, 177, 190
Brinkema, Eugenie, 20, 28
Bruno, Guiliana, 144, 167

The Cabinet of Dr. Caligari, 4
Cahiers du Cinema, 8
Calder-Williams, Evan, 154
cameras, 129, 137, 149, 161, 200–1
  and embodiment, 105, 138–141
  and found footage, 30–3, 37–40,
    46–8, 54–7, 62, 64, 71, 74–9,
    97–8, 101–2

and the perception-image, 82, 84–5, 87–93
and SEEKING, 111–13
and virtual reality, 175, 177, 182, 184, 186–7, 190
Cannibal Holocaust, 39
Carroll, Noël, 4, 31, 135
  cognitivist frameworks, 13–17, 26, 54–5, 98–9, 112
  impurity, 13, 36
  thought theory, 45
Cartesian Logic, 7, 25
Catatonic, 11, 174, 183
Chamarette, Jenny, 23–4, 28–9
Chion, Michel, 56, 59, 126–8, 146–7
cinema, 1–4, 8, 13–18, 20–2, 24, 26, 31–2, 37–9, 42–3, 46–50, 55, 59–62, 64–5, 69, 71, 75–84, 88, 91–2, 101–4, 106, 110–11, 124–5, 127–8, 135, 137–44, 147, 149, 152, 157–9, 161, 164, 168, 200–4
  and virtual reality, 6, 11, 173–82, 184–6, 188–96
  see also horror
Clover, Carol, 4, 31
Cloverfield, 39, 106
Coëgnarts, Martin, 103
Cogito, 84, 88, 90, 111
cognition, 8, 14, 16–20, 22, 26, 32, 36, 38, 43–4, 46–7, 49–50, 54, 58–60, 78, 80, 93, 101–3, 106, 109–12, 124, 136, 138, 202–3
  embodied, 101–3
  see also affect
cognitivism, 14–16, 20, 22–3, 26, 29, 44, 47–8, 50, 54, 65, 80, 85, 91, 98, 101, 110
Colebrook, Claire, 82
Colman, Felicity, 81
The Conjuring, 1, 41
consciousness, 6, 15, 21–3, 26–7, 29, 33, 40, 47, 69, 159
  camera-consciousness, 88–91, 93

cinematic consciousness and perception-image, 82–3
  see also Sobchack, Vivian
Creed, Barbara, 4, 15
Creep, 74–6, 84, 87–90, 94, 106
Cremin, Colin, 164–5
Crick, Timothy, 159
Cronenberg, David, 36
Currie, Gregory, 14, 17, 28, 45, 75
Cursed Kleenex Commercial, 122–3, 126
Curtis, Robin, 100

Damasio, Antonio, 22
DeJonge, Olivia, 98
del Rio, Elena, 1, 60–1, 81, 92, 143
Deleuze, Gilles, 3, 7–10, 28, 48, 74, 79–93, 127, 142–3, 202
  and affect, 21–2, 80–5, 106, 164–5, 204
  'becoming-with', 79–81
  'body-without-organs', 61
  the perception-image, 82–8
  and representation, 91–4
  sensory-motor schema, 127, 142–3
  spectatorship, 81–2
Denson, Shane, 3, 67, 121, 128–9, 151, 153–4
Deodato, Ruggero, 39
digital media, 116–17, 120–5, 127–9, 132, 135–7, 141, 144, 148–9, 174, 176, 180, 184–5
discorrelation, 3, 117, 128, 151, 154
Disney, 117–18, 174
distortion, 4, 11, 116–17, 122, 133, 141, 144–7, 150–1, 154, 157, 162–3, 165, 202
documentary, 32, 39, 41–5, 57, 62, 67, 71, 76, 98, 106–7, 122, 138, 184, 200
Dogme 95, 41
Dowd, A. A., 56
dread, 6, 10–11, 23, 40, 46, 48, 50, 57–8, 62, 123, 126, 148, 158–9, 165, 167–8, 192
  see also Hanich, Julian

Duchaney, Brian, 34
Duplass, Mark, 76
duration, 20, 32, 44, 120, 125, 137, 143, 148, 168, 179, 182–4, 189

Easter Eggs, 151
Egginton, William, 38
Egoyan, Atom, 60
einfühlung, 100
Elsaesser, Thomas, 29, 135
embodied simulation theory, 102–6
  see also empathy
embodiment, 2–11, 17, 22–3, 25–6, 28, 30–1, 33, 35, 37–9, 41, 43–7, 49–50, 54, 56, 59, 71, 75, 83, 87, 90, 92, 101–7, 109, 111–12, 125, 128, 133, 136–7, 139–40, 159, 167–9, 173, 177–80, 182, 191, 193, 202–4
emotion, 5, 14–17, 19–20, 26, 28–9, 45–7, 50, 65–6, 68, 77, 92, 97, 99, 101–4, 106, 109–11, 164, 179, 193, 196, 203
empathy, 10–11, 17, 65, 69, 75–7, 91, 97, 99–106, 192–3
  and embodied simulation theory, 101–5
epistephilia, 62
Eraserhead, 36
erotetic model, 16, 99, 112
Escape The Living Dead, 182–4

Facebook, 150
Flaxman, Gregory, 79
found footage, 4–7, 9–11, 30–4, 38–48, 50, 54–6, 58, 62–4, 66–7, 69–71, 74–9, 81–2, 85, 88–91, 93, 97–8, 100–2, 104–6, 109, 111–12, 116–18, 121–4, 133–5, 137–8, 144–5, 147, 149–50, 158, 161–3, 184, 186–7, 189, 200–3
Freud, Sigmund, 31

Gabriadze, Levan, 149
Gallagher, Shaun, 22, 25, 28–9
Gallese, Vittorio, 103–5
Glendinning, Simon, 25, 29
glitch gothic, 144
Gregg, Melissa, 4
Grierson, John, 42
Grisham, Theresa, 66
Grodal, Torben, 17, 101, 110
Gromala, Diane, 190
Grosz, Elizabeth, 80
Grusin, Richard, 124
Guattari, Félix, 7, 61, 79–81, 164
Guerra, Michele, 103–5, 139

Hagener, Malte, 29, 135
Hanich, Julian, 6, 10, 23, 28–9, 31, 65–71, 193
  cinematic dread, 66–70, 188–9
  temporality, 167–8, 177
  theatrical experience, 147
Hansen, Mark B. N., 81, 83, 88, 181–2, 185, 191, 193, 195
Hansen, Miriam, 107
Hantke, Steffen, 123
haptic visuality, 144–6, 177
haunting, 10, 20, 32–6, 40–1, 58, 66–7, 88, 116, 122–3, 134, 150–2, 161–2
Heidegger, Martin, 8, 91
Heller-Nicholas, Alexandra, 5, 39–40, 43, 46, 144, 149
Hight, Craig, 43
Himmelsbach, Sabine, 175
Hobbes, Thomas, 14
Hollywood, 10, 16, 35, 44, 75, 77–8, 127, 142, 149, 152, 174, 180
horror
  'art-horror', 13
  cinema, 1–9, 13, 18, 31–2, 64–5, 77, 102, 129, 158, 168, 176, 202
  New Horror, 49
Horrorshow, Kitty, 11, 159, 161
Huhtamo, Erkki, 195
Husserl, Edmund, 8, 25, 29

Ihde, Don, 139–140
illusion, 45, 77, 92, 109–10, 175, 178, 180–1, 189, 191
　illusionism, 38
immersion, 6, 64, 67, 69–70, 75, 104, 144, 147–8, 158, 173, 178–9, 187–9, 193
intentionality, 24, 65, 68
interactor, 186–9, 195
internet, 10, 117, 121–2, 133–4, 137, 147–8
Isaacs, Bruce, 181, 193

Jaunt, 184

Kant, Immanuel, 82, 86
Keller, James, 40
King, Geoff, 158
Kittler, Friedrich, 180
Knudsen, Eric, 134
Körper, 25
Kravanja, Peter, 103
Kristeva, Julia, 15
Krzywinska, Tanya, 158, 163
Kubrick, Stanley, 141
Kunzelman, Cameron, 159

The Last Exorcism, 32
Leib, 25
Leyda, Julia, 3, 66, 121
Lipps, Theodore, 100
Lovecraft, H. P., 192
Lumière Brothers, 180
Lynch, David, 36, 56

Manovich, Lev, 185
Marble Hornets, 7, 9, 11, 133–9, 141–3, 145–51
Marginalia, 11, 159–65
McConkey, Larry, 105
McLuhan, Marshall, 2, 127
McRoy, Jay, 35
Massumi, Brian, 5, 22, 28, 44, 50, 196
　affect, 19–20, 203–4

Mello, Cecilia, 41
Merleau-Ponty, Maurice, 8, 24, 26, 59, 81, 139
Metz, Christian, 34, 77–8, 83, 192–3
mimesis, 61–2,
mimetic innervation, 106–7
mind–body concept, 25
mirror neurons, 101–2, 104–5
Mitry, Jean, 82, 87, 90
Mitsein, 91
'molar plane', 143
'molar' spectatorship, 79–80
'molecular plane', 80, 143
'molecular' spectatorship, 61, 79–80, 91, 111
molecular thought, 8, 91, 111
monster, 7, 13–14, 18–19, 36, 48–50, 71, 135, 137, 143, 158–9, 163, 165, 180, 187, 191
Mulholland Drive, 56
Mulvey, Laura, 31
Münsterberg, Hugo, 15
MUVEs, 195
Myrick, Daniel, 39–40

Nagib, Lucia, 41
Nakata, Hideo, 35
Nannicelli, Ted, 103
narrative, 2–4, 6–7, 10–11, 14–18, 24, 31, 33, 35–6, 38, 41, 43–4, 48–9, 55, 63–4, 67, 71, 75–6, 78, 80, 85–6, 98, 100–4, 107, 109–12, 117, 119, 121, 123, 125, 127–8, 135, 141–4, 146, 148–52, 159–60, 162, 165–6, 173–4, 176–7, 179–87, 189–96, 200–1, 203
Ndalianis, Angela, 47, 49–50, 126, 203
neuroscience, 4, 7, 9–10, 22, 29, 47, 97, 109
Nichols, Bill, 42, 62
Noë, Alva, 22, 28

Oculus, 167, 174, 194
Olivier, Marc, 144

Panksepp, Jaak, 10, 109–12, 201, 204
Paranormal Activity, 9, 39–40, 64, 66–70, 76, 79, 88, 90, 128, 186
Paranormal Activity 3, 64
Pasolini, Pier Paolo, 82–3, 89–90
Peli, Oren, 66
Pepperell, Robert, 92
Perron, Bernard, 158, 163–4, 166, 168
phenomenology, 3, 4–8, 10–11, 23–6, 28–9, 31, 46–7, 59–60, 65–7, 81, 99, 101–2, 106, 117, 128, 159, 167, 177, 195, 204
philosophy, 8–9, 13, 79, 90
Pisters, Patricia, 92–3, 106–7
pixellation, 144, 151
Plantinga, Carl, 14–17, 19, 28, 106, 179
player, 11, 157–68
Poltergeist, 33
polyphony, 128, 146
post-cinema, 3, 11, 20, 66–7, 116–17, 121, 127–9, 135–6, 142, 146, 149–53, 202
POV, 32, 55, 186
Powell, Anna, 18, 21–2, 48, 61, 79, 92, 138, 143, 204
presence, 2, 4–5, 26–7, 31, 45, 49–50, 59–60, 64, 67–8, 70–1, 77, 85, 104–6, 112, 117, 123, 136–9, 158–9, 182
 in virtual reality, 176–80
Prince, Stephen, 42
proximity, 32, 46, 65, 68–9, 137, 148, 165–6, 176, 189, 201
psychology, 28–9, 185

Radford, Colin, 45
Raz, Gal, 106

realism, 4, 38, 40–4, 47, 126–7, 138, 140, 181, 185
representation, 14–16, 17–19, 21, 28, 38, 41, 44, 47, 54, 60, 66–7, 85, 91–2, 110, 125, 127, 144, 149, 151, 163–5, 202–4
Reyes, Xavier Aldana, 5, 34, 49–50, 179
rhizome, 34, 92, 164
rhythm, 147
Riegl, Alois, 144
The Ring, 34–37
Ringu, 35
Rizzo, Theresa, 82–3, 89, 91
Rizzolatti, Giacomo, 101
Rodowick, David, 24, 29, 184–5
Rombes, Nicholas, 66
Rosch, Eleanor, 22, 103
Roscoe, Jane, 43
Rushton, Richard, 81–6, 88, 111
Rutherford, Anne, 61–2, 107, 177
Rødje, Kjetil, 64, 76

Sánchez, Eduardo, 39–40
Sayad, Cecilia, 41, 55
Schmitz, Hermann, 68, 70
Schwartz, Louis-Georges, 82–3
Sconce, Jeffrey, 33, 123
Screenlife, 133, 149–50
Seeley, William P., 14, 26, 29, 54–5
Seigworth, Gregory J., 4
sensation, 20–1, 23, 30, 48, 50, 61, 84, 88, 92, 103, 128, 144, 146–7, 172, 178, 192, 203
Shaviro, Steven, 18, 20, 28–9, 66, 117, 125–7, 154
Shaw, Jeffrey, 174
Shaw, Spencer, 90
Sherlock, Connor, 159, 161
Shyamalan, M. Night, 97

Singer, Bryan, 56
Sinnerbrink, Robert, 8, 45–6, 99
Slater, Mel, 178–9, 181, 189
Slender Man, 134
Smith, Murray, 14, 17, 99–100, 102
Sobchack, Vivian, 24, 26, 29, 44–5, 65, 71, 139–41, 159
  'cinesthetic subject', 59–60, 65, 112
  consciousness and corporeality, 59–60
  documentary consciousness, 44
somatic
  alignment, 5
  empathy, 65
  response, 4–7, 13
sound, 4–6, 21, 44, 46, 56–63, 70, 100, 118, 126–8, 142–4, 146–7, 150–4, 161, 168, 175, 188
soundscape, 118, 127–8, 147
soundtrack, 97, 132, 146, 161
spatiality, 177–8
spectatorship, 1–2, 6–7, 9–11, 13–15, 17–19, 23–6, 30–1, 33–5, 37, 39, 41, 43–5, 47–50, 59, 71, 76, 79, 81–4, 91, 99, 102, 121, 125, 135, 143, 147, 157, 173, 177, 179, 195, 203–4
spectrogrammetry, 120–1
Spielberg, Steven, 174
Spinoza, Baruch, 4, 19
Stam, Robert, 77
Steadicam, 105
Storr, Anthony, 128
subjectivity, 3, 5, 23, 33, 76–8, 80–4, 88–93, 128, 153, 163, 165
Subramanian, Janani, 66
Suicidemouse, 117–19, 121–2, 125–6, 128
suture, 77
Suzuki, Noji, 35
synaesthesia, 4, 11, 117, 144–6, 154, 177, 202
synchresis, 127

Taberham, Paul, 103
Taussig, Michael, 61, 107
technology, 1–3, 6–7, 26, 35–9, 42, 46, 71, 93, 116–17, 122–4, 127–8, 137, 140, 147, 150–1, 173–4, 177–9, 190, 193–5, 200
  and horror, 10–11, 30–4, 37, 66, 123
Telotte, J. P., 64
temporality, 11, 24, 26, 32, 61, 66–8, 70, 86, 90, 99, 104, 107, 125, 142, 148, 151, 154, 159, 165, 168, 185–6, 188–9, 191, 193, 195, 201
tension, 57, 100, 107, 109, 128, 146–7, 151, 153, 159–61, 163
The Texas Chainsaw Massacre, 41, 68, 154
Thompson, Kristin, 78, 93
Tikka, Pia, 193
Tirrell, Jeremy, 35–6
transcendental, 83–8, 90, 93, 111

Unfriended, 11, 33, 128, 133, 149–53

Varela, Francisco, 22, 28, 103
Verbinski, Gore, 34
Vertov, Dziga, 177
video games, 49, 157–169
virtual reality, 2, 4, 6–7, 9–12, 167–8, 171, 173–87, 189–96, 202
vision, 30, 36, 46, 49, 56, 63–4, 76, 83, 89–90, 98, 109, 126–7, 138, 141, 143–4, 153, 159, 161, 166–7, 176, 180, 184–5, 188, 193–4
The Visit, 97–101, 106–9, 111–13
volumetric photogrammetry, 174, 189–90, 194

Webdriver Torso, 121
Weibel, Peter, 194–5
Wetmore, Kevin J., 39
Willow Creek, 9, 39, 56–61
Wojciehowski, Hannah, 104

Yacavone, Daniel, 24, 29
YouTube, 7, 9, 11, 116–25, 128, 133–4, 137, 203

Zacks, Jeffrey, 101
Zahavi, Dan, 22, 25, 28–9
Zemeckis, Robert, 180
Zimmer, Catherine, 39

EU representative:
Easy Access System Europe
Mustamäe tee 50, 10621 Tallinn, Estonia
Gpsr.requests@easproject.com

www.ingramcontent.com/pod-product-compliance
Lightning Source LLC
Chambersburg PA
CBHW070349240426
43671CB00013BA/2445